In Trace of TR

In Trace of TR

A Montana Hunter's Journey

DAN AADLAND

University of Nebraska Press • Lincoln & London

Publication of this volume was assisted by
The Virginia Faulkner Fund, established
in memory of Virginia Faulkner, editor in
chief of the University of Nebraska Press.

Library of Congress Cataloging-in-Publica-
tion Data
Aadland, Dan.
In trace of TR: a Montana hunter's
journey / Dan Aadland.
p. cm.
Includes bibliographical references.
ISBN 978-0-8032-1627-3 (cloth: alk. paper)
1. Hunting—Social aspects—Montana.
2. Roosevelt, Theodore, 1858–1919—Travel
—Montana. 3. Roosevelt, Theodore,
1858–1919—Homes and haunts—Montana.
4. Montana—Description and travel.
5. Montana—Environmental conditions.
I. Title.
GT5856.M9A23 2010
973.91'1092—dc22
2009038124

Set in Swift.

To those American hunters who honor the legacy of Theodore Roosevelt by pursuing game on foot and horseback while caring for the land; to wife Emily and sons David, Jon, and Steve, their families, their efforts to raise their children with an appreciation for open space and wild creatures; and, to the great ones of the past whose trails we follow.

Table of Contents

Illustrations

Acknowledgments

EVERYONE WHO HUNTS with me and who rides with me has contributed to this book. But, as with all my writing, this work owes most to the help and support of Emily, my wife of nearly forty-five years, my friendly critic, my number-one editor, my patient source of inspiration and encouragement.

Introduction

A Hunter's Heart

FIFTY YEARS AGO I sat on a wooden rail enclosing a large observation deck behind the visitor's center at Mount Rushmore. Encircled by a crowd of chattering siblings, so many of them that my father required us to count off military style each time we reentered the car, I watched a bedecked Sioux pose for pictures with admiring tourists. He was having a fine time, a mid-summer Santa Claus with headdress, surrounded by suitors—and so were the tourists.

Dad was in his meticulous stage as a photographer, camera perched on a massive varnished-oak tripod produced in his basement shop because rock-steadiness was required by the extremely slow slide film he preferred. We would be here a while. He would snap the famous rock faces from every angle possible, seeking branches with pinecones as foreground framing. We would wait; our initial "Wow's" on first seeing the stone presidents had been spontaneous and genuine but short in duration.

Ever the pensive one, I sat and stared, tuning out as best I could my siblings and, from the crowd, a cacophony of touristy comments that seemed to me, even at age thirteen, inane. Already too much the westerner, I didn't particularly like crowds of any sort, and these pudgy tourists in Bermuda shorts, clutching at children who ventured close to the edges of the deck, were too obviously creatures of pavement and suburbs in far-away places to which I'd rather not go.

But the four faces on the mountain did hold my interest. No stellar student, I was nevertheless secure enough in my knowledge of three of them. The stock but solid history drilled into us by elementary teachers in our stone Montana school-house had stuck rather well, and I'd begun to supplement my awareness of the past with more palatable stuff, historical novels I'd found during numerous sifts through our school's little library.

Washington, it seemed to me, was the most logical subject for sculptor's stone: Strong, a horseman and commander, but aware, too, of the limits of his role. Unschooled as a military man, he more than compensated with stubbornness and raw courage, while he led by example and had the class to step aside when it was time.

Jefferson was more like me, I thought, a reader and writ-er and perhaps a dreamer, but one who dreamed on a grand scale. He sent Lewis and Clark out to the good country, to my country, Clark's name having been lent to a branch of the Yellowstone River near our home. The Pryor Mountains, visi-ble when I climbed the hill behind our house, were named, I knew, for a soldier in his company.

From my early childhood, Lincoln's face invoked in me dumb admiration along with an impulse nearly to cry. I needed only a few minutes to memorize the Gettysburg Address (my school-ing occurred before teachers were taught that rote learning was unnecessary and destructive). I found the words beautiful in formal fashion, and the man lonely and tortured. I saw him pacing in his study, struggling for just the right word and just the right deed and coming to it as all great men must, alone.

And there, tucked back between the shoulders of his elders, was the junior member, the only one with spectacles and a mustache, Theodore Roosevelt. He was, in my father's politics, the "good" Roosevelt. Dad was nearly manic in his enthusiasm for national parks, and taking his brood to any one of them, homebuilt travel trailer in tow, was a task not daunting but relished throughout its yearlong anticipation. He thanked Roosevelt for the whole shebang, though as an admirer of Henry Ford, he said less about TR's stance toward big business.

Schoolroom clichés such as "trust buster" had stuck in my mind but meant little. I was vaguely aware that Roosevelt had some connection with the West beyond his advocacy of national parks. I did not yet know him as a hunter or horseman, though I suspect some seed had been sown, perhaps by a photo in a schoolbook or on the wall of a museum or visitor's center. My lexicon of historical hunters at the time was dominated by the likes of characters carved by Earnest Thompson Seton and, on television, Andy Burnett, the subject of the one Disney series I really liked. And, of course, there was Daniel Boone and *his* fictional Cooper counterpart whom I'd met in *The Deerslayer*. Perhaps a man who had been president of the United States was a bit too august to comfortably enter this fraternity.

But that would change. The small Montana town to which my minister father had moved the family when I was in the third grade was nestled in a valley between sage-covered foothills that beckoned to a small boy soon trusted with a .22-caliber rifle. The woods in the river bottom were equally magnetic. We cut and peeled fragrant willow, fashioning crude bows and arrows and slingshots powered by strips of truck inner tube scavenged from friendly mechanics.

The historian Frederick Jackson Turner would have been smugly gratified had he been able to observe our childhood tribe of preacher's kids. His thesis concerning the shaping effects of open space, the release provided by the availability of the West for the cramped and crowded soul, may still stand unproven in the minds of modern scholars. But for us, a decade before I heard Turner's name, the thesis was simple reality. And so it was, too, for Turner's good friend Theodore Roosevelt.

• • •

What is it that makes certain historical figures come out of their stuffy portraits and emerge from between the covers of musty books to live beside us as tangible human forms? Yes, we understand their influence. We understand that we are, in many respects, what they made. But that's not enough.

With artists it comes easily. To a devout child the tortured Christ of El Greco needs no explanation, nor does the mindset of the artist who saw his subject this particular way. Similarly, only someone with heart and soul made of wood could sit unmoved by the sounds of Bach's "Air on the String of G," and once hearing it, could ever again see the composer as merely a wigged stoic to be remembered for a quiz in a music appreciation class.

And no one who has ever watched a sunrise can fail to connect with one of Shakespeare's many descriptions of dawn. A favorite is when Romeo, turned realist by unfortunate circumstances, dreads the day but notes the beauty of its coming: "what envious streaks / Do lace the severing clouds in yonder east: / Night's candles are burnt out, and jocund day / Stands tiptoe on the misty mountain tops." The bard, businessman, director, theater manager, actor, and writer wrote mainly in the last hours of darkness, I'm convinced, and saw the russet dawn countless times. He seems to have looked for excuses to describe it, sometimes incongruously, through poetry from the lips of gruff men. And so a rancher—teacher—writer whose time for composition is squeezed into the last hours of darkness and the first hint of morning connects with him over four centuries, one workaholic to another.

It came later with Roosevelt. In many ways the "bully" stereotype masked the man. It hinted little of a life that contained tragedy of the most searing sort. It said less about the literary man, the president most published and prolific as a writer and insatiable as a reader. It did not depict Roosevelt the scientist, the ornithologist; and while crediting him for the politics of conservation, knowledge here came down to me in the same sort of fact-sheet format from which we learn—and are too often bored by—our lessons in history. Roosevelt's love affair with the natural world was not revealed.

I cannot cite a particular epiphany. The life of a New York blueblood could not have been more alien to a small-town Montana boy. Studied later in my life, Roosevelt's frenetic career in New York State politics, his life there as a shrill competitor, failed to attract. Indeed, the man emerged as someone I may not have particularly liked. "Hyper" personalities tend to crowd introspective ones. His life as a police commissioner and as a governor might as well have been, for me, on Mars.

As a military man he came closer. A little reading revealed the inaccuracies of the San Juan Hill stereotypes, showed them as fanciful as most artists' depictions of Custer at the Little Bighorn. In Roosevelt's own language I found the realities: fighting hungry, dirty, and hot; semi-lost most of the time; success through guts, determination and a little luck.

Equally telling of TR's character, perhaps more so, was his troops' handling of the mustering out, the dissolution of the Rough Riders, that all-American composite Roosevelt had assembled. As a farewell gift they presented their leader with Remington's sculpture of the Bronc Buster. Scouts, hunting guides, and West Pointers alike, welded by the bond of combat under a magnificent leader, wept openly. This was the leader who, because transport to Cuba had allowed room for only officers' horses, not those of the men, refused to ride while his men were made to walk. Whenever possible, the colonel marched on foot alongside them. And the former Marine in me, trained to believe that the very best leaders put mission first but the welfare of those serving under them a very close second, nudged me closer to the man behind the thick glasses.

• • •

It is, however, on horseback, rifle under my knee, listening to meadowlarks sing while I ride over sage and coulees, perhaps to find a deer or an antelope, that I've really met Mr. Roosevelt. Someday scientists may detect genes for warriors, horsemen, and hunters. I'm convinced there are those of us in whom the drive to go out to find meat, rifle in hand, bypassing feedlot, processing plant, and supermarket, is too strong to be denied.

So it is as a hunter and as a horseman that I have met him and that I have come to know him. His time in the West was a mere sliver of a life so full and varied that were he a character in a novel we would declare him beyond credibility. Yet without his time here, in my country, as a rancher, horseman, and hunter, he would never have been, by his own declaration, president of the United States. An intervening century prevents my riding with him, but I have felt under my horse's soft shuffle the ground over which he rode, smelled his campfires of pungent pine and acrid sage, and stalked with him the prairie goat.

I am not a Theodore Roosevelt groupie. I meet him not for an autograph but for a firm handshake, my gaze meeting his, our horses restive as the skyline beckons. I meet him as a rancher and horseman and most of all as a hunter. Through the shared experiences related in this book I have come to know him better while learning as well new things about myself, about his time and my time, about the things that endure.

Come along with us. It should be a good ride.

In Trace of TR

PART I
The Big Open

CHAPTER ONE

Pronghorns on the Powder

The cow camp; prongbucks TR style; Powderville, then and now; the young New Yorker and the buffalo bull; a "sadder man but wiser"; hunting in midday; Scooter and Partner; .30-30s and .45-70s; iron sights and eyeglasses; Partner's initiation; a satisfying single-foot

"HOLD ON, HORSES," she cried, but, of course, they couldn't hear her and in any case they lacked the tools to comply. I had been aiming the Dodge down the two-track, squinting through a windshield not yet wet enough to let the wipers mop up streaks of Powder River dust, the big gooseneck trailer bouncing behind us. We were doing our best to keep up with our hosts' pickup, trying to beat the rain that would turn this Jeep trail into the sort of gumbo that converts a macho four-wheel-drive vehicle into nothing more effective than a child's tricycle.

It was when the road dropped into a deep coulee that Emily shouted her warning to the horses. Our friends ahead slowed as if to consider whether the pelting rain had yet done its work, then accelerated into the coulee and blew up the other side. I brought our considerably heavier rig to a near stop, watched to make sure the vehicle ahead made it up the grade, then kicked the diesel down a gear and plunged. Trying to strike a balance between safe speed and enough momentum

1. Emily and Scooter at the Cow Camp.
Courtesy of Dan and Emily Aadland.

to help the slipping tires, I jockeyed the rig through the bottom, downshifted one more time, and poured on the coal. We cleared the rise with a sigh.

Ahead was our host's "Cow Camp" marked by a windmill that looked friendly in the gathering dusk. Rarely used for sorting cattle, the complex consisted of several low sheds, an adobe homesteader's cabin, and a series of neat, grassed-over corrals. A large fenced holding area would be the perfect camp for us, allowing our young geldings Scooter and Partner to graze freely without hobbles and to enjoy a stock tank full of clear water supplied by the windmill's quiet pulse.

Our hosts helped us through the steel gate into the fenced area and then said their good-byes. I backed the pickup and trailer into a north-south position to shield our new camp from the west wind and the driving rain. We watched the taillights of the ranch owner's pickup disappear, felt the soil under our rubber boots turn to gumbo, and knew that we'd be here until it dried. We were what eastern Montana ranchers call "mudded in."

I was soaked long before I'd completed our little camp, but the gas lantern was cheering, as was the wood smoke from the fire Emily constructed in the cast iron stove. We'd be sleeping in the nosecone of our gooseneck trailer. As the ground mushed we grew increasingly glad we'd abandoned the idea of our range tent. The weather forecast had suggested just this sort of scenario. Our sleeping area wouldn't be of the luxurious sort provided by horse trailers with built-in living quarters, but the oversized tack room of our gooseneck trailer, with woodstove installed, would certainly beat a tent in the mud.

Before long I had a tarp winged out from the trailer, a blue plastic lean-to, and under it a table and a propane cook stove steaming raindrops in the frying pan. Emily took over. Soon Polish dogs sizzled and the camp was home, the rain a mere inconvenience, the mud that would hold us away from highways and pavement now a friendly thought. No cell phone service, no television, no babble on political talk shows—this was hunting.

By the time we finished wolfing our hotdogs, the rain had stopped. We unfolded canvas stools, killed the lantern, and ventured from beneath the tarp, enveloped by a darkness total and, in its way, delicious. The blackness, undiluted by vapor lights, headlights, or neon signs, shielded us briefly from the vastness of the eastern Montana plains. It's a rare treat to be able to enjoy total darkness outdoors.

But what followed was even better. First, there were two cups of strong coffee, then bourbon and Coke mixed in paper cups. Just about the time my uncontrollable shivering from wet clothing subsided, the sky broke open, and the clouds, parting, let loose the Milky Way. Even without help from a moon still blanketed by clouds, the starlight, unpolluted by human light, made visible the low hills and buttes surrounding us. As if on a director's cue, coyote calls cracked the silence. We were in camp, and it was good.

• • •

We were here to hunt antelope TR style, horseback, with an iron-sighted lever action .45-70 riding in its scabbard under my knee. There would be no ATVs, no dashing pell-mell after fleeing herds, no field-dressed antelope carcasses bouncing around in the back of a pickup, wonderful meat progressing toward ruin on a hot hunting day. We would do it the old way, and also the best way (though it's a little-known secret), on horseback and on foot, looking for this critter of nearly bionic speed, whose eyesight is said to rival that of a human's through eight-power binoculars, and we would do it in this big, open, free country.

Modern boundaries precluded us from hunting antelope in TR's backyard, across the border in North Dakota, but here on the Powder River in Montana we were within his domain. Roosevelt's Little Missouri is the next major drainage to the east of the Powder River, and our location is one TR knew well. His trips to meetings of the Montana Stockgrower's Association in Miles City took him over the muddy Powder where it spilled into the Yellowstone River. On his first expedition to the Bighorn Mountains in northern Wyoming, his first true Rocky Mountain safari, he likely rode his wiry pony alongside the supply wagon through the Powder Valley not far from our camp, which is very close to a speck of a town named Powderville. Roosevelt's route seems to have taken him south up the Powder (which flows north) as he worked his way toward the higher ground of the Bighorns.

A couple of days' ride upriver from us, Roosevelt flagged down a passing cowboy and asked him to wait while he turned out a letter to his sister Anna: "I am writing this on an upturned water-keg by our canvas-covered wagon, while the men are making tea, and the solemn old ponies are grazing round about me. I am going to trust it to the tender mercies of a stray cowboy whom we have just met, and who may or may not post it when he gets to "Powderville," a delectable log hamlet some seventy miles north of us."[1]

Emily and I had passed through this "hamlet" named Powderville on the way to our friend's ranch. Marked by a community center (once a school) and a couple of additional old buildings, there is no real town, but we'll remember it most by its setting by the river, the willows flanking the long bridge across the Powder River brilliant yellow in mid-October.

Even if he had not been personally acquainted with this particular valley, it would qualify in every way as TR country: big, open, sprinkled with buttes and dry washes, and populated (heavily, we hoped) with pronghorns. And being here, listening to coyotes and watching the stars on the eve of a hunt as our horses munched hay nearby, was much the same, I am sure, as it was for TR at those many camps he enjoyed with the likes of Merrifield and Ferris, his friends and employees.

We stoked the woodstove and closed the draft in hopes of holding some fire through the night. Then, rife with anticipation, we crawled into our sleeping bags. We would ride tomorrow. We would ride, and we would hunt.

• • •

He came here in the fall of 1883, shortly before his twenty-fifth birthday, slim, smallish, squinting through the thick glasses that would prove a detriment not only to his interaction with westerners already inclined to be suspicious of New Yorkers, but to his marksmanship as well. He wanted to kill a buffalo. Anything that first impressions of Roosevelt's person failed to accomplish with Ferris and Merrifield, his wallet handled efficiently. He bought a buckskin mare named Nell and engaged his new employees as guides.

And so, the future president, the man universally considered the most influential conservationist the United States has known, began his western career pursuing an animal he knew to be on the brink of extinction. A few large herds of bison had indeed survived the relentless hunts for meat, hides, and bones following the Plains Indian wars of the 1870s. But according to the biographer Edmund Morris, most of these remaining animals—many thousands—had been slaughtered within a year of Roosevelt's arrival by Sioux released from the reservations for just that purpose by officials who knew that the buffalo, once gone, would cease tempting the Indian hunters.[2]

There is less paradox here than one might think. True, some of TR's conservation ethic was yet to be born. But he had been a naturalist since early childhood. The Roosevelt household, Theodore's room in particular, was a menagerie of dead critters, classified and studiously dissected by a boy who accepted his father's sober warning that life as a scientist would be less lucrative than one as a lawyer. He would have to learn to live on less.

The difference between TR as a twenty-something enthusiast and later as the Great Conservationist was tied to his growing stature as a leader. True, his conservation ethic sharpened as he aged, but equally important, so did the sense that he could do something about the plight of the several large animal species he so longed to hunt. The young hunter of 1883 had no inkling that the disappearance of the bison and the prairie elk was anything other than inevitable. In chasing down and eventually killing a grizzled old bison bull, TR was simply a miniscule actor in the last scene of a drama no human had the power to affect. Or so he probably thought.

And so we leave him here. In spite of his accomplishments as a New York politician, as an emerging author, and as an accomplished amateur scientist, he was, on this fall hunting trip for buffalo, still a bit of a boy. But he was a boy tough enough to make his sourdough companions rethink their first impressions. He, too, hunted in the rain. After he killed that lone bull, a prairie storm caught up with the exhausted men and their jaded horses: "They woke to find themselves lying in four inches of water. Shivering between sodden blankets, Ferris heard Roosevelt muttering something. To Joe's complete disbelief, the dude was saying, 'By Godfrey, but this is fun.'"[3]

June 1884. Still slim, still young, but perhaps now with a stronger set of the jaw, TR lopes a new horse, named Manitou, west across a treeless landscape briefly green from spring moisture. Much has happened. He has fought political battles in the New York legislature, losing some and winning many, and tied up loose ends before affording himself this great release, this reunion with the big sky and with prairie grass that he has never seen so green.

Ever tuned to birdsongs around him, the meadowlark today

is particularly beautiful—three descending eighth notes, a pair of higher sixteenths, then a lower resolving tone—and it's this song that will remain always a poignant reminder of the greatest single tragedy of his life. Just a few months earlier, on February 14, his mother and wife died in his house on the same day. Alice, the girl he'd met at nineteen, married at twenty-one, died of Bright's disease (a type of kidney failure) two days after giving birth to a baby girl. Mittie, TR's mother, had died of typhoid fever a few hours earlier. On that day, Theodore wrote in his diary, under a large cross, "The light has gone out of my life."[4]

He handled this crushing grief in a fashion that would prove typical through the remainder of his life. There was no discernable period of mourning. Instead there was a systematic putting in order of all unfinished business, political and otherwise. The little girl born two days before her mother died was safely at home in the hands of Roosevelt's sister. And hovering in the back of his mind, through both the pain and characteristic handling of it, was, I'm certain, this promised ride on a good horse pointed west over vast expanses of liberating space, the grass green, the buttes beckoning.

He was here to raise cattle and to hunt. The enthusiasm and the nearly manic pace he demanded of himself were not gone and never would be. But little of the boy remained.

• • •

When I set out from the ranch for a day's prongbuck hunting of a set purpose, I always rode a stout horse and started by dawn. The prongbucks are almost the only game that can be hunted as well during the heat of the day as at any other time. . . . There is therefore no necessity, as with deer, of trying to strike them at dawn or dusk. The reason why I left the ranch before sunrise and often came back long after dark was because I had to ride at least a dozen miles to get out to the ground and a dozen to get back.[5]

It is still true today. Much has changed in the 125 years that have passed between TR's first antelope hunting and this hunt of Emily's and mine on the Powder River. But the animals, though they have adapted to changing times in some ways (finding, for instance, the benefits of feeding on irrigated alfalfa fields and winter wheat), are the same pronghorns Roosevelt knew. They still don't require you to rise before dawn. Reserve that for elk hunting. Reserve that for icy mornings in the mountains, saddling in the dark, coping with recalcitrant frozen cinches and lead ropes, strapping your gear onto a horse that would rather be sleeping or munching hay, and then riding toward elk meadows in the dark over treacherous trails.

Antelope, unlike deer, are not nocturnal. They bed down at night like cattle. Across the United States, anywhere deer are abundant (and that's nearly everywhere) automobile collisions with deer are rampant. Drive through territory densely populated with antelope, however, and the sight of any killed in collisions with vehicles is relatively rare by comparison. The difference is that at night, while deer are traveling and feeding and playing chicken with oncoming headlights or, at the last moment, sprinting across the highway in front of a speeding car, antelope are bedded down. Often selecting a slight depression to protect them from the wind, pronghorns will bed in a tight group, sheep-like.

It's true that the hunter can take advantage of this tendency, if he's ambitious enough and if he has spotted a herd just before dark. I pulled such an early-morning surprise on a nice bunch back in the years I taught high school English in northeastern Montana. From the highway, at dusk, I saw a herd a half mile off, on the land of a rancher who had given me permission to hunt. I returned in morning darkness, hiked over a rise, and found them just at shooting light, bedded down at seventy-five yards.

But mobile as antelope are, "spot and stalk" is the usual game. Moving through antelope country on foot or on horseback, using the binoculars freely, eventually reveals the telltale white rump spots of a herd in the distance. With their incredible vision, the antelope are usually staring back at you from a mile or two before you've zeroed your optics on them. At this distance they may merely watch, not ready to flee. So, using terrain never quite as flat as it looks, you find a way to approach on low ground out of sight, exploiting any available dry washes or depressions or hills to mask your approach.

As TR says, most any time of day will do. I especially like looking west, with the morning sun at my back. The low, bright sun lights up the white rump patches. You usually spot in the far distance what looks like a sprinkling of dandruff on a brown suit. But it's not always that way. Sometimes you blunder into a herd unexpectedly at short range when you top a rise. The critters are where you find them, and once spooked they are not there for long.

Fortified by TR's statements about antelope hunting being feasible most any time of day, Emily and I on this first morning in camp retreated a bit deeper into our sleeping bags, enjoying a delicious half-sleep occasionally tempered by the innate guilt of hunters and ranchers at lying in bed as the world turns light. There were sporadic bursts of gentle rain hissing like handfuls of sand thrown on the sheet metal above us. I looked out the trailer window at a slate sky behind buttes to the east. But the clouds had thin spots through which filtered bright morning light, promise, perhaps, of a clearing day.

There was no standing puddle in the depression by the stock tank. This had not been a true soaker. The hunt would be a damp one, but the terrain I viewed was not awash. Much as we would have preferred leather boots and spurs, we would ride in rubber boots.

Breakfast smells soon mixed with the musty scent of wet sage. I fed the horses while Emily cooked, the black I had only recently christened Partner, and Emily's spirited little bay called Scooter. Still colts at four and five, the two geldings seemed a little awed by the scene brightening around them, the windmill with its grunt on each stroke of the pump, the bulls that strolled down to drink from the side of the stock tank that protruded through the corral fence. Both horses ate in short bursts punctuated by tactical checks of their surroundings, throwing their heads high, snorting, looking for potentially lethal spooks.

Emily's hunting experience had been pretty much restricted to the deer on our ranch. She announced that on this first morning, on her spirited colt, she would prefer not to cope with the complications of rifle and scabbard, that she'd be happier paying full attention to the behavior of her horse, and holding the two of them should I get a shot with the .45-70. It's true that hunting antelope on horseback is best done as a team. In a mostly treeless environment, rarely are you lucky enough to find a convenient place to tie up while you complete a stalk on foot.

Manitou, the powerful gelding TR repeatedly praised as the best hunting horse he ever owned, had the extremely valuable trait of staying put, contentedly grazing, where TR parked him. With other horses, TR, hunting alone, used three-legged hobbles. So fettered, a horse can't take the characteristic hops of one that has learned to travel well when hobbled only by the front feet. Emily and I had the usual phobia of horsemen of the Plains, that one's horse might run off and leave one afoot.

The Crow and Cheyenne warriors who called the Powder River country home kept a favorite horse near their lodges while they slept, often running a thong from his halter under the tepee skin, and then attaching it to the owner's wrist. Sounds a bit risky to me, a potential wreck, a spook, a stampede, a rather rude interruption of your sleep as the horse skidded you out of the lodge and through the village. But these were trusted horses, of course, and the warriors probably considered the risk relatively mild compared to the many they faced daily, and in any case, worth it to prevent loss of their favorite animal.

Saddled up, we secured the camp against the wind that is always blowing across this open country. I slid the octagonal barrel of the long Marlin into my saddle scabbard, first checking that the folding tang sight hadn't loosened. There is nothing quite like sliding a good rifle into a saddle scabbard. That simple motion, the smell of oiled leather, the shifting of the horse that, with his nearly 360-degree vision, eyeballs the rifle's stock as it sinks into the scabbard, the saddle shaped for your body, the horse, the original all-terrain vehicle, ready and willing: it's a syndrome, a sensual composite. He knew it well, that small, tough man who did much to change the world.

Emily mounted first. Her Scooter, a little snorty on this wet morning, finally stood for her after she turned him around several times briskly, murmuring in his ear exhortations to be good. I had a brief moment of concern as Scooter, on his toes, appeared to contemplate actions that would not match that description. But he succumbed to Emily's cue, her firm insistence that he move forward. Impulsion is the great corrector of much equine misbehavior. The two circled the corral at a brisk running walk, Scooter's neck arched, his eyes looking for a suitable butte to climb. "He'd take you to Wyoming and back," I said.

"Yeah, and faster than I'd want to go." They stopped, and Scooter sighed his relaxation. I mounted, cussing my colt's continuing determination to grow taller as I grow older. Then we were off.

We rode southeast. In the center of a ranch of many thousand acres there was little danger we'd stray onto the land of our host's neighbors, and chances of finding antelope seemed about equal for each of the cardinal directions. We headed down a two-track, which was just muddy enough to cool the horses' impulse to get all their traveling done during the first fifteen minutes. The road took us through several gentle coulees, past stoical bulls that Partner eyed warily. Raised with cattle, Partner knew that these were not *his* cattle. But the bulls had ended two months earlier that one mission for which they exist, and now, pulled away from their cows, seemed resigned to seven months of bachelorhood on winter pasture.

It's strange how life in the West has changed the connotation of many words. "Pasture," to the easterner, may mean a ten-acre enclosure. Here it means several sections (square miles) of sparse grass of deceptively high nutrition if only it's not abused. Roosevelt the rancher soon learned a fact that John Wesley Powell tried unsuccessfully to shove down the craws of disbelieving easterners: the lifeblood of the West is water, there's never enough of it, and all eastern agricultural truisms must be discarded. It takes vast acreage to sustain cows in this country, but the grass is high in protein, evolved for grazing by bovines and elk, and is sustainable if cared for.

We rode casually, enjoying the horses and the day, the slight drizzle having ended. We were hunting, yes, but our quest for antelope was far from intense. Better to share the exhilaration of these fast-walking horses, the privilege of riding under Montana's big sky over butte-studded terrain with few fences, feeling the same sense of freedom TR craved after the smoke-filled caucus rooms of Albany and the house newly marred by death.

In the distance was a stock reservoir, a standard feature of eastern Montana cattle country, created by constructing a dirt dam over a coulee. The pond backed up by this one looked large, five or six acres perhaps, testimony to relatively good moisture during the preceding spring. But before we reached the little lake, Emily spotted to the east a sprinkling of white flecks on a patch of ground greener than that surrounding it.

Partner stands relatively still when asked, but glassing from the back of a horse, even a well-behaved one, is tenuous at best. I dismounted to peer through my binoculars. The large patch of green was new grass emerging where a fire had blackened the sagebrush, leaving it skeletonized. Enjoying the resulting growth was a small herd of antelope does and fawns, perhaps a dozen pairs, along with a very decent buck. He was already looking at me, as were the older and wiser does. I wasted no time in mounting Partner and hissing to Emily, "We'll just keep riding. They're not that spooked."

Avoiding anything more than a furtive glance in their direction, we continued southeast toward the reservoir, feeling the pronghorns' big, telephoto eyes on our left shoulders, knowing that if we simply went on our way we might be taken for cowboys who meant the critters no harm. Soon we dropped into the coulee, safely now in defilade, and crossed the dam. Partner eyed flocks of ducks, watched them flush, and did not spook. This was progress in the education of a horse destined to accompany me into old age.

A mile ahead of us, the rolling grassland was broken by a small grove of cottonwoods. We would turn north before reaching this inviting oasis, staying low, riding in front of a low ridge that should keep us out of the antelopes' sight. We rode at an easy walk now, the colts just tired enough to cooperate.

On a good horse there's a powerful temptation to stay in the saddle just a moment too long. Twice I've cost myself an easy elk when I've failed to dismount and pull out my rifle as I approached likely clearings, each time riding instead into the middle of a herd that scattered into the timber before I could get into action. But we did the right thing this time. We dismounted, leading our horses to lower our profile, and edged up over the ridge at approximately the point we thought they'd be.

There's nothing stealthy about pronghorns. They don't pussy-foot through timber like whitetail deer. When suspicious they simply relocate, and they do that with amazing speed, even in their lower gears. Our herd had spotted us in the distance, two working cowboys, perhaps, but maybe cowboys with evil intent. So they had moved, probably in an easy lope that took them a mile in a couple of minutes. Looking as nonchalant as ever, they now grazed along a fence representing the eastern boundary of the land on which we had permission to hunt. Several of the older does and the big buck eyeballed us between snatches of grass. The message was clear. Make one move toward us and we'll accelerate off your allotted land and out of your lives forever.

There was nothing to do but smile. My suggestion was my usual one when getting busted a couple hours into a hunt: take a break, drink some water, and eat a snack. The ground was too wet to invite sitting, so we stood on the low ridge holding our horses' reins, water bottles in hand. The tension was gone. Chapter one in our antelope hunt now over, we could look over this vast landscape and marvel at how far we'd come horseback in a very short time. The buttes near our camp far to the northwest were now diminutive, the windmill a mere dot of shiny metal.

We remounted and rode casually north through the bare sagebrush of the burn, the short regenerated grass green under our horses' hooves. In less than a quarter mile, we saw him, facing us, watching us, a pronghorn buck of modest size staring at us through the sage. At 350 yards his tan and cream markings were distinct and beautiful, his behavior, no doubt that of a satellite buck ghosting the herd we'd spotted earlier, too young to take on the big buck that owned it. Now he was eyeing two people horseback who could be cowboys but for their bright reflective hunting vests. He was no trophy, but I was hunting with an iron-sighted .45-70, and he looked just fine to me.

This was the classic Mexican standoff. He was too far a-way for a shot with the rifle I'd brought, and moving closer seemed impossible. There was just one possibility. "Antelope can't count," I hissed to Emily. "You stay here and hold the horses. I'll ease down into the coulee and circle. Maybe he'll just watch you."

It almost worked. Bent at the waist, I started my circle headed directly away from the buck, Emily and the horses between us, then gradually angled toward the lower ground to the west. After a hundred yards I'd dropped far enough to be out of the antelope's sight, so I cruised along at a near trot. And then he was in sight again, the distance 250 yards, according to my rangefinder binoculars (an innovation coming a century too late for TR), and he was watching Emily and me alternately, puzzled at what was being pulled on him.

Buffalo hunters, armed with rifles similar to mine and equipped with ammunition far inferior to the hot stuff I was using, regularly made kills at five hundred yards and beyond. But their tactics and the animal itself were considerably different. The usual scenario involved spotting a herd of bison from a high point, getting down into a prone position, estimating range, and firing an initial shot. The big, slow bullet arced toward the critters and threw up a substantial dust cloud where it hit. Like an artilleryman fed information from his forward observers, the buffalo hunter then adjusted his sights.

The bison, meanwhile, milled around. The animals primarily knew a different sort of hunter, one who chased them on horseback. Confused, they held their ground as the second shot rang out, this one smashing into a member of the herd. Instantly there was the smell of blood. Unlike deer, antelope, and horses, which are flight animals, bovines are inclined to stand and fight. Domestic cattle have much of this bred out of them, but not all—I've faced many protective mother cows that show their wild genes.

With a member of the herd down, thrashing, bawling, and smelling of blood, the bison continued to mill, and the buffalo hunter, the tall tang sight on his Sharps now adjusted for range, continued to put them down one by one. Then the skinners moved forward.

If I missed I would not get a second shot at this antelope buck that stood directly before me. He would be gone in a flash. Facing me directly he offered a very slim target, and the sagebrush made prone position impossible. A high kneeling position just cleared the intervening growth. With my best breath control I kept the dancing front sight on the critter as well as I could. Practice at home dictated the "Kentucky elevation" required. Nagged by this violation of my hunter's ethic—the shot was too far for my equipment and my ability—I squeezed the trigger. My justification for this marginal action was simple: the animal's position was such that wounding him was extremely unlikely. He would probably either be hit solidly in front by a 300-grain hollowpoint bullet or be missed clean.

Still, I was relieved to see the buck spin away from where the big bullet crashed through sagebrush a whisker to his side, then lope to the east. I had no temptation to chase him with additional lead, but reflected that TR would have done so. Often he mentioned that in antelope hunting more ammunition is expended per animal than in any other sort of hunting. The new Winchester lever actions with their tubular magazines and fast, repeating actions, made it possible to send fusillades toward distant critters.

But the oft-quoted judgment that Roosevelt was a terrible shot is unfair and not quite accurate. Yes, he missed much, but he also connected often, and when he did so it was with iron sights and, during his ranching years, black-powder calibers with rainbow trajectories. When the .30-30 appeared, Roosevelt commented on its flat trajectory, although today the caliber is considered a short-range proposition. Later, when TR acquired his "little Springfield," the bolt-action rifle he took to Africa, chambered for the .30-03 (forerunner of the .30-06), he was astounded by its long-range ability.

Roosevelt's nemesis as a marksman was, of course, his eyes. His thick glasses compensated only partially. Open iron sights beg your eyes to focus on the rear notch, the front blade, and the target all at the same time. Add poor vision and you have a nearly impossible scenario. Roosevelt would have profited immensely from peep sights on his early lever actions, since they reduce the focal points to two. Letting the rear peep fuzz out in one's vision allows one to focus only on the front blade as it lies on the target. The eye automatically centers the sight picture in the center of the rear peep.

Given TR's boyhood training with small-bore rifles and shotguns, his love for shooting, and his vast accumulated experience on game, it's likely that a telescopic sight would have converted him into a sharpshooter. Such sights existed in his day, and they were used by some buffalo hunters as well as by early military marksmen. However, the scopes were long, fragile affairs, the adjustable mounts beautifully made, but sensitive. A rifle so equipped was not a tool for the ranchman, to be bounced in and out of saddle scabbards, to be carried horseback through dust and rain and snow. Besides, mounting one on the top-ejecting lever-action Winchesters wouldn't have been feasible. Such scopes were most often used on single-shots.

Perhaps, then, TR deserves more credit for his shooting. He certainly brought home the bacon. One wonders how modern hunters addicted to rangefinders, scope sights, bipods, and flat-shooting calibers would stack up by comparison if forced to use TR's tools. Would they be as successful as he was at keeping the staff of a ranch headquarters supplied with fresh meat, the most popular source of which was this critter, the pronghorn, a specimen of which had just shrugged off my shot and loped casually east toward parts unknown?

I walked back to Emily and the horses. I had no real disappointment at missing a shot I shouldn't have taken anyway. But we had now approached the northeast boundary of our friend's land, so it was time to circle back and see some alternate territory. We rode along, recapping the excitement. "Did the horses jump when I shot?" I asked her.

"Barely; just a start. All that shooting you and the boys do around the ranch probably has made them pretty used to it." We angled down a shallow coulee, the horses, perhaps affected by our careless conversation, relaxing as we did so. The sky was now brighter, though still mostly gray, the sun teasing us with cameo appearances on this grand stage of the Big Open. Meadowlarks sang.

In hunting, sometimes one is given gifts. You can work your butt off on an elk mountain for days without seeing a track, then stumble into a herd by a county road. You can stay tactical and stealthy for hours, then jump a big whitetail buck while you're strolling along visiting with a friend, the hunt finished in your mind. And today, as we rode over a gentle rise, the gift came in the form of the young antelope buck I'd missed earlier, now feeding his way through the sage within reasonable range.

It is a smooth blur in my memory. I swung off my horse, pulled the rifle from its scabbard, and handed the reins to Emily, saying, "Hold the horses!" Then there were a couple of quick steps forward, a kneeling position, and a boom from the .45-70. The rifle rose in recoil, its stock dealing out the customary slap to my cheek, and the antelope buck went down as if struck by lightning. I glanced back at Emily, concerned that the horses might have pulled away from her, and saw that all was well, even though, as she characterized it later, I'd shot "practically under their noses."

Curious and a little shaky, I took time to examine the buck through the rangefinder binoculars. A hundred and ninety-two yards. As I took Partner's reins, I found myself awed at the effectiveness of the rifle I now slipped back into the saddle scabbard.

• • •

My first big-game rifle was a Sears .30-30 made by Marlin, the action the venerable Model 336, virtually the same as that of .45-70 I carried today. I earned the rifle harrowing a grain field on a ranch, a task I remember mainly for the jarring punishment the tractor dealt out while crossing the furrows, for the dust, and for the biting gnats that accompanied me in a cloud and from which there was no protection.

But when the rifle arrived in the mail, its box smelling of new gun oil, I quickly forgot the torture on the tractor. Even at age fourteen I knew that the .30-30 wasn't the ideal caliber for wide-open Montana, that someday I'd have a Jack O'Connor special, a scope-sighted .270. But I killed many deer with the lever action. Finally, just before I left for Vietnam as a young Marine lieutenant, I purchased for a last-minute hunt with Emily a left-handed Savage 110 in that caliber and mounted it with an inexpensive four-power scope. I never looked back.

But in the meantime I'd had a course in the tremendous effectiveness of rifles mounted with proper peep sights. The instruction, courtesy of the United States Marine Corps, was called the "A-Course" in rifle marksmanship, taught during the least torturous week of my officer candidacy at Quantico, Virginia. The Marine Corps was in transition to the M-16 (a mistake the U.S. military has spent forty years trying to rectify by successive modifications to that wretched little rifle). But in 1967 Marines still qualified on the rifle range with the M-14, a more traditional semiautomatic chambered for 7.62 NATO, the military version of the .308 Winchester.

If I recall correctly, firing was offhand at two hundred yards, kneeling and sitting at three hundred, and prone at five hundred, each position assumed with proper form and a tight sling. We were taught intricate methods for doping our peep sights for each range, counting clicks of elevation. When all went well we had the satisfaction of seeing the bull's-eye disappear behind the white disk held up in front of it by the crew "pulling butts" below the target. When it went badly, when we missed the target completely, a red flag ("Maggie's drawers") was waved. Scores for shots between these extremes—on the target but not in the bull—were indicated by a red disk held up in one of three positions.

I was plagued by the TR problem, but not nearly to the same degree. Nearsighted, I refused to admit it and thus wore no glasses, but I still managed to fire that first time in the middle category, "sharpshooter." It's a trait of the Marine Corps that even generals wear shooting medals on their dress uniforms because Marines never outrank the need for marksmanship, though after a certain rank, officers no longer need to qualify yearly with pistol and rifle. Thus I was pleased after admitting my visual deficiency and acquiring glasses to begin regularly scoring "expert," the top category, on the range.

As a hunter I became as addicted as anyone to flat-shooting calibers and scope sights. But the military training had taught me just how effective peep sights can be and that the fundamentals of good shooting—breath control, trigger control, and the necessity of solid shooting positions—apply to all rifles and sighting systems. And, after many quests for antelope while carrying scope-sighted .270s and various 7mm magnums, taking to the field with a long-barreled .45-70, peep sight mounted behind its hammer, seemed a reasonable challenge.

• • •

We led our horses carefully toward the downed buck. The colts had never been hunting, had never smelled blood, and

2. Partner sniffs antelope taken with .45-70.
Courtesy of Dan and Emily Aadland.

although they had grown up sharing their hay with whitetail deer, antelope were new to them. Any fears we had of uncontrollable spooks, of snorting horses showing the whites of their eyes, were quickly allayed. Scooter ignored the buck completely, even stepping on the pile of entrails after I removed them. Partner sniffed the buck without snorting, then began searching for tidbits to graze around the carcass.

Whenever I stand by a game animal I've killed, I feel a sense of satisfaction mingled with affection for the animal, regret for the ending of his life, and thanks to the animal and to the terrain that has offered me the opportunity. I do not feel guilt. The animal has played out its natural role, and so have I, mine being that of predator. I have acquired my meat directly and honestly without the involvement of a middleman.

I've often wondered just what TR felt. During his lifetime he killed countless animals. As a boy fascinated with biology and ornithology, he collected specimens the only way it was done at that time—he killed them. After his presidency he went to Africa and hunted for two museums, each of which desired both sexes and all ages of the animals collected. Total score from the meticulous records he kept was 512 animals (not counting birds taken) on a safari that encompassed a year and traversed much of the continent on horseback. Perhaps because his hunting had garnered some criticism during his recently completed presidency, he felt just apologetic enough about the high number, and about taking female and juvenile specimens, to frequently remind his readers of the museums' requirements: "Kermit and I kept about a dozen trophies for ourselves; otherwise we shot nothing that was not used either as a museum specimen or for meat—usually for both purposes. We were in hunting grounds practically as good as any that have ever existed; but we did not kill a tenth, nor a hundredth part of what we might have killed had we been willing. The mere size of the bag indicates little as to a man's prowess as a hunter, and almost nothing as to the interest or value of his achievement."[6]

As to his personal feelings upon killing an animal, he gives us slight indication. But he was a product of his time. Men avoided expressing emotion. That he was a sensitive human being is immediately evident to anyone who reads his writings with perception. But directly expressing his emotions in work meant to be read by the public was completely alien to him. We know of his crushing grief at the death of his wife and mother by the observations of others, but from his own hand there was only the single diary entry about the light having gone out of his life, a confession of grief intended for his eyes alone.

As I looked at the downed antelope buck, I felt very much in TR's mode as meat collector for his ranch and roundup camps. The work starts when the animal falls. I cannot take a big-game animal, even in leisurely circumstances, without thinking of that wonderful Charlie Russell painting of the packer on the ledge trail, rifle in hand, looking over a cliff at the mountain sheep he has killed. Its caption: "Meat's not meat until it's in the pan."

This buck had fallen on ground we could easily reach with our four-wheel-drive pickup, but we would leave ruts, or at least marks, a prospect distasteful to us. The nature of western grasses is such that, even were the terrain completely dry, the rancher would be able to spot for a year or more just where we had driven. Perhaps, given the permission he had granted us, he would have no problem with that, but to us it is an unseemly thought. We are ranchers, too. Each set of visible vehicle tracks on our ranch is, to us, an intrusion.

So Partner, the friendly but challenging colt I'd been training, would have the duty. He could carry the buck. I would lead Partner back to the two-track road by the reservoir, then drop the buck for retrieval by vehicle. TR's usual procedure was to carry the antelope tied securely behind the saddle:

> In packing an antelope or deer behind the saddle, I cut slashes through the sinews of the legs just above the joints; then I put the buck behind the saddle, run the picket rope from the horn of the saddle under the belly of the horse, through the slashes in the legs on the other side, bring the end back, swaying well down on it, and fasten it to the horn; then I repeat the same feat for the other side. Packed in this way, the carcass always rides steady, and cannot shake loose, no matter what antics the horse may perform.[7]

It's the "antics" part that bothers me. Partner has always shown some tendencies in the direction of "antics," and at sixty-three, a trifle top-heavy, I'm not the horse trainer I once was. Perhaps I'll one day pack an antelope on Partner using

TR's method, but for his first meat-packing experience, I would not share Partner's back with the now-bloody, field-dressed, pronghorn buck. Instead, the buck would go over the saddle, secured to the saddle strings and to the cinch rings with poly rope from my cantle bag.

As always, easier said than done. The ground sloped slightly, so Emily held Partner's reins and kept him on the downhill side of me. I bear-hugged the buck, gave a heave partway up, then horsed the animal up to the balance point, holding him briefly at that point while allowing my complaining lungs to catch up.

Roosevelt, when he first came west, did this often. He weighed at that time approximately 130 pounds. I weigh 225. I'm not young, but no one accuses me of being weak. A lifetime of ranch work has seen to that. Since TR tossed antelope onto horses' backs relatively frequently, I can only judge that his famous devotion to physical fitness was well underway by the time he reached Medora. The thickly spectacled easterner made believers of his ranch hands when he once walked into camp leading Manitou, his favorite hunting horse, with one antelope buck tied across the saddle and two behind it!

Securing the buck's legs as rapidly as I could on the near side, I ducked under Partner's neck and began working on the other side. I was almost finished when the horse noticed something amiss. One of the antelope's front legs stuck stiffly off to the right, and in his nearly 360-degree vision, Partner caught this unusual sight. His right eye whitened and he startled forward.

There were a few moments when things teetered in uneasy equilibrium. I had a vision of a colossal wreck, an antelope dragging from the horse's side like a rider caught in the stirrup, a black horse dashing across the sagebrush, bucking and kicking and trying to shake off this strange bloody appendage glued to him. But it didn't happen. Eyeing the protruding leg, Partner lunged around me in two quick circles while

3. Partner packs an antelope. Courtesy of Dan and Emily Aadland.

I held the reins, hoping the partly tied antelope would stay on his back. On the third or fourth "whoa!" he stopped. And that was that, his spook for the day.

Emily, at my insistence, mounted up. She'd suggested that she should walk with me, but I reminded her of Aesop's tale about the man, the boy, and the donkey. When the boy rode, the passersby berated him for causing his feeble old father to walk. So the man rode, and the people they met chastised him for making his poor little boy walk while he had the luxury of the donkey's back. Then the two rode double for a spell, only to be crucified by what must have been budding members of the ancient Greek Humane Society for putting so much weight on the unfortunate donkey's back. So, as a last ditch effort to please everyone, both walked and led the donkey, only to be called idiots for wasting the strength of their useful animal by leaving him unladen.

We soon reached the reservoir. Although we'd ridden to it cross-country, not on the two-track that wound its way down to the earthen dam, we were sure that we could drive the pickup to this point. But for some reason I didn't want to drop the buck off Partner's back. I was in a nice rhythm walking along, the exertion a pleasant warmth, the feel of my feet on soft soil beneath the prairie grass something I wanted to preserve for a bit longer. So I walked a second mile, and then a third, and then it was Emily reminding me of Aesop as a blister rising on my right foot under the rubber boot seconded her suggestion that I finally drop the buck and ride the rest of the way to camp.

I found a nice grassy spot next to the road between clumps of sage. I untied the buck on Partner's right side, then on his left, finally gently lowering the buck to the ground. I found myself very possessive of this animal so recently beginning his journey to meat in the pan. I've shot a good number of antelope bucks, most with horns more impressive, but this one, I knew, would always stand out because of the manner in which we took him.

In camp I would hang the buck to cool overnight, skin him in the morning, and put the quarters on blocks of ice in the giant cooler we'd brought. Treated with that sort of care, the meat of the pronghorn is superb.

I mounted up. Given their heads, Partner and Scooter picked up into smooth, swift, running walks, their hooves single-footing a rat-tat-tat on the two-track road. This was how TR traveled while hunting and on frequent jaunts over the forty miles between his north and south ranches, a trip that took approximately five hours. The ranch horses of his day, before highways and horse trailers, were built like ours, to cover ground. "My foreman and I rode beside the wagon on our wiry, unkempt, unshod cattle-ponies. They carried us all day at a rack, pace, single-foot or slow lope, varied by rapid galloping when

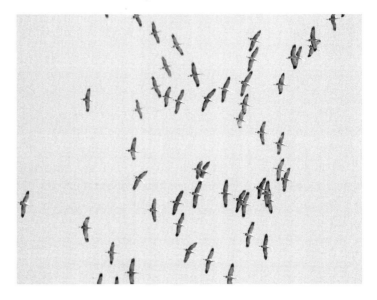

4. Migrating sandhill cranes filled the air.
Courtesy of Dan and Emily Aadland.

we made long circles after game; the trot, the favorite gait of eastern park-riders, is disliked by all peoples who have to do much of their life-work in the saddle."[8]

For fun, I pulled out my GPS unit. We were traveling just TR's speed, the GPS odometer hovering around 7.9 miles per hour. There was a .45-70 in the scabbard, blood on the saddle, and meat for the camp. If he could have seen us, TR would certainly have smiled.

In the morning coyotes again sang a prelude to the dawn. The sun rose, and shortly afterward, thousands of migrating sandhill cranes, in countless successive V formations, flew over, against a big sky of royal blue. TR saw them, too: "Great flocks of sandhill cranes passed overhead from time to time, the air resounding with their strange, musical, guttural clangor."[9] The bulls came down to the stock tank to drink, and the horses munched hay. Life was good in the Big Open.

CHAPTER TWO

The Elkhorn Ranch

On the road with Redstar, Partner, and Emily; Miles City and beyond;
Medora and the Maah Daah Hey; Black Gold on TR's ranch; a pleasant
porch on the Little Missouri; meadowlarks and mountain bluebirds

ALTHOUGH I KNEW that little remained on the actual site, I
needed to see it. On the banks of the Little Missouri, pleasantly shaded by stately cottonwoods in summer and protected by
the high bluffs framing the valley when winter's winds blew
in from the Montana prairies, the Elkhorn Ranch was TR's
western home. Built of cottonwood logs by Sewall and Dow,
the two woodsmen he had known back east and who had con-
sented to come out and try life in the Badlands, the house no
longer stands. But its site is protected in an alcove of national
park land about halfway between the north and south units
of Theodore Roosevelt National Park.

So in early May we head east, pulled by the throaty Dodge
diesel, a new if Spartan camper in the truck bed and a two-horse
trailer behind. The horses, of course, have to be with us. To be
in TR country with only wheels, to look at the Badland bluffs
on TR's ranch without a horse to saddle is unthinkable. We
will ride those bluffs, see the Little Missouri from them, briefly taste on horseback the cattle country that hooked Roosevelt
upon first visit and made him a rancher.

We have left our home ranch in south-central Montana, our spirits buoyed by the first moisture we've seen after a cold, dry spring and a winter nearly devoid of snow. There's only a hint of green in the Yellowstone Valley, the cottonwoods budded and trying to break free of a frosty April featuring mornings that plunged nearly to zero. The weatherman has promised more moisture after a few clear days. Our calving is under control, the calves branded, the daily feeding still required but in the hands of a helper.

To be ranchers, to have an extended family of horses and cows and dogs and cats, means never leaving home with an entirely clear conscience. But we've come remarkably close. Partner and Redstar have seemed equally anxious, stepping briskly into the cave-like trailer and diving into the oats I've left in the feed bunks for them. Their health papers and brand inspections, western passports for horses heading over state lines, reside in the visor of the pickup, current and correct.

Only half believing that we're actually getting away for this gig, we bypass the Billings exits with glee. There will be no stops today for the usual supplies, bulk food at Costco, steel posts at Shiptons, ink cartridges at the office store to satisfy the insatiable appetites of our computer printers. We may not be Huck and Jim setting out on the raft, but we're about as close to that as workaholics can get.

Interstate 94 roughly parallels the Yellowstone River as it drops toward Miles City and Glendive, the highway and the river parting only at the eastern edge of the state where the river bends north before eventually mating with the Missouri. The cottonwoods along the river have been slow to leaf this spring, their branches only now showing a hint of green, tinted slightly by their buds, the grass under them still mainly brown.

We parallel, too, the railroad, which spawned most of the towns along this route, each growing up where the railroad work paused before pushing west. The line across southern Montana was completed in 1883, the same year TR first saw the Big Open. You can readily see the railroad's mark in another way, the layout of typical towns across prairie America, a long main street running east and west, paralleling the tracks, the old buildings of commerce on the north side of the main street face south toward the railroad, the poorer sections of town gradually having grown up on the south side of the tracks.

I-94 occasionally shortcuts through the hills on the southern side of the valley. The diesel asks for a downshift from overdrive when we encounter the bluffs called the Hysham Hills, adjacent to the town of that name. These hills are known for their mean winter storms.

At Miles City we stop for fuel on a street that looks all too much like Grand Avenue, America. There are the usual brand names on billboards and the typical complement of fast-food restaurants. The exceedingly high population of cowboy hats and diesel pickup trucks is the only real clue that we're in Cowtown, USA. Make that Army Town (named after General Nelson Miles), Buffalo Hunter's Town, and Railroad Town, as well, for Miles City was all of those things in its more than colorful past. (According to the historian Mark Brown, Miles City was once home to some ninety-odd cathouses.)

Here lived TR's friend L. A. Huffman, the photographer who preserved each of Miles City's successive eras. The cowboys he captured in crisp black and white ride horses like those described by TR: smallish, lean, high-withered, and narrow, with builds favoring endurance and the ability to cover mile after mile after mile.

East of Miles City the exit signs are sparse, but those that exist are an interesting mixture of authentic western redneck and realtor appeal. Subdivision still lacks a major toehold in this part of Montana, but many of the ranches have been purchased by the out-of-state rich. Exits for "Whoopup Creek" and "Bad Route Road" are softened for realtor brochures by roads named "Pleasant View" and "Home on the Range." And, in one of the towns, California asserts itself with a motel named "El Centro."

At Glendive, I-94 dives straight east, leaving the Yellowstone River, and as we enter North Dakota we discover I've somehow left at home the one map we really need, the one that traces a gravel route north from the interstate through a labyrinth of county-road junctions up to the vicinity of Roosevelt's Elkhorn ranch. So we stay on the interstate for another twenty miles to Medora, catching the visitor's center at the headquarters of Theodore Roosevelt National Park just before closing time and securing a copy of the misplaced map from employees who are friendly, though with quitting time in their eyes.

Then we backtrack west on the interstate, exit north, and drive thirty miles of dusty roads that have gained junctions and side turns since the map was made, the result of oil development now occurring at a frantic pace. But along with the oil wells there are ranches that still function as ranches, irrigated alfalfa fields, cattle, and the boneyards of discarded equipment that distinguish working ranches from what I call "land yachts": ranches purchased by wealthy folks for status and occasional retreat.

And there are TR's "prongbucks." A bachelor group of seven nice antelope bucks scoot off the road in front of us, then pick up speed and outrun Emily's camera. More are off in the distance, their rumps flecks of white against the hint of green showing on the flanks of the many little buttes that dot the area.

Finally, the road takes us down a coulee that drains west toward the Little Missouri. We've seen the river at Medora, and there's nothing little about it, thanks to a huge wet spring snowstorm in southeastern Montana that flattened power lines and buried farm equipment. Melt from this storm has made the Little Missouri a muddy tide that surges along above its banks. Emily, seeing it, has flatly announced that we won't be crossing it with the horses, and I have no motivation whatsoever to argue.

Then we find it, up a short stretch of side road into a coulee, a tidy forest service campground, horse-friendly, with hitching racks and a hand pump, the gravel road harrowed, the place absolutely empty in pre-tourist early May. And very quickly, it seems like home.

• • •

It is only after the horses are watered, Partner hobbled and turned out to briefly graze, Redstar picketed by the front foot with a long line to the horse trailer, that I think about our dash through Medora. With miles of gravel roads yet to travel, we'd been limited to the map stop at Park headquarters and a quick stop at a "quick stop" whose droll proprietor spoke of the coming tourist season with the same anticipation she'd have shown for a pending root canal. The fact that the incoming crowd was also her paycheck seemed of little consequence to her.

What was it like for TR here? New York was written all over him. His thick glasses broadcast "Eastern Dude," a snap judgment from Medora's motley crew of disparate western humanity. This was a place so different from upstate New York that it might as well have been the surface of the moon.

During the brief interval between Roosevelt's late-1883 arrival in search of a bison bull and June of 1884, when he came to ranch, hunt, and combat his grief, Medora had grown into a bustling frontier town of nearly a hundred buildings. The beef business was good, the Marquis de Mores's grandiose scheme of a slaughter plant and shipments of beef quarters east in refrigerated train cars having come to fruition. (The enterprise would be a brief one, but no one in this bustling, optimistic frontier town yet realized that.)

We're told that TR's grief at the loss of his mother and his beautiful wife, so rarely expressed, frequently plunged him into the depths of depression. Hunting and riding seemed the only tonic. There were circles in the saddle of seventy miles, TR relishing the task of supplying his hired men with fresh meat while they built his house and tended the stock.

The tough folks of Medora must soon have begun to revise their first impression of the little four-eyed dude from the East. Harassed by a drunk who was packing two cocked pistols, Roosevelt knocked the man on his back with a quick right-left-right combination. Both guns fired, missing anything significant (the drunk had already aerated the barroom clock in a belligerent session of target practice).

And there was the standoff with the Marquis himself, who asserted that he had already laid claim to the land to which Roosevelt had purchased rights. None of the big cattle ranches were deeded at this time. The land was merely claimed and occupied. In *The Rise of Theodore Roosevelt*, Edmund Morris details TR's conflict with this illustrious individual, who promenaded through Medora frequently with his red-headed wife, both of them known and feared as deadly shots, their money the well from which Medora grew. TR's conflict with the Marquis grew to the point of intimidation. Sewall and Dow were visited by the Frenchman's men while Roosevelt was absent, and there were even hints of a duel between the two principals. But Roosevelt stood his ground, the ranch was his, and the conflict ebbed toward cool acquaintance and eventually smoothed into an uneasy friendship.

But always, through this first plunge into ranching life, there was the grief encapsulated for him into the omnipresent song of the meadowlark. The pretty Baby Lee, born so close to her mother's death and tended by TR's sister, was the subject of only infrequent inquiry from the stricken father, and of visits, when he was east, deliberately brief. He could see too much that was painful in the blue eyes and blond curls of the baby girl. And the only successful medicine for sleepless despair was the West, the Big Open, and long, hard hours in the saddle.

• • •

In the morning there were eggs and Italian sausages, cooked in the unaccustomed luxury of the camper's kitchen, along with my requisite quantity of black coffee. As Emily straightened things up, I short-tied Redstar and Partner to the horse trailer. We loaded our cantle packs with sandwiches and cameras and prepared for a ride on the Maah Daah Hey Trail. The official National Park Service translation of the trail's Mandan name is "an area that has been or will be around for a long time." The Mandans must have been masters of linguistic economy.

The recently completed trail is a magnificent achievement. Ninety-six miles long, running generally north-south, the Maah Daah Hey connects the north and south units of Theodore Roosevelt National Park while running through many miles of national grasslands administered by the U.S. Forest Service. We were not planning to tackle it all, fine a challenge as that would be. Maybe someday we'll do that with a packhorse in tow. This time we had come to ride the heart of it, the section adjacent to the Elkhorn Ranch, TR's headquarters, to taste firsthand his backyard, the buttes and hollows where he ran his cattle.

So there was no saddle scabbard under my knee that morning as I swung into the saddle on patient Partner. I could have carried a rifle, since we wouldn't be venturing onto national park land that day, but I had no need to do so. Hunting during season is allowed on the national grasslands, and there's much heartburn among wildlife managers and hunters who believe it should be allowed in the national park itself. Bison and elk are overrunning and overgrazing the park named after America's most famous hunter, and control of them has proven virtually impossible without hunting as a tool.

On an earlier visit Emily and I had been appalled, too, at the proliferation of prairie dogs within the national park boundaries. Like all critters, the little rodents have their place. However, they've now become politically correct darlings, cover children for magazines, and the fact that they're inveterate over-grazers seems blissfully ignored by people who decry livestock grazing on public lands because of alleged damage to the resource. Prairie dogs graze grass right to the roots, converting fodder for elk, deer, bison, and domestic stock into bare dirt. I'm not suggesting the Park Service do what TR would perhaps have done—grab a sack of poison oats—but some sort of management of this species would seem in order. Pretty little valleys within Theodore Roosevelt National Park look like bare, pockmarked vacant lots, thanks to the little prairie rats.

Yes, I'm talking here like a rancher, and on this particular sojourn into TR country I found my rancher's mentality, not my hunter's, to be dominant. I raise cattle on a relatively small ranch straddling a valley. On our ranch the dryland ranges on each side of the valley are fenced, and the valley bottom features irrigated alfalfa fields that produce some hay even in drought years.

Such fences and hayfields were largely absent in TR's ranching environment, although a certain amount of "wild hay" (uncultivated, naturally occurring grasses) was put up for the horses and milk cows kept close in. The cattle were managed without fences by good cowboys and good horses. Water sources and the placement of salt troughs regulated the animals' movements to a degree, and in any case, the spring and fall roundups sorted out the details. Cattlemen banded together in associations with strict rules. Branding was done at the spring roundup, the owners sorting cow-calf pairs by the brand of the mother cow, and then branding the calf accordingly and castrating the bull calves to convert them into steers.

Winter feed consisted of sections of range saved for the purpose, cowboys in line shacks keeping the herds within their respective territories:

> The camps are established along some line which it is proposed to make the boundary of the cattle's drift in a given direction. . . . The camps are usually for two men each, and some fifteen or twenty miles apart; then, in the morning, its two men start out in opposite ways, each riding till he meets his neighbor of the next camp nearest on that side, when he returns. . . . In riding over the beat each man drives any cattle that have come near it back into the Bad Lands, and if he sees by the hoof-marks that a few have strayed out over the line very recently, he will follow and fetch them home.[1]

It was a hard life in those line shacks, some of them merely tents or dugouts banked with snow. But this system of leaving cattle on range all winter worked well—for a while. The stiff prairie winds bared off the steeper ground so that cattle could reach the brown but potent winter grass. South slopes, warmed by the southern winter sun through dry western air, quickly melted off after a snowstorm.

But this was a good thing that came to an end. Ability to manage a large number of cattle with few helpers without fences and hay feeding during winter came to a frozen halt during the infamous winter of 1886–87. A drought the previous summer had dried up water sources and pushed cattle closer to the creek bottoms, where they consumed the feed normally saved for winter. Then, unrelenting winter set in with November. In a cruel late-winter twist, a chinook wind melted deep snowfall before the air again turned bitter, freezing a layer of ice over the remaining feed. Cattle starved, froze, and died.

The cattle industry was broken. Losses ranged from 30 percent for the lucky ranchers to 60 percent for those, like Roosevelt, who fared the worst. During the spring rise the Little Missouri in front of his cabin was choked with the bloated carcasses of cattle killed by this terrible winter.

Riding the Maah Daah Hey Trail in early May, Emily and I can't help but admire the cattlemen past and present who cope with this particular environment. Alternating with bad-land buttes are pretty little hollows with grassy bottoms that catch and hold the moisture, the lush grass contrasting with the bare dry buttes above. No quarter section of land could be ignored during roundup time. Each little basin over the many square miles would have to be physically checked for the small band of cows it would likely hold. "On the level or rolling prairies the cattle can be seen a long way off, and it is an easy matter to gather and to drive them; but in the Bad Lands every little pocket, basin, and coulee has to be searched, every gorge or ravine entered, and the dense patches of brushwood and spindling, wind-beaten trees closely examined."[2]

Water, of course, was everything. Springs were developed by hand, by digging into their source and installing perforated pipe that ran to a collection box, then into a tank. The same method is used today, though with more sophistication and the help of backhoes to do the digging. After using the hand pump in the campground to bucket-water Redstar and Partner, we found, just a half mile from camp, a modern spring development, two big stock tanks brimming with clear, cold water.

But there were older springs in the coulees above, as well, some with the rusted remains of stock tanks that might have dated nearly to TR's era. That the trail winds through these coulees is no accident, of course. Today the route conveniences the recreational rider, but earlier trails, made by cattle and, before them, bison, would have converged on these natural springs.

5. Emily and Redstar above the Little Missouri on the
Maah Daah Hey Trail. Courtesy of Dan and Emily Aadland.

We rode past the entrance to the national park parcel that
houses TR's cabin, reserving our entrance into it for the next
day, and ascended the trail onto the high bluffs that overlook
the valley of the Little Missouri. Dry, the trail was mild by our
mountain standards, though there were occasional ledges on
nearly vertical hillsides. But we speculated that we'd rather
not venture onto parts of it right after a rainstorm. The trail's
powdery surface would quickly turn into the region's famous
gumbo, slick as grease through segments of the trail where a
misstep could mean a long fall.

Of course, the cattleman hasn't the leisure to choose his
weather when there's work to be done. TR and his men rode
these bluffs on, and, of course, off, similar trails made by bovines. During spring roundup, wet weather was common, and
the riding not for the faint of heart.

In the Bad Lands the riders unhesitatingly go down and over places where it seems impossible that a horse should even stand. The line of horsemen will quarter down the side of a butte, where every pony has to drop from ledge to ledge like a goat, and will go over the shoulder of a soapstone cliff, when wet and slippery, with a series of plunges and scrambles which if unsuccessful would land horses and riders in the bottom of the canyon-like wash-out below. In descending a clay butte after a rain, the pony will put all four feet together and slide down to the bottom almost or quite on his haunches. In very wet weather the Bad Lands are absolutely impassible; but if the ground is not slippery, it is a remarkable place that can shake the matter-of-course confidence felt by the rider in the capacity of his steed to go anywhere.[3]

"No thanks to any of that," Emily and I agreed. We've done our share of rough-country riding. We, too, have searched steep coulees and thick brush for recalcitrant bulls and loped over slopes during adrenalin-driven chases for uncooperative cows, but we came to TR country with a thoroughly recreational mindset. Neither of us had a desire to test the limits of Redstar or Partner off trail in the Bad Lands; riding through this terrain we readily deferred to the horsemanship of those sinewy young men of the past who rode steeplechase style over treacherous terrain and enjoyed every minute of it.

Enjoyment of the trail for us was in the special beauty of the place. The route wound through patches of aromatic flowering shrubs I couldn't identify by name (my knowledge of botany and ornithology is embarrassingly scant compared to TR's). Would that the average hunter or outdoorsman today had 5 percent of TR's knowledge of and enthusiasm for the myriad species of birds and animals *not* considered hunters' quarry.

We rode high up the west valley wall, the Little Missouri a muddy thread far below us, TR's ranch domain, which straddled the river, spreading around us. Topped out, we found civilization in the form of a gravel road, a good one, recently improved to service the oil wells now sprouting like dandelions throughout the border country between Montana and North Dakota. We watched a helicopter land on the pad next to one oil well a quarter mile to our left and a service truck pull into another site to our right.

The trail crossed the road, resuming at a wooden post bearing the logo of the Maah Daah Hey, the image of a turtle. Such posts are placed wherever there might be doubt about the course of the trail. It would be exceedingly difficult to get lost.

Then it was down a knife ridge and back into buck brush; below was an inviting grove of cottonwoods and a small stream along which we progressed through grass belly deep on the horses. This would have been a fine place to camp. The trail here was relatively level, a dirt path that made us wish for wind in our faces. The horses, pleased, picked up a running walk alternating with a canter that brought us to still another road and an oil well nestled in the valley bottom. This time the trail skirted close to its plunging iron boom, and the smell of sulfur was pungent in our nostrils. Would the horses spook at this iron monster, its looming, moving mass, its strange sounds and smells?

Surprisingly, no. Though we tightened our legs in anticipation, Redstar and Partner studied the fenced compound and its strange machinery but continued to march. We relaxed a quarter mile beyond, when we reached a gate and a salt trough, the smell of the cows that had recently congregated there a welcome replacement for the alien air we had briefly breathed.

What would TR think? What would he make of his home ranchland sprinkled liberally with roads, oil wells, and helicopter landing pads? Who knows, really? In this year of a presidential campaign we heard the name "Teddy Roosevelt" frequently invoked. Politicians take joy in aligning themselves with the great leaders of the past. Few presidential candidates fail to claim themselves direct intellectual and moral descendants of Thomas Jefferson, though at least half of them are really children of Jefferson's great philosophical antagonist Alexander Hamilton.

In this particular election year, TR's star seemed to have risen again, perhaps because the candidates claimed an ability to shake up the status quo, to bust the trusts, to take on the special interests. But it's so easy to cherry-pick the past, to adopt those particular qualities of a given historical figure that support one's present agenda. Yes, TR was the Great Conservationist, the man who more than any other we should thank for the preservation of undeveloped space, for origination of our system of national forests and expansion of our national parks, for the saving of wildlife habitat. And, yes, TR was perfectly happy to help eradicate the wolf, to defeat intruders into what he considered "our" space on the globe, and to "improve" nature with massive projects such as the Panama Canal as great exercises of Man's ingenuity and ability.

He was many things. Perhaps he would see this development as the ruination of a land he loved. But it is just as likely he would rejoice at the thought that the rich black crude pumped on his very ranch was fueling some of the engines that moved the world.

The western loop of the Maah Daah Hey ended soon after we passed the oil well, the trail edging east again and across a flat section of cattle range. We worked our way through the scattered cattle, Partner demonstrating his usual suspicion of any that weren't black. A half mile to our south were irrigated alfalfa fields. The previous summer must have been a good one for hay production, since a big stack of round bales remained, having not been used during winter. A tractor was loading bales onto a flatbed truck, work familiar to me.

6. Partner and author on the Little Missouri.
Courtesy of Dan and Emily Aadland.

Then it was time to drop back into TR's valley on a ledge trail that would have been precarious if wet. But first we had to simply stop and look—the view from above the tops of the cottonwoods was grand, the trees themselves a bit stark so soon after the cold spring, the buds on their branches just edging toward friendly green. A pheasant squawked below us. We plunged down to the trees, the horses spirited in anticipation of a rest and a bite of grass, their riders equally ready for a rest and a sandwich while sitting on a big cottonwood log and staring at the big brown Little Missouri.

• • •

We returned after our sixteen-mile ride to find the campground still pleasantly deserted. Going farther north on the Maah Daah Hey would have involved swimming the flooding river, and that held no appeal whatsoever. (Emily's resolution in that direction had only been strengthened by reading TR's description of the flooding river in *Ranch Life and the Hunting Trail*.) We planned instead a leisurely morning, perhaps with a short ride south, and then a hike into the national park acreage to the site of TR's Elkhorn cabin.

But nature, at dawn, planned otherwise. It had been building during the night, a screaming west wind, and though morning was sunny the wind was of the sort that would send your hat in the direction of Minnesota. The idea of another ride to the tops of the bluffs, this time south of the Elkhorn, had little appeal. Yesterday, even before this wind event, the breeze above the valley had been formidable.

So, basking in the luxury of recreationalists who had no real *need* to ride, we altered our plans. We would have a good breakfast, then ride the low ground in the valley bottom and visit TR's home.

With the wind at our backs it wasn't bad, though I soon cursed my decision to stay with my cowboy hat rather than swap it for a baseball cap. The result of that decision was that I had to ride much of the time with my right hand clamping the hat more tightly on my head and often simply removing it and tucking it under my arm. At least I could be pleased that Partner's neck rein was finished enough that two-handed riding was never required. The horses' tails blew toward the vertical, and the sagebrush and buckbrush sang in the wind. We watered our geldings at the stock tanks, then crossed the flat on which, the afternoon before, while returning to camp, we had enjoyed a quarter-mile lope.

In scrub timber near the National Park gate we tied our horses securely, grabbed our cameras, and walked through the gate into the Elkhorn enclave. In the cottonwoods of the river bottom, the wind was all but gone. After a pleasant ten-minute walk, we stood at the cabin site, easily discernable (even without

the help of park signs) by the big sandstone boulders that described the perimeter of TR's cabin.

The early ranchers did not have access to concrete. Portland
cement and the mixers necessary to combine it with sand, gravel,
and water, were a luxury that came later. The alternative to
laying a solid foundation was to assemble big sandstone boulders and skid them in on a stoneboat, a flat, sled-like affair,
pulled by a team of horses. These boulders were dug in and leveled, fine tuning being done with wood blocks atop the rocks,
to bear the weight of floor beams. Many old barns and houses, including the ancestral home on our ranch, were built this
way, with no continuous foundation.

Built of cottonwood logs by Roosevelt's Maine imports Sewall
and Dow during the winter of 1884–85, the structure was large
for its time, thirty by sixty feet, with eight rooms.

> My home ranch-house stands on the river brink. From
> the low, long veranda, shaded by leafy cottonwoods, one
> looks across sand bars and shallows to a strip of meadow-
> land, behind which rises a line of sheer cliffs and grassy
> plateaus. This veranda is a pleasant place in the sum-
> mer evenings when a cool breeze stirs along the river
> and blows in the faces of the tired men, who loll back in
> their rocking-chairs (what true American does not en-
> joy a rocking chair?), book in hand—though they do not
> often read the books, but rock gently to and fro, gazing
> sleepily out at the weird-looking buttes opposite, until
> their sharp outlines grow indistinct and purple in the
> after-glow of the sunset. The story-high house of hewn
> logs is clean and neat, with many rooms, so that one can
> be alone if one wishes to. The nights in summer are cool
> and pleasant, and there are plenty of bear-skins and buf-
> falo robes, trophies of our own skill, with which to bid
> defiance to the bitter cold of winter.[4]

The line that sticks with me is "so that one can be alone if one wishes to." A man torn by grief, living in a day when showing emotion was unseemly, even "unmanly," needed a place to be alone. And doing so grew increasingly difficult, for Sewall and Dow soon moved their wives and children to the Badlands, and the ladies eventually presented their husbands and their patron with baby sons. The log house at the Elkhorn ranch became a lively place indeed!

And that private room in the ranch house was needed as well for writing. Theodore Roosevelt was (and is) our most published president. Beginning with his first published work, at nineteen, *Summer Birds of the Adirondacks*, which concerned a subject that would always remain dear to him, TR wrote (and read) incessantly. Written partly while TR was still in college, his first scholarly work, *The Naval War of 1812*, was so respected that it became required reading at the Naval Academy.

Indeed, part of TR's motivation for the move north from the Maltese Cross cabin was his constant compulsion to write. The Medora area was not Grand Central Station, but the location of TR's first cabin was an invitation to the passing cowboy, the neighbor who wanted to visit. Social as Roosevelt was, he had the writer's need for quiet. So he set out horseback looking for a spot to build a new ranch headquarters. On the advice of a neighboring rancher, he looked north down the Little Missouri, where he found a pretty meadow and, in it, locked together from an earlier fatal combat, a pair of elk antlers. He would build the Elkhorn Ranch on this spot.

Since TR's residence at Elkhorn, the river has meandered east, so that the home site, on a nice little flat elevated above the floodplain, could no longer be considered to be "on the river brink." Although the river was at flood stage during our visit, the old channel in front of the house was dry. Rivers on flat valley bottoms will meander, given a chance, the curves and oxbows nature's way of slowing the flow. Flood control is

7. TR's Elkhorn cabin. Courtesy of the Boone and Crockett Club.

already built into natural rivers. The trouble starts with Man's dikes and dams and his penchant for building in spots Nature reserved for the river.

The view, however, is little altered. There are still sand-bars and mudflats, and a pretty grassy meadow across on the east side of the river, bordered behind by rugged bluffs. Yes, it would be pleasant here, and if Roosevelt had been a man for whom a pleasant life was the ultimate objective, he might have lived out his days on this spot. But as the world knows, he was not such a man.

• • •

We untie Redstar and Partner from the scrubby trees where biting flies have harassed them. Glad to see us, they shift nervously, reluctant to stand still while we mount. Headed into the wind, we tighten our reins, and the horses arch their necks, collecting into a swift single-foot, anxious in the manner of all horses everywhere on windy days when dust rises from the sagebrush and the crows overhead quarter into the wind and let it take them.

I scold Partner for threatening to spook at shapes stirring behind a board fence at a cattle guard, movement he can see only through the slits between the boards, telling him, "They're just cows, damn it, Partner, just cows!" He straightens out with a parting snort.

The wire gate by the cattle guard is problematic now. Dismounted, I must hold Partner's reins, along with my hat, then open and close the tight gate with one arm, dust blowing in my face. Partner stands while I clamber aboard, and we turn toward our camp, marveling that throughout all this the meadowlarks still sing in the sage, their songs cut short when the wind steals some of their notes. I love the birds, always will, but I'm afraid that knowing what they meant to TR might have forever sobered their song for me.

> The meadow lark is a singer of a higher order [compared with the plains skylark], deserving to rank with the best. Its song has length, variety, power and rich melody; and there is in it sometimes a cadence of wild sadness, inexpressibly touching. Yet I cannot say that either song would appeal to others as it appeals to me; for to me it comes forever laden with a hundred memories and associations; with the sight of dim hills reddening in the dawn, with a breath of cool morning winds blowing across lonely plains, with the scent of flowers on the sunlit prairie, with the motion of fiery horses, with all the strong thrill of eager and buoyant life. I doubt if any man can judge dispassionately the bird songs of his own country; he cannot disassociate them from the sights and sounds of the land that is so dear to him.[5]

We stop at the two brimming stock tanks; the water into which our horses plunge their noses has been converted by the wind into a microcosm of a wavy lake replete with mini-whitecaps and spray. Partner and Redstar drink in the manner of all horses, all animals that have once been prey, by intermittently throwing their heads into the air to check for any danger that may have crept up while their heads were down. Then they drink again.

We're to camp in a flash. Here it is quieter, the shelter of the coulee having taken some of the edge from the wind. We slow to a walk up the gravel road toward our camper. "Look!" Emily whispers, pointing toward the barbed-wire fence to our right. On it are a dozen mountain bluebirds flitting above the wires, then landing again, their blue the gorgeous saturated tone of the Montana sapphires I once saw emerging from drab gravel being washed in a geologist's office. The birds brighten the tall yellow grass behind them like Christmas lights against dark spruce. These birds, too, are TR's.

CHAPTER THREE

Horses, Rifles, and a Man Named Magnus

Rosie and Elmer; mule deer in the sage; TR's arsenal; the New Yorker
and the Dane; Partner and Paycheck, Manitou and Muley

ROSIE, THE FIRST HORSE I could truly consider my own, could
run like the wind. After some learning, she could cut out a
cow quickly enough to jar your teeth. She was also given to
unreasoning upsets, and she absolutely refused to be tied up.
She'd break any lead rope, halter, or reins with which you attempted to hold her, and when my father-in-law, Elmer, tried
a three-quarter-inch nylon rope tied with a bowline around
her neck, a rig with which you could pull a truck out of the
barrow pit, she strained and bucked and squealed until Elmer, convinced she'd ruin every muscle and tendon in her
body, cut her loose.

But Rosie's imperfections were minor to me. I carried a
set of rawhide hobbles tied to the saddle strings. A sucker for
this type of restraint, she would turn her attention to grazing
whenever I stopped to fix a fence or stalk a deer. I'd pile off,
slip on the hobbles, and go about my business, knowing she
would never stray very far.

And it was with Rosie I first felt full rapport with a horse.
My earlier experiences working on various ranches tended to
involve the last pick from the rancher's remuda, the horse the

hired kid could ride because no one else particularly wanted to, the crow-hopper, the one that balked or lagged. My town-kid lack of skill no doubt exacerbated any such deficiencies.

Even then, though, during my teen years, when I worked summers on ranches, there were good experiences with equines, and I rode whenever I got the chance. There were recreational town rides with my friends on horses we borrowed from a tolerant retired rancher who boarded them nearby. And there was a solo triumph horseback that sticks in my mind from fifty years ago—a half-day battle with a bull, a running contest through a brushy creek bottom that left me bloody and exhausted.

The rancher had trusted me, at age fifteen, to be in charge of his place during a brief vacation. I milked the small dairy herd—twenty cows or so—and did the irrigating. Too small in the dairy business to mess with artificial insemination, the rancher maintained a Holstein bull to service his dairy cows. The bull in question was a three-year-old that would be sold that fall, because dairy bulls become big and quick and dangerous in maturity.

Beef bulls, Angus and such, are no match in size, speed, and agility for a Holstein bull, and the bull in question loved a good fight. He had begun sojourns up the valley that resembled military campaigns, destroying the fences in his path, bawling his challenge to any bull foolish enough to take him on. He'd whip each defender thoroughly, then, bored with the lack of competition, head up the valley to look for a more worthy opponent. He chose to launch one such rampage when I was alone on the ranch.

So I caught the big black horse whose name I've forgotten, jumped on bareback for what I thought would be a brief ride, and commenced a seesaw retrieval attempt. Several times I found the bull, bluffed him out, and got him headed back to the ranch only to have him duck into nearly impenetrable

8. Elmer. Courtesy of Dan and Emily Aadland.

brush and manage to outflank us and head up the valley again. Finally I triumphed. The bull was in the corral, my clothes were torn, and my arms were covered with dried blood from the many scratches I'd sustained charging through brush. Worse, my face was a mess from a nosebleed I got when I leaned too low over the horse's neck as I ducked brush. The horse spooked and threw his head into the air, and the top of his unyielding neck bashed my face. But I felt good. With the help of a good horse, I had won.

Once we got to know each other, Rosie, in spite of her imperfections, showed me the meaning of "becoming one with the horse." An unsophisticated rider, I knew of leg cues and lead changes only from books. What I did know and feel was that Rosie went where I wanted her to go with the slightest movement of the reins in my left hand, that she lifted into a lope at the smallest squeeze from my legs, that she could cut a cow so quickly she'd nearly step out from under me. And there was satisfaction in realizing that although she had arrived at the ranch with basic training, I had since taught her many of these things.

She never quite received Elmer's approval, even though he had picked her out at an auction and had eventually given her to me on the agreement that I wouldn't commence raising colts. Born in 1903 (during TR's presidency), mounted on arch-necked Brownie, the last of his single-footers, Elmer would shake his head at Rosie's occasionally irrational antics and mutter, "hot blood," a reaction I always found ironic. By any comparison I could divine, Brownie was the "hotter," exuding spirit even in his late teens. But Elmer knew him, had trained him, had lived through a nearly fatal accident with him. Brownie was an extension of his own body.

And, of course, Rosie was not gaited in any fashion, a serious deficiency in Elmer's mind. Like his father Magnus before him, Elmer believed no horse qualified as a complete saddle horse unless it possessed a smooth, four-beat intermediate gait, all of which (though he knew them individually) Elmer lumped together under the term "single-foot."

"You've got to ride a gaited horse some day, Dan," he told me often. "There's nothing so keen." Brownie, of saddlebred lineage a couple of generations back, had little gaitedness left, but he'd rein back into a rack if you spurred him and collected him just right. And even his trot was silky smooth compared to Rosie's.

But I do remember one genuine smile of approval directed at Rosie and at me as her teacher. We had noticed a cottonwood perhaps a foot in diameter blown down and now straddling the irrigation ditch west of the river. We rode on, Elmer mentioning that he would drag it off the ditch the next time he passed by with the Jeep. There was no hurry; the tree lay well above the water's surface, so it was not damming the ditch.

I suppose my ego was involved, along with my steadily advancing admiration for this mare that was revealing herself to me. I was tired of hearing her criticized, particularly by a man so gentle he rarely said a negative thing. Each day it was my job to ride across the river to change the irrigation dam, to spill crystal water from the Rosebud River across the hayfield in a new location. The day after discovering the fallen tree, I grabbed a stout rope, climbed into the saddle, and spurred Rosie across the river at our ford, then lifted her into a lope toward the fallen tree at the ditch.

Using a "rolling hitch," a way of tying onto a log so that a pull tends to rotate the log initially, making it easier to drag, I secured the rope, then remounted. Carefully plotting the likely path of the tree trunk so that it wouldn't hit Rosie in the rear when it moved (I was not confident enough in the mare to relish that idea), I took two dallies around the horn and moved Rosie forward until the rope was taut. Angling my pull to break the tree trunk loose on one end, I tightened my legs. Rosie lowered her head and pulled without panic. The tree moved as if on grease. We dragged it well off the ditch, then changed our dam and went home.

I said nothing. A couple of weeks passed. Eventually work took us toward the place on the ditch where the tree had been, and I noticed Elmer downshift and steer the Jeep to the right. I knew what he had in mind, but I played dumb. He stopped the Jeep and stared through its streaky windshield for an instant. "Why, it's been dragged off!"

"Oh, yeah," I said, trying to be as nonchalant as possible. "I dragged it off with Rosie a while back." I said it as if it were an afterthought, a minor matter I'd nearly forgotten.

"No kidding!" he said. And then he smiled. Nothing more was necessary.

• • •

Nearly a half century has gone by since I rode Rosie alongside Brownie carrying Elmer while doing ranch work and on other occasions alongside the same brown gelding carrying Emily for rides to the hills, our favorite pastime. Today, riding up the side of our east valley wall on the black colt named Partner, I reflect on just how a good horse cuts through time, through decades, even centuries. Partner is not yet the cow horse Rosie became, but only because of his aging trainer; I've taken him very slowly, in a way that now suits me, and he is coming along. He is bigger and stronger than Rosie ever was, and he has the running walk Elmer coveted during those late years when arena horses transported by trailer became the local rage.

The marriage of a good horse and a good rifle with game for the taking, winter meat on the hoof, is in my blood as it was in Theodore Roosevelt's and in that of all early men of the American West. Just when I first thought that straddling a horse, your knee touching a saddle scabbard, was simply *the* place to be, I can't recall. I can't recall ever thinking any other way.

But for my very earliest hunts I had the rifle and the horse but not the scabbard, a luxury out of reach for a cash-poor college student. No matter. From webbing purchased at an Army–Navy store, Emily sewed me a serviceable sling, not adjustable but sized to allow carrying the Marlin 30-30 slung crosswise on my back, bandito style. I'd found money to buy a cheap $2\frac{1}{2}$-power scope, and this, mounted on a rifle I'd earned working my first ranch job at age fourteen, seemed an effective outfit indeed.

I remember the pungent sage of October, the blue Beartooth Mountains to our south, the smell of horse sweat, the sight of mule deer lining out on their pogo-stick legs as they burst out of buckbrush turned scarlet with fall. Emily, with no desire to become a hunter at that stage of her life, was often along. Two tags were standard Montana issue with one's hunting license in those days. Having grown up in a preacher's family where meat and money were in short supply, I had nothing against using my first tag on a doe, then trying for big antlers on the second.

Perched on the highest point of our east range, we would spot the deer from afar. Then, using the terrain, we would duck our horses down into the coulees and approach on low ground, out of sight of the deer, often getting nearly in range. Emily then held the horses while I sneaked over the last rise, ready to assume a sitting position and fire away. Sometimes I was greeted with the sight of deer spooked and lined out a half mile away. Other times, they were within two hundred yards, and I was able to put one down.

Then there was another smell, not unpleasant, from the rising heat of a deer field dressed, the recent life in her replaced by movement to the food chain, to the promise of Swiss steaks simmered by Emily or floured ones fried by her mother, Nora.

We did not attempt to pack deer down to the ranch buildings on our horses in those years. When hunting on the ranch it was quicker and easier to ride home after the field dressing and get my father-in-law's Jeep. Elmer usually came along as well, jolly at the thought of new meat in the larder. We'd cram ourselves into the tin cab of the Jeep and pick our way up the ledge two-track through "Big Coulee," then thread our way through sagebrush to retrieve the deer.

I'm a lucky man in that most of these things are still with me, though I recall with some envy those young days of easy satisfaction with simpler things. Emily still hunts with me some of the time, occasionally with rifle in hand, and the ranch and even the Jeep are still here. There are fine memories of her parents, of early horses, of good times. And the rifle, the Sears version of the Marlin Model 336 chambered for the .30-30, rides today in the overhead rack of my pickup.

For handiness, I replaced the scope with what is known as a "ghost ring" peep sight, a sight with a fairly large rear aperture. The ring blurs out while you look through it so that you are hardly conscious that it's there, thus the term "ghost ring." I was reminded last fall of just how well some old things work. I had already shot a decent buck and now had an antlerless whitetail tag to fill. When a fat yearling doe ran over a rise at 175 yards I dropped to one knee just as she saw me and screeched to a halt. The .30-30 barked and she went down, hammered in place by a caliber more than a century old and a rifle that I've owned for fifty years.

Even in those early years I knew that for our open country this rifle was not the flat-shooting left-handed bolt action I craved. The scoped .270 was a few years away. But trajectory is a relative thing. Theodore Roosevelt's first encounter with the .30-30 was an eye opener. After years of hunting with big-bore black-powder cartridges, powerful enough but with rainbow trajectories, the new smokeless round was a revelation. "In the fall of 1896 I spent a fortnight on the range with the new ranch wagon. I was using for the first time one of the new small-caliber, smokeless-powder rifles, with the usual soft-nosed bullet."[1]

So different was the trajectory of the new cartridge that TR tended to "take a coarse bead" (hold the front sight too high in the notch of the rear) and miss by shooting over the animal's back.

The band [of antelope] had just reached the ridge crest about 220 yards from me across the head of the valley, and had halted for a moment to look around. They were starting as I raised my rifle, but the trajectory is very flat with these small-bore smokeless powder weapons, and taking a coarse front sight I fired at a young buck which was broadside to me. There was no smoke, and as the band raced away I saw him sink backward, the ball having broken his hips. . . .

The last shot I got was when I was out with Joe Ferris, in whose company I had killed my first buffalo, just thirteen years before, and not very far from this same spot. . . . Toward midday, after riding and tramping over a vast extent of broken, sun-scorched country, we got within range of a small band lying down in a little cup-shaped hollow in the middle of a great flat. I did not have a close shot, for they were running about 180 yards off. The buck was rearmost, and at him I aimed; the bullet struck him in the flank, coming out of the opposite shoulder, and he fell in his next bound. As we stood over him, Joe shook his head, and said, "I guess that little rifle is the ace;" And I told him I guessed so too.[2]

Roosevelt was as much a progressive where rifles were concerned as he was politically, and he lived in an age of rapid advancement in the design of guns available for hunters. Rifles for both hunting and for military use took quantum leaps forward between the Civil War and the turn of the century.

Before the Civil War, the only accurate shoulder-fired weapons available in America were the Kentucky rifle and its larger-bore successors. Built primarily by German gunsmiths in Pennsylvania, these legendary rifles were individually crafted masterpieces, rifled one groove at a time, steel impeccably mated with wood and brass. Their cost must have been extremely high. The rifle of a frontier family probably represented as large a chunk of the budget as an automobile would today. When Boone of A. B. Guthrie's novel *The Big Sky* runs away west after stealing his father's rifle, he's administering a mighty financial blow not only to his abusive father but to the rest of his family as well.

Big, tough western animals—bison, elk, and grizzly—tended to shrug off the relatively light balls fired by rifles of only .36 caliber. A lead ball of this diameter weighs only around 80 grains, and propelled with black powder at only 1,200 to 1,400 feet per second, their energy was comparable to cartridges such as the .32-20, a round we'd consider today to be suitable for only small game. Lewis and Clark recorded the number of hits a grizzly could take from such weapons and still keep coming. Roosevelt called them "pea-rifles."

Enter the Hawken brothers and other gunsmiths like them. The western need for sizeable chunks of lead was answered by big bores. There was really no other way to increase power. The projectile could be made heavier and the corresponding powder charge greater, but the velocity ceiling tied to black powder as a propellant was still there. Velocity was going to stay under 1,500 feet per second, for the most part.

Meanwhile, across the pond, the British, Germans, and other colonizers were running into the same problem in Africa and India. In response to the size and ferocity of elephants, rhinos, Cape buffalo, and lions, gun makers in these nations were producing massive muzzle-loaders that killed on both ends. One reads of "four-gauge" bores—a caliber of a size to throw a ball weighing one fourth pound—and of recoil so fierce that nosebleed (and worse) was the usual result for the poor man who pulled the trigger. And, of course, on all these continents, we're still talking about single-shot muzzle-loaders, or in the case of the British, double-barreled muzzle-loaders. With a nasty animal, one had better shoot well or at least be able to count on cool marksmanship from a small army of similarly armed buddies surrounding him.

The Industrial Revolution and the Civil War (and nineteenth-century warfare in other parts of the world) changed all this.

Breech-loading rifles and repeaters began to appear, the battlefield a primary testing ground. Cartridges with paper casings were tried first, but they were eventually replaced with brass. The earliest repeaters tended to be chambered for wimpy cartridges, the reason the U.S. Army stuck with the Trapdoor Springfield single shot .45-70 through the Plains Indian wars of the 1870s. That decision is much berated by history buffs who claim repeating rifles in the hands of the Sioux and Cheyenne had much to do with Custer's demise. But that's an unlikely scenario.

The army had tried and rejected the Spencer lever actions unveiled during the Civil War. The long-range effectiveness of their lightweight rimfire cartridges was nil. The Springfield .45-70, by contrast, was effective as far out as its 405-grain conical bullet could travel, and reloading was far more rapid than it was in the muzzle-loader days. Thus the Springfield stayed in the army system for some additional years, and a number were still in use during the Spanish–American War. The Custer argument fails to hold up for other reasons, too. Although it's true that the Plains tribes had acquired some repeating rifles, the bodies of most of Custer's men were found bludgeoned to death. And the Sioux sniper who did much to help keep Reno's men dug in on a hilltop several miles away from Custer, who was shooting accurately at five hundred yards, was using the army's standard, a Springfield .45-70!

On the civilian front, the years after the Civil War saw development of heavy breech-loading single-shot rifles like the Sharps, specifically developed for long-range bison hunting, and the first of the big lever actions from Marlin and Winchester, fast repeaters that eventually became TR's favorites.

It was just seven years after Custer's demise that the young Roosevelt arrived to hunt, carrying a battery of firearms that was varied and interesting.

When I first came to the plains I had a heavy Sharps rifle, 45-120, shooting an ounce and a quarter of lead, and a 50-calibre, double-barrelled English express. Both of these, especially the latter, had a vicious recoil; the former was very clumsy; and above all they were neither of them re-peaters; for a repeater or magazine gun is as much supe-rior to a single or double-barreled breech-loader as the latter is to a muzzle-loader. I threw them both aside: and have instead a 40-90 Sharps for very long range work; a 50-115 6-shot Bullard express, which has the velocity, shock, and low trajectory of the English gun; and, better than either, a 45-75 half-magazine Winchester.[3]

In the caliber nomenclature of the day, the first number designated bore diameter, the second the grains of black pow-der used to propel the bullet. Sometimes a third number was added to designate the bullet weight in grains: .45-70-405. The last rifle mentioned, the .45-75 Winchester, became Roosevelt's favorite, and he extols its virtues for use on everything from "grizzly bear to big-horn." This rifle, which he called, "by all odds the best weapon [he] ever had" was a Winchester Mod-el 76 lever action.

Introduced with much promotion in the year of the nation's centennial, the Model 76 was Winchester's attempt to produce a lever action capable of handling the big, tough game of the American West. The company's earlier lever actions, like the Spencer and Henry repeaters, had been chambered for mod-est calibers. Winchester wanted to market a rifle with similar power to the military's .45-70, but needed a somewhat short-er cartridge to fit their new design. The .45-75, a bottleneck cartridge, was short enough to fit, yet flung a 350-grain bul-let with enough authority that the Model 1876 became the first repeating rifle to gain respect out West on game as large as bison.

Of course, big game was only part of TR's hunting picture.

9. TR with son Kermit in Africa, after presidency.
Courtesy of the Boone and Crockett Club.

For the ducks and geese of the Little Missouri and the grouse of the sage, he had several shotguns, including his "little ranch gun," what the Europeans call a "drilling," a double-barreled sixteen-gauge shotgun with a .45-70 barrel underneath.

But TR was ever tuned to advancements by the makers of sporting firearms. The successor to his beloved Winchester Model 76 was the Model 1886, a heavy, powerful masterpiece created by John Browning, perhaps the greatest designer of firearms both civilian and military that the United States has ever produced. The '86 could handle the big, powerful cartridges, the .45-70 and the slightly longer .45-90, most often mentioned by Roosevelt. But he wasn't done yet. Still to come was the little but impressive smokeless round, the .30-30 discussed above, and the big .405 Winchester caliber chambered in an innovative lever action, dubbed the Model 1895. This was his "big medicine" gun on the African safari that followed his presidency, his favorite rifle for lion.

But on that safari Roosevelt, continually the pioneer in adopting the latest firearms for hunters, ushered in as well the era of the bolt action, along with the world's favorite hunting caliber, the .30-06. His "little Springfield" was chambered for the prototype cartridge labeled the .30-03, which evolved with slight changes into the caliber that became the American standard in military use from World War I through Korea. Certainly, a president's advocacy of the .30-06 did much to jumpstart its popularity among hunters.

But through this succession of hunting arms, Roosevelt kept his perspective on rifles, that they are mere tools of the hunter, that power and rapidity of fire will not make up for lousy marksmanship. In an age of iron sights, his poor vision was more problematic than it would be today, when most rifles carry optical sights. TR shot badly quite often, but well, too, and he knew better than to blame the rifle when things went south. More than once he reminds readers that the man behind the gun is the all-important factor.

And I suspect he would add, in looking back at a lifetime in hunting, that the horse under that hunter was equally important. There were no ATVs (thank God) in TR's time. His lifetime saw the growth from invention to proliferation of motorized vehicles, but he never thought of them as tools for the hunter. Yes, a train carried him into his first hunting territory, but it was the horse that took him on the hunt itself, and that was true throughout the United States and even in Africa in those days before the Land Rover or Toyota.

• • •

So today as I press Partner into a running walk up the old two-track, once a spur of the famous Bozeman Trail, my thoughts have turned from horses to rifles and back to horses again. And as I look down into this south-central Montana valley, at the site of the second Crow Agency, home to that tribe until 1892, at the ranch house occupied from the 1890s by Emily's family, I think of another man, a Danish immigrant named Magnus. And I marvel at his influence on me, even though he died before I was born and did not leave writings for me to read in the way TR did. And yet I feel I know him. And in spite of vast differences between Magnus and Theodore, the two somehow relate for me.

Magnus did leave a journal, and I remember seeing bits of it before it was destroyed in a fire. I remember leather binding and yellowed pages covered mostly with records of purchases and expenses, milk cows bought and horses sold, the neat handwriting first in Danish, then in a mixture of Danish and English, and finally primarily in the language of his new homeland, though in a broken version of it. His name started out as Magnus Jensen but became Americanized to Johnson, not a change, really, but a translation.

Born in 1868, ten years after Theodore Roosevelt, Magnus hailed from the Danish Island of Bornholm, a rolling piece of volcanic rock in the Baltic Sea, closer to Sweden than to Denmark, its real estate having been a bone of contention between the two countries through history. Magnus, like many in Bornholm, was a dairyman. He grew up with none of TR's wealth or educational opportunity but sought it by coming to America at sixteen after finishing the Danish version of high school.

The mid-1880s saw him in the Helena, Montana, area, then near White Sulphur Springs, Montana, where he capitalized on mining ventures by producing a different sort of white gold—dairy products, milk, butter, and cheese so craved by miners that, with his cousin as a partner in the enterprise, Magnus thrived. TR, who kept a milk cow or two at the Elkhorn ranch, mentions how scarce milk was in the West, how fine an addition to the larder a milk cow provides, and how few ranches bother with one. Such must have been doubly true of the bustling mining camps in Montana. Magnus's business appears to have been very successful.

The trails of the two men briefly crossed in 1885. Traveling through St. Paul, Minnesota, on his return from a couple of months in the East, TR remarked to a reporter that he was on his way to Helena, Montana, after which he would return to Medora.[4]

Magnus bought during this time a saddle made in Helena, one we still own and have restored, a Sam Stagg double-rigged A-fork (swells did not appear on western saddles until around 1900) with a Cheyenne roll on the cantle.[5] And he *used* that saddle. Family lore has it that he found the location for his dream ranch during trips to the Crow Reservation to buy horses. Traveling by rail to what is now the town of Columbus, saddle (no doubt) over his shoulder, Magnus would look over the Crow horses, buy a dozen or more untrained ones, then, picking out one with a single-foot and an easy way of going, break it over a couple of days. Finally, he would use it to drive the herd of new acquisitions back to the White Sulphur Springs area, where he would break them for sale to nearby cowboys.

Today, this matter of herding horses on a green broke animal so recently part of a free-running herd boggles the mind and tightens the belly of any true horseman. I can see it: a corral at the Crow Agency grounds near which Magnus eventually settled; a horse but three days along in training, humpy under the saddle; Magnus, his powerful right arm gripping the saddle horn, his left pulling the bridled head around to him in a tight arc, then swinging aboard, ready for those first tight bucks, followed by a gradual lining out until the animal could circle the corral once in each direction. From another compartment of the corral the Crow horses pour out, and Magnus, on a bronc half bucking, half loping, gets south of them and chases them north, not worried about the exact direction, simply staying with them at a headlong gallop for mile after mile until all are tired and consent to be driven by a man on horseback. And then, two hundred more miles!

And so we have two horsemen, an eastern blue-blood becoming a rancher, not without bumps, bruises, and worse, and a Danish dairyman who must have suffered the same until becoming so competent with horses that his son Elmer told me that if Magnus could get one hand on the saddle horn and one foot in the stirrup, no horse could get rid of him. That was strength, brute strength, and it shows, even in the older Magnus overweight from a condition that sounds like diabetes, in the power of his arms and shoulders. And it shows as well in the older TR, formerly the sickly but turbocharged child whose father told him, "You have the mind, but not the body. You must make your body."

And did he ever, bulking up to 225 pounds during his presidency. We are told that most of that was solid muscle from a regime of weight lifting, boxing, and forced marches to the top of any high ground he could find. Still boxing as president, TR was permanently blinded in one eye by his opponent of the day, a young army captain. Who can imagine such a scenario today?

And although JFK is sometimes cited as our first "physical fitness" president, his efforts to shape up the American public, though laudable, pale next to TR's. Roosevelt, discovering that many of the high brass of the military were in woeful physical condition, unable to either hike or ride long distances, cracked the whip. Riding ability among military officers was a standard requirement. Inability to handle a horse at a stiff trot for long distances was shameful. So TR instituted the first officers' physical fitness test, and it was a simple one: all

officers were to either walk fifty miles or ride a hundred over
the course of three days. In his autobiography, TR details the
vehement reaction of a press that had apparently grown as
soft as the officers in question. Beginning with a statement
that would not pass standards of political correctness today,
Roosevelt expresses his belief that the test requirement was
relatively mild:

> This is, of course, a test which many a healthy middle-
> aged woman would be able to meet. But a large portion
> of the press adopted the view that it was a bit of capri-
> cious tyranny on my part: and a considerable number
> of elderly officers, with desk rather than field experi-
> ence, intrigued with their friends in Congress to have
> the order annulled. So one day I took a ride of a little
> over one hundred miles, myself, in company with Sur-
> geon-General Rixey and two other officers. The Virginia
> roads were frozen and in ruts, and in the afternoon and
> evening there was a storm of snow and sleet; and when
> it had thus been experimentally shown, under unfavor-
> able conditions, how easy it was to do in one day the task
> for which the army officers were allowed three days, all
> objections ceased.[6]

But resistance to the order remained. TR details how a one-
armed Marine captain along with two of his lieutenants, following their leader's example, chose to walk the fifty miles
in one day rather than three, only to be reprimanded by the
Navy Department for having disobeyed the president's order
to walk the course in *three* days.

Equally famous (or infamous, depending on one's physical
condition) were President Roosevelt's early morning forced
marches, cabinet members, press corps, and visiting diplo-
mats in tow. These normally culminated with a swim across
the Potomac, even in at times of year when ice crystals clung

10. Magnus. Courtesy of Dan and Emily Aadland.

to the banks. The French ambassador, disrobing for the swim, told a reporter from the (obviously male) press corps that he would retain his gloves "in case they might meet the ladies" on the other side.

Magnus's strength, of course, came from sheer, backbreaking labor, not from any idea that physical strain would be somehow good for him. There were postholes to dig, logs to move, and a dozen big cottonwood trees to saw up and split each winter to answer heating and cooking needs. Elmer told me the trees were cut in winter, when the sap was down, sawed into blocks with a two-man crosscut saw, then, when frozen, split to dry and be burned the following winter.

11. President Roosevelt in 1905 on Colorado bear hunt with
Springfield rifle. Courtesy of the Boone and Crockett Club.

But for all of these differences between the man who became president and the Danish immigrant, there is a similar-
ity about the proud way they sit a horse. Cowboys of their day
would be appalled at the modern image of the "western pleasure" horse, butt in the air, head in the dirt, the horse looking, by their standards, as if it were ashamed of itself. In this
era the saddle horse was the equivalent of a man's sports car
today. It should arch its neck and "look for the next town."
Magnus's, in the photo, is not one of his prettier ones, but one
can imagine that it was a tough customer.

Magnus's spirit and drive, his ability to take command, were similar to TR's but in microcosm. There was no world stage for Magnus, no accomplishments on a grand scale. None were sought. There was the simple immigrant's desire to make a wild chunk of real estate into a home for himself and his family, to continually make his ranch and his region better places. He furnished the land for the first church in the area, then tended it. He did likewise for the first post-reservation school. When he heard that a young child was being abused by two aunts of questionable sanity who fought over the girl, each stealing her away in succession from the other's homestead, he took matters into his own hands. He rode over, picked the child up, placed her on his saddle horse, took her home, and adopted her. She became the Norwegian sibling, my wife's aunt Gert, a lady I remember with a continual laugh in her eyes.

I cannot know whether Magnus was a hunter, but I suspect he was, like nearly everyone in his day, a hunter for sustenance if not for sport or pleasure. We do have his shotgun, a Parker twelve-gauge with exterior hammers, the barrel (unfortunately) of the Damascus type, made by forging a spiral twist of metal around a mandrel instead of boring it from a solid block of steel. Such barrels cannot be trusted to withstand the pressure of modern cartridges.

We do have one story concerning that shotgun, a touching one, and it came from Elmer. I had noticed a small board shelf, perhaps a foot long, high on the gable of the old log barn shown behind the photo of Magnus on page 70. Since the shelf connected to no door or opening in the wall of the barn, I was curious about its purpose. Elmer chuckled when I asked him.

"During the Depression we ate pigeons. Shotgun shells were expensive and scarce, so my dad would sprinkle a little grain on that shelf. When a whole flock of pigeons would crowd onto it he'd let go with one barrel of the twelve-gauge and get the whole bunch." A different time, a different world.

Had Magnus cowboyed in the eastern half of Montana, I could

entertain the fantasy that he just may have met TR, but Magnus's region was farther west. Nor would Magnus have been a delegate to the Stockgrower's conventions in Miles City, frequented by Roosevelt. But there is one time their trails may have crossed.

Magnus, with the common immigrant's determination that each successive generation should enjoy opportunities his own did not have, sent each of his children to a private boarding high school named Billings Polytechnic Institute. There was a new high school in a nearby town, but Magnus wanted something better. The "Poly" offered much more, and students could earn tuition and board by working on the school's farm and in its dairy and kitchen.

During 1918 Theodore Roosevelt, his desire to raise a military unit and lead it to World War I having been turned down by President Wilson, embarked on a different patriotic endeavor. He toured the country giving speeches that urged citizens to support the war effort by buying bonds. His son Quenten, a fighter pilot, had died in France the summer before TR gave his last speech on a campus, at Billings Polytechnic on October 15, 1918. Elmer, my father-in-law, was there in his first year as a student. He once pointed to an upscale condominium cluster south of what is now Rocky Mountain College and said, "To think I plowed that field on my sixteenth birthday when I was a student at the Poly." That would have been the following spring, April 16, 1919.

So Elmer may have been there on the campus that day to hear TR's stirring words. He's no longer here to ask, and one has to speculate as to whether a fifteen-year-old cowboy would have been drawn to that speaker's platform where the famous man was scheduled to appear. Magnus, even, may have been there, for the visit of a famous former president to Magnus's home turf was accompanied by great fanfare and publicity, perhaps justifying a sixty-mile trip in his family's first automobile.

12. TR on October 15, 1918, at the "Poly" in Billings, Montana.
Courtesy of Rocky Mountain College.

Hermann Hagedorn wrote that "the town was filled with the crowds who had come from near and far to see the man who, everybody said, was sure again to be President of the United States."[7]

I cannot know if this happened. I cannot know whether the solidly built Dane stood on a fine fall day under the cottonwoods on campus, turned their brilliant October yellow, stood in that crowd, perhaps with his wiry fifteen-year-old son in tow. But on Partner, on a fine day, threading down through sagebrush as we return to the valley floor, on a ranch that was Magnus's, under a western sky that helped make TR the incredible man he became, I like to think that the two men may have met that day.

• • •

My wife has named the colt "Paycheck," for reasons she won't allow me to disclose. He's a charcoal gray, destined to lighten in color over time, as all gray horses do. He is barely past his second birthday, just old enough to start in training, assuming great care on my part. Although Partner is only five years old, I find myself hankering to start another colt for myself. I'm sixty-four. I can't help asking myself how many more colts there will be for me, started from scratch by me and me alone, and the sheer joy of the process is such that I find myself in genuine need of it.

Working for me is a fine, young horse trainer who does stellar work. But there is something about training one's own from scratch. It's a bit like buying a new pickup truck even though a slightly used one, early depreciation having passed, might be a better investment. You know exactly what that new one has been through from day one.

Roosevelt liked starting his own colts under saddle as well, and he, like me, hedged his bets by picking from among the gentler ones to begin with. He recalled, "When I had the opportunity, I broke my own horses, doing it gently and gradually and spending much time over it, and choosing the horses that seemed gentle to begin with. With these horses I never had any difficulty. But frequently there was neither time nor opportunity to handle our mounts so elaborately. We might get a band of horses, each having been bridled and saddled two or three times, but none of them having been broken beyond the extent implied in this bridling and saddling."[8]

Here and elsewhere he shows his awareness that there are two basic approaches to horse training, and he refutes the present-day stereotype that in the cowboy West all horse training was rapid and forceful. And, like me, he relishes the thought of a few weeks after roundup when he can spend time with his books and a couple of colts. "I would go back to the ranch to turn to my books with added zest for a fortnight. Yet even during these weeks at the ranch there was some outdoor work; for I was breaking two or three colts. I took my time, breaking them gradually and gently, not, after the usual cowboy fashion, in a hurry, by sheer main strength and rough riding, with the attendant danger to the limbs of the man and very probably ruin to the manners of the horse."[9]

In both quotations TR implies the superiority of slower, gentler methods of training, but he is not judgmental, either. He writes at length of the sort of training necessary to prepare large numbers of horses in a very short time, of the professional horse trainer who makes his rounds of the ranches, puts a few rides on each colt, "bucks them out," then turns them over to the cowboys, who put them to immediate work with considerable risk to life and limb. Such training, TR points out, is required by circumstances, by need, by economics. But it's better, when you can, to enjoy the luxury of time. And the end result, too, will likely be superior.

Paycheck seemed to immediately like me. It is nice to be liked. He doesn't sulk after any of the more rigorous increments of training I use, but instead follows me to the corral gate, and if I'm gone for a few moments, comes to the gate to meet me when I return. So tickled am I with him thus far that I remark to Emily that in a couple of years with Partner, Paycheck, and Ruthie, our gaited mule foal, I'll be able to go almost anywhere. She suggests she may have to put a "Running-W" on each of us![10]

During the very first session I taught Paycheck to lead by each foot. On the second he was introduced to the saddle, on the third to the bridle, and on the fourth to ground driving with long lines. Whatever the drill, when moved faster than walking speed he picks up a perfect running walk, head nodding, each foot touching the ground singly in four-four time. He will soon be ready for our first few tentative rides. As I look at him, I see in my mind's eye this pretty gray colt filled out and grown, dapples emerging on his coat, the arched neck proud. And I can see, too, just where the saddle scabbard will lie, and I think of hunts down the trail.

• • •

She was a buckskin mare named Nell, and TR's writings do not tell us a great deal about her. It's likely she had some special place in his memory, however, if only because she was his first western hunting horse, his Rosie, and she carried him faithfully through a hunt that would have been abject misery to most. This was the hunt during which Theodore's enthusiasm for even the soggy worst of it was astounding to those around him.

TR acquired Nell simply because on that first trip west in late 1883, on the quest to find and kill one of the very few buffalo that remained along the Little Missouri, the guides he had hired refused to lend him a horse. Joe and Sylvane Ferris and their friend Merrifield had a profound distrust of Easterners in general and those wearing glasses in particular. They said later that for all they knew the stranger might just ride off over the horizon on any horse they might lend him.[11] So they proposed consigning TR to the wagon for the buffalo hunt, but Roosevelt would hear none of it. He *must* have a horse to ride. He had not come west to hunt buffalo from the seat of a buckboard.

The simple solution for Roosevelt was one he used frequently during his first western endeavors—cash. If these men would not lend him a horse, how about selling him one? Thus came Nell, the first animal he owned out west, and in a sense, his first stake in this wide-open country.

I have seen it written that Roosevelt was not a particularly accomplished horseman, but I beg to differ. He grew up with horses. Before he came west he had ridden to the hounds over fences after foxes. Younger still, on a world tour his family had ridden across the desert sands of Egypt, TR enjoying the gallop of his hot-blooded Arab. In Edmund Morris's words, "Riding eastward . . . Teedie began to get the feel of his horse. 'He has some Arab blood in him, and is very swift, pretty, and spirited.' After so many summers spent on the placid back of an American pony, it was thrilling to crouch over his lean body as it drummed tirelessly across the plain."[12]

Few families with children would undertake such a horseback journey today, but those were different times. TR's own modest statements about his level of horsemanship must be put in context. By today's standards he would be considered expert, even before he turned west.

Western riding among the cowboys and professional hunters was a different story, of course, and TR frequently writes of the differences between the two styles. He was convinced that one who had grown up with flat saddles and fences in the Eastern tradition would never be fully accomplished as a Western rider, but that the reverse was equally true. Contrasting hunting quail in the East with the very different pursuit of Western big-game hunting, Roosevelt contrasts the riding styles as well:

> As it is with hunting, so it is with riding. The cowboy's scorn of every method of riding save his own is as profound and as ignorant as is that of the school rider, jockey, or fox-hunter. The truth is that each of these is best in his own sphere and is at a disadvantage when made to do the work of any of the others. For all-around riding and horsemanship, I think the West Point graduate is somewhat ahead of any of them. Taken as a class, however, and compared with other classes as numerous, and not with a few exceptional individuals, the cowboy, like the Rocky Mountain stage driver, has no superiors anywhere for his own work; and they are fine fellows, these iron-nerved reinsmen and rough-riders.[13]

Unlike most cowboys and most West Pointers alike, Roosevelt had "been there and done that" in both camps by the time he wrote those words. And it is interesting that he uses the term "rough-riders." When he helped form the famous unit by that name he drew on riders of both sorts. The group he trusted with his life in combat featured horsemen from the Great Plains, hunting guides, and young army officers of the West Point tradition. And he said, "The qualities that make a good soldier are, in large part, the qualities that make a good hunter."[14]

Roosevelt once quoted, with self-deprecating good humor, his foreman's statement as he overheard it, that the boss was no "bronc-buster." Privately, TR admitted that he had an abject fear of bucking, but that didn't get him out of the experience. As boss, he got first choice of new horses for his remuda, but it was done round-robin style, so he acquired some animals that were broke in name only, and he bore the requisite number of bruises and broken bones.

Each of us in succession would choose a horse (for his string), I as owner of the ranch being given the first choice on each round. . . . The first time I was ever on a round-up Sylvane Ferris, Merrifield, Meyer, and I each chose his string in this fashion. Three or four of the animals I got were not easy to ride. The effort both to ride them and to look as if I enjoyed doing so, on some cool morning when my grinning cowboy friends had gathered round "to see whether the high-headed bay could buck the boss off," doubtless was of benefit to me [!], but lacked much of being enjoyable. The time I smashed my rib I was bucked off on a stone. The time I hurt the point of my shoulder I was riding a big sulky horse named Ben Butler, which went over backward with me.[15]

Ben Butler, it seems, was named after the presidential candidate of a minor political party to whom, in Roosevelt's eye, the horse bore a remarkable resemblance! TR was warned that the horse was treacherous. I am a horseman who believes an animal that repeatedly flings itself over backward is fit to ride no more, and I find it surprising that the Ben Butler did not succeed in killing the future president. No antic by a horse is more dangerous. TR was lucky to escape breaking only the point of his shoulder, but that was painful enough, and, like most frontier injuries, had to be endured while it healed without medical attention.

But horses for cowboy tasks and those for hunting were in a different category. It was bad enough to get bucked off among cowboys and friends where medical help was distant or nonexistent. But alone, on wilderness sojourns for wild game, trust in one's horse was paramount, just as it is today. And if there was a single horse to which Roosevelt owed absolute allegiance, it was an animal named Manitou.

TR's constant mention of Manitou speaks of more than "first love" for a horse that was truly his, a companion for a number of years. This was an animal that seems to have been exceptional, replete with the range of qualities necessary in a horse with which one trusts his life. With Manitou TR formed the type of bond that can come only with shared adventure, with tackling as a single man–horse team tasks that involve distance, danger, and adverse circumstances.

There was Manitou's oft-mentioned willingness to stay put, contentedly grazing while Roosevelt stalked game on foot. In an environment where being rendered horseless could be inconvenient at the least, fatal at the worst, Roosevelt's trust of Manitou in this regard is astounding. The frontier saying was, "Better to count ribs, than tracks." Better to see your horse suffer from feed deprivation than to trace his tracks over the next ridge. With other horses, TR used "Scotch hobbles," which restrict three feet and make much movement very difficult. With Manitou no such restraint was necessary.

This remarkable attribute was only one of many. One cannot read TR's hunting stories of the Badlands without knowing Manitou.

My own hunting horse, Manitou, is the best and most valuable animal on the ranch. He is stoutly built and strong, able to carry a good-sized buck behind his rider for miles at a lope without minding it in the least; he is very enduring and very hardy . . . even growing fat when left to shift for himself under very hard conditions; and he is perfectly sure-footed and as fast as any horse on the river. Though both willing and spirited, he is very gentle, with an easy mouth, and will stay grazing in one spot when left, and will permit himself to be caught without difficulty.

The list of virtues goes on, along with that of the vices possessed by many of the horses on the ranch, vices from which Manitou is free. TR ends with telling sentences that speak volumes on the best in horse–human relationships: "Manitou is a treasure, and I value him accordingly. Besides, he is a sociable old fellow, and a great companion when off alone, coming up to have his head rubbed or to get a crust of bread, of which he is very fond."[16]

It was on Manitou that TR placed three antelope, then led the horse into camp, and on a different occasion, two large mule deer bucks. The horse was completely unflappable: "The buck was packed behind good old Manitou, who can carry any amount of weight at a smart pace, and does not care at all if a strap breaks and he finds his load dangling about his feet, an event that reduces most horses to a state of frantic terror."[17]

It was the steady nerves of this favorite horse that increased TR's confidence in standing off five young Sioux warriors in his only encounter with American Indians that could have turned violent. In relating the event both in his autobiography and

13. TR and Manitou. Theodore Roosevelt Collection,
Harvard College Library.

in *Ranch Life and the Hunting Trail*, TR lavishes praise on Manitou. The small band of warriors may have been merely determined to intimidate, but as TR learned later, their previous actions with another party, an encounter that involved the theft of two horses, were genuinely hostile.

Their charge came as a surprise. In the middle of a wide plain, perhaps a half mile across, TR saw the five men, and when they spotted him, their reaction was immediate and aggressive:

> The second they saw me they whipped their guns out of their slings, started their horses into a run, and came at me full tilt, whooping and brandishing their weapons. I instantly reined up and dismounted. The level plain where we were was of all places the one on which such an onslaught could best be met. . . . The fury of an Indian

charge, and the whoops by which it is accompanied, often scare horses so as to stampede them; but in Manitou I had perfect trust, and the old fellow stood steady as a rock, merely cocking his ears and looking round at the noise.[18]

When the warriors had come within a hundred yards, Roosevelt drew a rifle bead on the one in front, and the effect was "like magic. The whole party scattered out as wild pigeons or teal ducks sometimes do when shot at." After doubling back, the Indians consulted and then sent one man forward, but Roosevelt stopped him at fifty yards, refused to let him come farther to show his reservation pass, and told him that no, he did not have any sugar or tobacco to give him. The Indian rode off shouting profuse "Anglo-Saxon profanity."

TR takes pains to call the incident minor, to assure the reader that the Sioux may have simply been bluffing, but it's clear he believes otherwise. And he continues his thanks to Manitou as he reports leaving the scene pushing "tough, speedy old Manitou along at a rapid rate."

But the incident with Manitou that makes my horseman's blood run cold, one that shows what I'd call a foolhardy trust in an animal TR must have considered a "superhorse," was a river crossing that by all rights should have killed the young man. The notorious Marquis de Mores had built a low dam across the Little Missouri, which, at low water, made a slippery ford, useable for brave riders. More cautious horsemen crossed the river on the railroad trestle, on a narrow path between the rails, a dicey prospect in itself.

During the spring breakup one April, when the river was high and brown and laden with huge chunks of ice, Roosevelt arrived on Manitou. An ice jam at the bend below Medora had backed up the water so that nothing of the Marquis's dam could be seen. According to Hermann Hagedorn, TR inquired, of a man named Fisher, just where the dam began.

Fisher, astounded that Roosevelt would consider using the dam when it was invisible under brown, ominous water carrying chunks of ice downstream, told TR that he'd certainly want to cross the river on the railroad trestle, but heard in reply that if Manitou could get his feet on the dam, they'd make it across just fine.

Fisher continued to argue. Certainly the dam would be mostly washed away by now, anyway, but the reply was equally firm. Manitou, he was told, was an excellent swimmer, so it wouldn't really matter whether or not the dam was still there. Fisher, seeing that he could not talk the young Easterner out of his plan to ford, pointed out where the dam began. What followed was witnessed as well by Roosevelt's friend Joe Ferris watching from the steps of his store:

> Anxiously, he watched [Roosevelt] pick his way out on the submerged dam. Manitou, meanwhile, was living up to his reputation. Fearlessly, yet with infinite caution, he kept his course along the unseen path. Suddenly the watchers on the east bank and the west saw horse and rider disappear, swallowed by the brown waters. An instant later they came in sight again. Roosevelt flung himself from his horse "on the downstream side," and with one hand on the horn of the saddle fended off the larger blocks of ice from before his faithful horse.
>
> . . . if Manitou drifted even a little with the stream, Roosevelt would never get ashore. The next landing was a mile down the river, and that might be blocked by ice.
>
> The horse struck bottom at the extreme lower edge of the ford and struggled up the bank. Roosevelt had not even lost his glasses. He laughed and waved his hand to Fisher, mounted, and rode to Joe's store. Having risked his life in the wildest sort of adventure, it was entirely characteristic of him that he should exercise the caution of putting on a pair of dry socks.[19]

To Joe's question as to whether Roosevelt was afraid, the young man replied quietly that no, he was not afraid because he was riding Manitou. It was that simple. Manitou, to him, was a machine. To Fisher's accusation that the act was reckless, Roosevelt pleaded guilty, but added that it was "lots of fun."

Well, it was reckless, indeed crazy, even, but it was also an act only possible because of total trust in a tremendous horse—trust earned, and it worked both ways, the two forming a powerful team. Roosevelt violated a basic principle in staying on the downstream side of his horse. Whether the heavy object is a swamped canoe, a log, or a horse, basic doctrine, when caught in current, is to stay *above* the object, lest you get pinned between it and a rock or fallen log.

Many years ago while canoeing on the mighty Yellowstone River with a minister friend, we had the canoe literally yanked from under us by a side current under a bridge. I could think of just one thing, this basic doctrine—get above the canoe, keep my friend there, too, grab the rope situated to spill and trail the canoe in just such an occurrence, and do this before the canoe smashed us into the concrete abutment with tons of force, drowning or crushing us. It went well. We swam fifty yards to a shallow bar where the swift water was only thigh deep, and leaning into the current, managed to pull the errant canoe back to us.

Roosevelt, having crossed the Little Missouri dozens of times (his ranch straddled it), must have known this basic principle. No matter. He was going to help his horse by shoving pieces of ice out of his way. There are times, I confess, that Roosevelt's story, from his first arrival in Dakota territory all the way to the infamous "River of Doubt" in the Amazon basin, prompts me to believe in guardian angels!

There were many other horses for Roosevelt, for even when away from the West, he hunted foxes, jumped horses for pleasure, and, when war beckoned, commanded troops in cavalry formations. But the horses of his days in the Badlands seemed most indelible in his memory. There was a small Indian pony named White Eye, very fast when speed was called for, and possessing great endurance.

Another favorite was "Muley," who greeted TR in the fall of 1896 on one of his last hunts in the Medora area:

> I was mounted on Muley. Twelve years before, when Muley was my favorite cutting pony on the roundup, he never seemed to tire or lose his dash, but Muley was now sixteen years old, and on ordinary occasions he liked to go as soberly as possible; yet, the good old pony still had the fire latent in his blood, at the sight of game—or indeed, of cattle or horses—he seemed to regain for the time being all the headlong courage of his vigorous and supple youth. . . . [I]t was two or three hours before Sylvane and I saw any game. Our two ponies went steadily forward at a single-foot or shack, as the cow punchers term what Easterners call a "fox trot."[20]

It may come as a surprise to modern equestrians that TR's favorite cutting pony was a gaited horse, an animal with a smooth, fast four-beat gait that replaced the trot. But really it should not. I've many times referred to differences between western horses of TR's time and those so designated today, particularly where gait and ability to cover ground efficiently and smoothly are concerned.

The noted equine physiologist Dr. Deb Bennett says that a classification of horses by use is more valid than by breed. All horses are the creations of humans. "Wild" horses are really feral horses, equines bred to look as they do by humans even though they have run wild, perhaps for generations. Bennett, who has studied thousands of horse skeletons dating from prehistoric times to the present, tells us that had horses never been domesticated, they would scarcely be recognized by us today. The animals would be small, heavy-boned, shaggy, and, by our standards, quite ugly.

Thus most equine traits that we find pleasing to the eye today were bred there by humans, and the same can be said for horses' physical abilities. Just as pointing dogs, herding dogs, and sled dogs were bred for their respective uses, so have horses been as well. The sloping shoulder we find attractive in a horse was originally bred there to make the pull of a harness trace directly perpendicular to the collar, important for efficiency.

Of the uses Bennett describes for horses, two involve riding, and she labels these categories as the "saddle type" and the "racing type." The two have always overlapped, of course, speed being important both recreationally and tactically, should an enemy be on your tail. But in areas where civilization has outstripped the building of roads and railroads, where there was much ground to cover on horseback, the saddle type has always prevailed. The early West, much of South America, the vast panoramas of Mongolia—such areas favored the "saddle" build over the "racing" one. And that, quite simply, is why TR found fast-walking horses of endurance build when he went west.

The photos taken by TR's friend L. A. Huffman, of horses ridden by cowboy and Indian alike, show moderate to narrow builds, good bone, high withers, and long, hard muscle. For those seventy-mile rides, for the forty-mile commute between Roosevelt's two ranches, the need was for endurance, speed, and, in spite of the toughness of the men, comfort. I could find only a couple of mentions, in all of Roosevelt's writings, of the most popular western horse of today, the Quarter Horse. Each was in lower case, indicating a type rather than a breed, and each comment was in a simile, such as "The deer burst out of the brush and streaked away like a quarter horse." Obviously, Roosevelt was familiar with quarter-mile racing, and of the horses involved in it, but he and his hands did not normally ride this sort of animal.

Heavy quick-twitch muscles are terrific for acceleration and lateral movement, but not for endurance. They weigh an animal (or human) down and require much nourishment and oxygen. One would not choose a weightlifter's build for a human marathon runner. Modern cowboys and participants in western events trail their horses to arenas over the highways. In TR's time you rode, whether to a roundup, to a branding, or to the mountain hunts a hundred miles away.

Manitou, though described by Roosevelt as "stoutly built and strong" appears in photos to be moderate in build, with ample bone, but he is certainly not heavy and muscular like a 1950s-era "bulldog" Quarter Horse. I've seen just one photo in which Roosevelt sits a horse of relatively heavy build, the one on the cover and on page 71. The white horse (probably an aging gray) may show some "cold blood" (work) lineage, but he is still the "saddle" type. Dated during Roosevelt's presidency, apparently on his 1905 Colorado bear hunt, this photo shows TR at 225 pounds, a weight that he believed limited a horse's performance. Roosevelt holds a military Springfield bolt-action rifle, and the horse is probably one furnished by his Colorado hunting hosts. One suspects, when furnishing a mount for the President of the United States, the hosts chose the safest, most sure-footed, but possibly not most spirited, animal they owned.

The importance to Roosevelt of equine partners shows in his diary, which is sprinkled throughout with the name of whichever horse he happened to be riding that day:

> June 18 [1886]. Rode to Medora on Sorrel Joe. . . .
> July 2. Rode out with Bill Rowe after calves; got them into corral and branded them. Rode little black horse.
> July 3. Rode up to Medora on Manitou.[21]

Affection for equine partners is a major motif in Theodore Roosevelt's life. Perhaps "love" would be a more accurate word, but not the love one feels for a lap dog or a house cat, though there is an element of that when TR mentions rubbing Manitou's face and feeding him favorite treats. The bond, however, is stronger than that, more like that of a dog musher who comes through a hazardous journey and hugs his lead dog at the end of it. The bond is similar to that among humans who share military combat, the strongest sort of attachment because it is born of total reliance upon each other.

And to see such equine partners suffer or be in some way mistreated is intolerable. Roosevelt was known to never swear, but even that sterling standard was broken when he witnessed the unloading of his two mares named Texas and Rain-in-the-Face from a ship during the Rough Riders' excursion to Cuba. Unloading the horses and mules posed a great problem, since there was no suitable dock or ramp. All but Roosevelt's were simply pushed over the side into the water, after which they swam to the Cuban shore without difficulty. A few of the animals swam in the wrong direction until a bugler already on the beach, seeing the problem, sounded a cavalry call. The horses and mules promptly turned at this call to arms and swam onto Cuban soil!

However, in a misguided attempt to treat their colonel's horses in a more delicate fashion, the men unloaded Roosevelt's mares with slings on a boom. Rain-in-the-Face was engulfed by a wave and drowned. Edmund Morris quotes Albert Smith, a cameraman who witnessed the scene: "Roosevelt 'snorted like a bull, split the air with one blasphemy after another.' [Then] the terrified sailors took such care with Texas that she seemed to hang in the air indefinitely, until Roosevelt, losing his temper again bellowed, 'Stop that goddamned animal torture!' This time there was no mishap, and the little horse splashed safely to shore."[22]

It might be hard to understand for those who have never known it, this nearly prehistoric connection between humans and some of the first animals they domesticated, animals that lent their four strong legs and big hearts to Man, to carry him and pull his loads and push his civilization along. Roosevelt knew it well, and it is primary among the things that bind us together over an intervening century. During all his political bombast, during his harrowing and frustrating experiences with the hardship of ranching on the range, I do not recall another reference to Roosevelt losing his temper and shouting oaths. But witnessing the suffering of his horses was enough to do the trick.

PART II
The Mountains

CHAPTER FOUR

The Big Horns

David, Jon, Justin, and TR; a pretty park; alibis; tenderloins in camp; ATV
jockeys; ranchers and dudes; compass and GPS; TR's tally; Old Ephraim;
Jedediah Smith; grizzlies through the canvas; a big, big buck

THE PARK STRETCHES for eight hundred yards east and west, a
ragged open cut through the timber, long and narrow, perhaps
a hundred yards wide. It is far from level, its east end a couple
of hundred feet lower in elevation than its west. Because of its
length and the scattered bunches of aspen that crop up here
and there within the park there is no way I can survey the entire thing and hope any elk emerging from the black timber
will necessarily be within rifle range, or even visible at all. The
best I can do is take this stand behind low bunches of buckbrush on a shelf of rock so precisely contoured that it looks
man-made, carved from granite as a doorstep for a giant.

My perch is on the north side of the park, approximately
in its middle, and a dozen feet above the grassy floor. I'm well
hidden, but I'm worried about the thermal winds. There seems
no rhyme or reason to them, no doping them as upslope part
of the day and downslope the rest. Indeed, they blow hard one
direction for half an hour, pause as if to rest, then commence
rustling the aspen leaves from the other direction. There seems
little choice but to wait here behind the screen of buckbrush,
for other methods have proven unproductive.

I've been hunting for several days now with three young guys (sons Jon and David, along with David's friend Justin) from our relatively comfortable vehicle camp at 8,800 feet in the Big Horn Mountains. The campsite is windswept and a bit too close to a county road—in October at this elevation you stay close to routes reputed to rate snowplows in the event of a storm—but it has served well nevertheless. We have a wall tent and a smaller spike tent, both with woodstoves; a tarp-covered cooking area; and a corral consisting of portable steel panels winged out from the gooseneck horse trailer. I've brought four good geldings, tough, ranch-raised Tennessee Walking Horses of my own breeding. In their talent for covering rough ground in smooth, fast gaits, they're much like the single-footing cow ponies Theodore Roosevelt praised as endemic to the West.

The Big Horn Mountains lie primarily in Wyoming, though the northern end of the range juts across the Montana border onto the Crow Indian Reservation. (The spelling of the mountain range has been standardized since TR's time as two words, while the second word in the name of the river—the Little Bighorn—remains one word.) Like the Crazy Mountains in south-central Montana, the Big Horns lie in a generally north-south line and are detached from the more extensive ranges nearby, isolated by prairie and rolling foothills from the spine of the Rocky Mountains, which runs through several states along the Continental Divide. Flanked by the city of Sheridan on the northeast side and the town of Lovell to the west, the Big Horns rise proudly from the prairie, beckoning to anyone with hunting in the blood.

To a rancher living in the gumbo breaks along the Little Missouri River in what is now western North Dakota, the Big Horns were the closest and most accessible range of the Rocky Mountains. Certainly there was much rough country near Roosevelt's two ranches, and there was much game as well. Roosevelt and his ranch hands practically lived on the flesh of the pronghorn antelope, preferring it to the beef they raised, and there were deer, both mule deer and whitetails aplenty. But the bigger, more exciting creatures were nearly gone.

The bison, the elk, and the grizzly bear, the scattered survivors of these species, still occasionally touched Roosevelt's land, but occurrences were rare. During his early years in the West, Roosevelt was convinced that elk were headed for extinction. He was aware that these big members of the deer family were native to both mountain and prairie environments, but were most vulnerable in the open country rapidly being settled by cattlemen and homesteaders. Certainly the desire to hunt mountain country where there were still concentrations of elk was a primary reason for Roosevelt's first trip to the Big Horns in 1884 with his foreman Merrifield, a teamster ("a weather-beaten old plainsman"), and a wagonload of supplies. He must have craved a true expedition to high country where bull elk whistled through the yellow aspens, where grizzly bears roamed free from competition with cattlemen like himself.

Those of us today who fight tight schedules, who scarcely dare take a week of vacation time, can't help but be envious. Roosevelt and his two companions, we're told in *Hunting Trips of a Ranchman*, having completed some cattle business in southeastern Montana and northern Wyoming, find themselves at "the foot of the Big Horn Mountains," and treat themselves to "a fortnight's hunt through them after elk and bear." A *fortnight*! Justin, Jon, David, and I have managed to schedule a week.

Some things, however, like the beauty of the Big Horns, do not change. I can't top TR's description:

> The Bighorn range is a chain of bare, rocky peaks stretching lengthwise along the middle of a table-land which is about thirty miles wide. At its edges this table-land falls sheer off into the rolling plains country. From the rocky

peaks flow rapid brooks of clear, icy water, which take their way through deep gorges that they have channeled out in the surface of the plateau; a few miles from the heads of the streams these gorges become regular canyons, with sides so steep to be almost perpendicular; in traveling, therefore, the trail has to keep well up toward the timber line, as lower down horses find it difficult or impossible to get across the valleys. In strong contrast to the treeless cattle plains extending to its foot, the sides of the table-land are densely wooded with tall pines. Its top forms what is called a park country; that is, it is covered with alternating groves of trees and open glades, each grove or glade varying in size from half a dozen to many hundred acres.[1]

The description of the plateau, while it could apply to many locations atop this rocky chain, fits perfectly the junction between Highway 14A and a gravel road onto which Jon and I turned a few days before my vigil for elk on the flank of the long, narrow park. Roosevelt and his companions abandoned their wagon at the foot of the mountains and proceeded horseback with four packhorses. Climbing the 10 percent grade of Highway 14A, the powerful diesel humming at capacity, a gooseneck trailer laden with four geldings and our camp supplies, hearts in our throats at the sight of runaway truck ramps that terminate in concrete barriers perched on cliffs, it occurred to me that Roosevelt's trip to the top was probably considerably more pleasant.

But he was human, too, and his difficulties with the pack string recall my very earliest days as a packer: "No one who has not tried it can understand the work and worry that it is to drive a pack train over rough ground and through timber. We were none of us very skilful at packing, and the loads were all the time slipping; sometimes the ponies would stampede with the pack half tied, or they would get caught among the fallen logs, or in a ticklish place would suddenly decline to follow the trail, or would commit some one of the thousand other tricks which seem to be all a pack pony knows."[2]

We've considered, and rejected, packing into one of those big, beautiful parks Roosevelt described. To do so would have required a couple more horses, a somewhat less luxurious camp, and more meticulous planning. The load in the gooseneck trailer would have pushed capacity.

On our first morning in camp we chose not to leave before daylight. Justin and David had met Jon and me late the previous afternoon, and setting up camp gobbled the rest of daylight. At first light I adjusted stirrups, and unfamiliar with Justin's experience with equines, gave him a quick review. With the sun already several notches above the ridge to our east, we departed camp, worried we'd been laggard.

It's when you're only half ready that it happens, when, as we former Marines say, "you're not being tactical" that all hell breaks loose. Because we hadn't followed the usual elk-hunter's routine of saddling up well before daylight and riding in the dark to the most likely spots, hoping to catch elk still feeding, we were taking a relatively leisurely ride, exploring as much as hunting. My companions insisted I ride in the lead, since I had the only bull tag.

Justin reminded me that the first small park was just ahead. I should have dismounted, extracted my Ruger #1 single shot from its scabbard, loaded it, and walked slowly toward the park, leading my horse, rifle in hand. I did none of these things. Thus we rode right into a small park full of elk. I vaulted off my horse, grabbed the rifle, barked to Justin to hold my horse, and ran in a half crouch toward a small rise past which I'd seen a bull, antlers high and nose raised in the most alert posture, steam rising from his nostrils in the cold morning air. The little ridge hid us all, now dismounted, from the elk's line of sight, but it wasn't enough. I crested it, took a kneeling position in the snow, and watched the bull's rear end disappear into the trees, the herd of cows and calves crashing through the brush ahead of him.

I'd blown it, and I knew it. I threw the boys a few lame excuses, alibis. Much as I love my single-shot rifles, they have a disadvantage on horseback, because one mustn't ride with a round in the chamber. Thus, you must load the rifle, rather than merely work a bolt or lever when dismounting. The difference is really but a matter of a split second. So I faced up to the simple truth. "Justin, I should have gotten off when you reminded me that the clearing was just ahead," I said.

It is strange how similar spheres of experience tend remind us that even the great ones in history were human, too. Roosevelt's first encounter with elk in the Big Horns was strikingly similar to mine: "The lowest glade was of some size, and as we reached it we saw a small band of cow elk disappearing into the woods on its other edge. I was riding a restive horse, and when I tried to jump off to shoot, it reared and turned round, before I could get my left foot out of the stirrup; when I at last got free I could get a glimpse of but one elk, vanishing behind a dead trunk, and my hasty shot missed."

Roosevelt's horse, my single-shot. And he, too, indulges in a little face-saving: "I was a good deal annoyed at this, my opening experience with mountain game, feeling that it was an omen of misfortune; but it did not prove so, for during the rest of my two weeks' stay, *I with one exception got every animal I fired at*" (italics mine).[3]

• • •

It has been a fine hunt. Warm weather and lack of snow have slowed things a bit, yet one or more of us has seen elk every day. Hunters on four-wheelers have frequently stopped at our camp to compare notes, have complained about the dearth of elk, and we've chuckled, after they depart, about their primary problem: butts epoxied to the seats of their ATVs.

We have split our forces, each day going out in separate pairs, the better to survey the terrain and find elk. We have also switched companions each day to prevent getting into any sort of social rut. One day Jonathan and I ride up a high ridge south of our camp, exploring several old logging roads. Two young bull moose grazed in a clear-cut, their manner blissfully unconcerned. We decide no one camped in the vicinity has one of the highly sought moose permits allotted this area. (The Big Horns, not yet reached by the introduced Canadian wolves, still have plenty of moose.)

But Jonathan and I are entertained by the presence of a bright-orange suit high in a tree dead center in the clear-cut. We learn later that a Wisconsin deer hunter has made himself a tree stand there, and it's hard for us to understand why, with thousands of acres to hunt for mule deer, he would elect to fix himself in one spot, in the open, a few hundred yards from a county road. But habit is a strong thing. Perhaps, we think, he's hunting the only way he knows how. Perhaps, too, this environment frightens him, and he feels most secure here near camp.

One evening Justin and I ride south and, at nearly nine thousand feet watch until dark a beautiful but elkless snow-covered park. Riding back down, the trail dimly illuminated by our headlamps, we encounter spotlights shining on us from the trailhead past which motorized vehicles are banned. Confused, their night vision shot, our horses threaten to spook, but after much shouting we convince the men in front of us to cut the lights.

These men, too, are out-of-state deer hunters. They have parked their four-wheelers, walked in a short distance, and shot a modest mule deer buck. They are tired from dragging it out, but very proud. We lavish congratulations on them. Then we head rapidly down the trail.

As we break out of the timber onto a treeless plain that

leads the last mile down to camp, the moon, too, breaks out. And in night light so brilliant it casts our shadows in fantastic, elongated forms, El Greco silhouettes, we have a ride I'll never forget. Our horses, anxious for camp, require a tight rein. We fly down the hill at a running walk, the chilled night air in our faces, the gas lantern in camp a promising pinpoint of light on which to fix our sights.

Each day some of us have seen elk. But it is David and his brother Jonathan who finally connect. They see the shapes of elk moving through the timber, and sprint; it's David who has the shot, a quick one through a gap in the timber, his .35 Whelen flattening the young cow on the spot. Jonathan, whose high school years allowed more hunting trips with his dad, has shot several elk, but this is David's first, and it's good to see the delight written equally over both brothers.

We've been able to get the horses right to the cow for packing out the quarters. Elk tenderloins for supper have spiced and sealed the deal. I've not given up on shooting a bull, but I'll take any elk at this point, my last night of hunting, and I will not be crushed if it does not happen. So I sit on the slab of rock, hiding behind buckbrush, watching for elk.

The minutes of remaining daylight tick away. The park turns golden with the setting sun. I find myself wondering if Roosevelt watched this park, too, hoping for another bull or perhaps for another of the giant grizzly bears he killed in the Big Horns. I think of our comfortable camp, of a cold beer, food, and laughing companions. Roosevelt, on his first trip here, was about the same age as my youngest son, Steve, who, regrettably, can't juggle time from his graduate studies to be with us. And it seems as if I've barely missed TR, as if he, Merrifield, and the "weather-beaten plainsman" were hunting here mere days or weeks ago. A century and a quarter is a mere skip in time between hunters' hearts.

There is much time to think while watching a park as the

day runs out, just as there is when sitting on a stool staring into the campfire. Sometimes thoughts turn away from the joking and ribbing of laughing companions. Here in the Big Horns, at a camp similar to ours, TR's grief caught up with him, and his biographer Edmund Morris related that in a rare moment he spilled it all: "One night in the Big Horns as bull elk trumpeted their wild, silvery mating calls, he blurted out to Merrifield the details of his wife's death. He said that his pain was 'beyond any healing.' When Merrifield, who was also a widower, mumbled the conventional response, Roosevelt interjected, 'Now don't talk to me about time will make a difference—time will never change me in that respect.'"[4]

The breeze turns cold. And then, in the last of the fading light, on the far lower edge of the park, well out of range, mere dots of yellow against the black trees, the elk are there. The binoculars show them, mixed cows, calves, and bulls, already restive, probably having scented me in the wind that now blows defiantly straight from me to them. And, very soon, they are gone. And so is my hunt. But the lack of meat and horns in camp, the lack of tangible evidence of "success" on elk, seems to me a very minor thing. It's been a fine hunt, and a privilege to watch for elk in a pretty park.

I stand, stretching muscles cramped by my long vigil. The walk back to my vehicle through dense timber in the dark is oddly pleasant, fulfilling, and far from lonely. The boys will have the fire burning in camp.

• • •

Two years later we returned, sons David and Jonathan and I, but not Justin, whose new business would not allow it. We found our old campsite and made it home with a wall tent and stove and a portable corral for the horses. Little Mack, in his teens but still a tiger, and Redstar accompanied Partner, on his first expedition to the mountains.

All trips, especially with sons, are fine, and this one was no exception. But on this trip values other than meat in the pan *had* to be paramount, because the elk were nonexistent. Oh, yes, there was sign, but it was all old. From what we could tell, the elk had been there, but when the vehicles started arriving—and the chainsaws kicked, and the ATVs roared on their scouting trips up and down the gravel roads—the elk had simply said, "No, thanks. Been there, done that, it's time to leave."

Our hunting camp, on a high plateau, at 8,800 feet, was near maximum elevation for the Big Horns, so the situation was the opposite of the more common one, where spooked animals head for the high country. In our area, security for the elk was gained by going down, down into the black timber on the sides of the mountains away from the open parks. Early in the year, with feed aplenty, security was paramount for the elk. There was no need for the risk involved in grazing these high open meadows and clear-cuts. During late season, when the snow deepens and cold temperatures kick up the metabolism required to survive, many of these elk head lower still, onto private ranches below, where they'll hammer haystacks if allowed.

But we tried hard. We scoured the parks where we had spotted elk on the previous hunt, and we rode hard, too, Little Mack more turboed for David than ever, as if the mountain air contained a surplus rather than a dearth of oxygen. Partner, initiated on the recent antelope hunt in Powder River country, was game and curious, as if each bend in the trail held something possibly scary, possibly only interesting.

One morning we rode west down a semi-open valley along a small creek that dumps at the bottom into the Little Bighorn, which at this elevation is a crystal-clear brook running north toward Montana, where in 1876 it became famous. Theodore Roosevelt arrived just seven years later, Magnus Johnson following close behind. What event in my life was a mere seven years ago? For Roosevelt and Johnson, the death of Custer and the men around him, the last powerful spasm of the Plains Indian tribes before they were engulfed by a westward tide they could not hope to deflect, must have seemed nearly as fresh in time as yesterday's headlines.

My father-in-law, Elmer, born in 1903, talked uneasily of Indians, though he was very cordial to the Crows who stopped by one day and asked to look for evidence of graves they thought could have been located near the creek east of the ranch house. During his boyhood those last wars with the Sioux and Cheyenne were as close in time to him and his parents as the Vietnam War is to my sons and me. The transition of the land Elmer ranched from Crow ownership to white was a very recent one.

Halfway down the valley, details of the terrain became more distinct as the lingering dawn broke into a cloudy morning, grudgingly brightening. To our left across the valley was a double row of posts set into the ground, which at first looked like a corral fence, but was clearly a different sort of structure. A closer look showed them to be the remains of a sluice for mining, two parallel rows of posts that had once borne an open-topped wooden flume. There would have been small battens across the bottom to hold up any flecks of yellow conveyed by the water from the small tributary creek above. I wonder whether anyone got rich. It's not likely.

Even with a dearth of elk, it's hard not to love a morning ride in the mountains. Our descent on the right side of the valley kept us in just the right area, on the fringe of the timber but with the open meadows below us. The cattle that graze here during summer had been removed during roundup of several weeks ago. Near the county road to the east of us, on top of the mountain, is a spot called simply "Cow Camp," a base camp of long enough standing to be recognized on all the official maps. David and I had driven past it on a scouting trip several years earlier. We saw a dozen big wall tents, at least that many horse trailers, a cook tent, all the trappings, with forty or fifty cowboys and cowgirls readying themselves for the ride, their bright, yellow slickers making them stand out like canaries against the dark timber.

We got the distinct impression that some of the riders we saw were ranchers and cowboys, the others guests paying for the privilege of spending a week scouring these mountains for cattle of many brands, to sort them so that each rancher could trail his own down to his home place for winter. And that business, too, dude ranching, started during TR's time. After the disastrous winter of 1886–87, brothers Howard and Alden Eaton, friends of Roosevelt's, could no longer survive as pure cattle ranchers. Talented and congenial hosts, they had been entertaining friends and relatives from the East for many years, and now it was time to be honest with them. They could keep doing that, they said, but they would have to ask the guests to chip in for their keep. Enjoying their yearly sojourns west, the guests were happy to do so, and dude ranching, as we know it today, was born. The Eatons later moved their dude-ranching operation to Wyoming, to the foot of these Big Horn Mountains.

It was near the bottom of the valley, close to where the trail forded the Little Bighorn, that we had the only near miss on elk of this trip. New tracks in old snow showed that a half-dozen head, mixed cows and calves with "maybe" a bull, had fed in the open along the creek. As daylight approached they had eased back into the timber, probably spooked by the headlights of a pickup on a rough-terrain road across the north-south valley of the Little Bighorn. Two spots of hunter orange flanked the vehicle, their binoculars pointed our way.

I conferred with my sons. Would it make sense to tie the horses and head up the densely timbered ridge in hopes of catching up with these elk, or would time be better spent exploring our way north, downstream, in hope there would be others feeding their way up out of the drainage? We decided on the latter. I've rethought it since, but hunting, like quarterbacking, is easier after the fact.

The next day we all set off on foot, my own route to the south of those taken by David and Jon, through heavy timber and much downfall. Guided by compass I quietly still-hunted my way to the top of a ridge, my course planned for gradual descent toward the end of shooting light to that same park I'd watched two years earlier to good effect. It was a fine hike. I walked uphill until my heart thumped, then sat for a minute or two on one of the many fallen trees and listened to the squirrels chatter and to the breeze in the trees. Ravens squawked.

Walking through deep timber, compass in hand, brought back memories of Marine training in Quantico, Virginia, the part of it I found almost fun, hiking alone through the woods for a land navigation test and emerging at just the right spot. The Virginia woods were beautiful, too. There were pines like those here in Wyoming, but also many oaks and maples hanging onto some of their color even when the snow flew, and a host of deciduous trees and shrubs I could not have identified to save my soul. I am as far behind TR in this respect as I am in bird identification, a deficiency I'm not proud of.

It was in narrating his first hunting trip to the Big Horns (in *Hunting Trips of a Ranchman*) that Roosevelt instructed the reader on avoiding getting lost, which he characterizes as "very uncomfortable."

> In hunting through a wild and unknown country a man
> must always take great care not to get lost. In the first
> place he should never, under any conceivable circum-
> stances, stir fifty yards from camp without a compass,
> plenty of matches, and his rifle; then he need never feel
> nervous, even if he is lost, for he can keep himself from

cold and hunger, and can steer a straight course until he reaches some settlement. But he should not get lost at all. Old plainsmen or backwoodsmen get to have almost an instinct for finding their way, and are able to tell where they are and the way home in almost any place. . . . But most men cannot do this.[5]

TR follows this with much more good advice. Pick out prominent landmarks when in new country, and learn how they look from different sides. Keep looking behind you as you travel, retaining a sense of just how different your return route will look to you, and additionally, increasing the likelihood of seeing game that has allowed you to pass before moving. Locate camp in your mind in reference to a line, not to a certain point, so that you can "strike back to this line" and follow it home.

When hunting in a new region, hunt up a creek drainage so that simply following it down will take you back to camp. It doesn't work the other way, he says, because in returning upstream it would be hard to tell which tributary to follow each time the creek forked. And don't lose track of where you've left your horse. TR confesses that once, worried that someone might meddle with his horse, he hid the animal so well that he spent the better part of a day looking for it.

Like TR, I am a fan of the compass, but I have, too, a device he may well have envied, the tiny GPS unit now tucked into a small pocket of my orange vest. With it I had marked our base camp as one waypoint, the place I left our vehicle as another. Punch the right keys, and presto, an arrow points to the location I seek. The same unit can tell me the distance I've traveled, elevation, time, location in either UTM grid or in latitude and longitude, and, for that matter, a host of additional information I've not yet had time to discover.

But there is a downside, too. Many hunters today become lost because their GPS units' batteries fail. Or the units are unable to fix upon the required number of satellites because of a thick tree canopy or an extremely heavy storm. So, not wanting to succumb to the Emersonian judgment that we have "built a coach but have lost the use of our feet," I hang onto my map and compass. Modern devices are wonderful, but they make one dependent on them, and the more elemental skills are too often lost.

I emerged from the timber just where I wanted to, the Marine Corps pride renewed. It was just a little early, so I found a convenient stump and watched a small clear-cut first before descending the rest of the way toward the park. Nothing stirred but the wind. Soon I grew stiff and just a little cold, so I eased along the fringe of the clear-cut down into a position where I could watch the park, hoping for a repeat of the sight I had seen two years earlier. But it did not happen. I did hear from over the ridge an unwelcome murmur, then a soft undercurrent, and finally, as the sound drew closer, the unmistakable roar of a convoy of all-terrain vehicles making their way up the logging road. Certainly the elk could hear them, too, and from far greater distances than I could. And certainly they had learned, too, that the coming of the engines in October was also the coming of the hunters.

Darkness near, shooting light past, an orange vest showed itself on a rock ledge across the park. It belonged to Jonathan. We linked up, a little discouraged, and walked out together.

But then there are those intrinsic values that have nothing to do with animals collected. So we had a lovely evening in camp, a meal of pork chops barbecued on the tiny propane grill I'd brought, savored with two sons and beer and bourbon around a card table in the wall tent by the woodstove, its warmth aromatic with pine. And while we shared stories, the snow began. It was warm, heavy stuff, but by late evening it threatened the tent enough that we knocked it off the sagging roof. There would be decisions to make in the morning.

14. Tough weather in the Big Horns.
Courtesy of Dan and Emily Aadland.

We were hampered by our individual schedules and by the nature of our high-altitude campsite. Although we had allowed a full additional day for our hunting, in this region tales of snowbound hunters abound, of vehicles deserted until spring under four-foot drifts. The doctrine preached was always to get out quickly at the first sign of a major storm. Ironically, of course, it is major storms that sometimes change elk hunting drastically and for the better. But when we emerged from the wall tent before dawn to find at least a foot of heavy, wet stuff, the air still filled with flakes, safety concerns trumped our hunting desires. We were already into tire-chain territory, and if we managed to pull the big gooseneck trailer the eight miles to the highway, we would certainly head west down the somewhat less white-knuckle grade into Sheridan. (We learned

15. David in the Big Horns. Courtesy of Dan and Emily Aadland.

later that the 10 percent grade of the western route to Lovell had been closed.)

So our second Big Horn saga ended with the usual regrets at striking the tent, hitching to the trailer, and loading the horses. There would be other times and other hunts, but maybe not here. We left convinced that this spot was a victim of its own fine attributes, that like many good places it had been altered by the number of people it now drew. And although the behavior of hunters driving ATVs had been lawful and courteous toward us on our horses, there were simply too many of them. Too much noise, too much activity, and because of that, too few elk.

• • •

An excess of hunters was not a problem for TR in 1884. Nor, for that matter, was there any shortage of game, or worries about herds of elk holing up on inaccessible private land. The

Big Horns seem to have teemed with elk, bear, and birds. Although a myth exists that elk were once strictly creatures of the plains, fleeing to the mountains only when pressured by settlement, the truth seems to be that they always existed in both places, probably migrating to wherever they found feed. True, Lewis and Clark nearly starved in Montana's western mountains, but Osborne Russell, one of the very few mountain men who wrote of his adventures, killed the largest bull elk in his storied career around 1840 within sight of Old Faithful in what is now Yellowstone National Park. Indeed, Russell's party seems to have lived on elk during their travels in the Yellowstone and Grand Teton regions.

Roosevelt saw firsthand that the prairie elk, apparently slow to adapt to the tactics of white hunters with firearms, were among the first wildlife to be decimated. A few still existed around his Medora ranch, but for the hunter it was slim pickings indeed. Thus the call to the mountains, where the elk had been relatively unmolested.

Here again we have the paradox: the father of American conservation, the man we know as having had not only the ethic but the political power to effect changes that have given the modern American hunter nearly everything he or she currently enjoys, seems no better than the exterminators of the bison when you consider his total take of game on this one trip to the Big Horns. Edmund Morris cannot help waxing sarcastic when he quotes from a letter TR wrote to his sister Bamie about this trip, about its positive effect on his mental state.

> "I have had good sport," he wrote Bamie, on descending from the Big Horn Mountains, "and enough excitement and fatigue to prevent overmuch thought." He added significantly, "I have at last been able to sleep well at night."
>
> Readers of Roosevelt's diary of the hunt might wonder if by "excitement" he did not mean "carnage." A list

culled from the pages of this little book indicates just how much blood was needed to blot out "thought." (Since Alice's death his diaries had become a monotonous record of things slain.)[6]

Morris tallies TR's total take of animals and birds on his forty-seven-day Big Horn safari, including those shot on the return trip to Elkhorn, at 170 critters! This certainly doesn't match the excesses of the Irish nobleman Sir George Gore, guided by Jim Bridger (who was soiling his own nest), a generation earlier. Gore, whose entourage required two large wagons dedicated to carrying his massive arsenal alone, shot perhaps five thousand animals in a killfest that sickened Indian and White alike.

No one accuses Roosevelt of a similar bloodlust, but modern hunters, limited to a deer tag or two and strict limitations on their daily take of birds—all this in short, restricted hunting seasons—can only gape at TR's tally. Ironically, were it not for Roosevelt and others, founders of the Boone and Crockett Club, and arguably founders of the entire modern wildlife-management philosophy, such restrictions would probably not exist, and for that matter, neither would the game we hunt.

But no matter how one glosses it over, no matter how the later deeds of the Great Conservationist rub out the hunting excesses of his youth, the early TR must still be classified with the beaver trapper and the buffalo hunter, with the "get some first before it's gone" philosophy of nearly everyone who went west in the late nineteenth century. (Homesteaders, who for the most part came intending to stay, may have been a notable exception.) Roosevelt knew the game was disappearing. As we have said, he did not know he would be able to effect powerful policies to stem the tide. So, young in his conservation ethic, he killed nearly as much game as he could find. His one prohibition was against shooting females of each species, unless meat was truly needed.

By my count TR killed six elk and seven deer during the forty-seven days of his Big Horn excursion. By no stretch could the three men in his party consume anything close to that, assuming salvage of the meat, even with a nearly all-meat diet. Since the hunt took place during the second half of August and the first half of September, keeping the meat from spoiling was problematic. When the ponies were packed up for the trek down the mountain to the stashed wagon, TR referred to their being laden with hides and horns, the stuff needed for mounted trophies, not with meat. (It takes two packhorses to carry the quarters of a large elk.)

So was the young TR a game hog? I'm afraid so. Like so many early westerners, he was consumed with the idea that he had to hit while the iron was hot, enjoy the last of it. Huge admirer that I am, I have to assert that gluttony entered in. One thinks of Faulkner's character Boon in the last pages of "The Bear," distraught at the disappearance of the Southern wilderness that has been host to the hunters each year, and his attempt to possess a tree full of squirrels.

There was a gum tree, alone in the middle of a clearing. A favorite squirrel hunter's trick was to charge it rapidly, marooning the squirrels, which had no other trees to which they could jump. As the narrator, Ike, approaches the clearing looking for Boon, he hears a hammering sound:

> It grew louder and louder that steady savage somehow queerly hysterical beating of metal on metal, emerging from the woods into the old clearing, with the solitary gum tree directly before him. At first the tree seemed to be alive with frantic squirrels. There appeared to be forty or fifty of them leaping and darting from branch to branch. . . . Then he saw Boon, sitting, his back against the trunk, his head bent, hammering furiously at something on his lap. What he hammered with was the barrel of his dismembered gun, what he hammered at was

the breech of it. The rest of the gun lay scattered about him in a half dozen pieces while he bent over the piece on his lap his scarlet and streaming walnut face, hammering the disjointed barrel against the gun breech with the frantic abandon of a madman. He didn't even look up to see who it was. Still hammering, he merely shouted back at the boy in a hoarse strangled voice: "Get out of here! Don't touch them. Don't touch a one of them. They're mine!"[7]

Boon's wilderness was disappearing, having been penetrated by a railroad. Its borders were being gnawed by the axes of settlers and would soon be logged commercially by a company set to move in. Although Roosevelt approached the inevitable disappearance of western game with none of Boon's hysterical possessiveness, the myriad western hunters of the late nineteenth century did have something in common with their southern fictional brother. Take what you need while it is abundant, then some more, because all of this may soon be gone.

But critics of what is sometimes called Roosevelt's "bloodlust" miss the point. Having seen for himself that wildlife populations were vulnerable, having been himself an agent of their disappearance, Roosevelt knew firsthand what had to be done to assure game populations in the future. Like a big-city cop whose boyhood was spent on the margins of the law, TR was all the better equipped to enforce it. The rest, as they say, is history.

• • •

The Big Horn Mountains of today retain much of the beauty Roosevelt found in 1884. Well known for its elk hunting, the area is even more coveted by hunters for its healthy moose population, hopeful hunters faithfully applying each year for a once-in-a-lifetime tag, with odds of drawing exceedingly scant.

Interestingly, moose are a species Roosevelt did not shoot or mention seeing on his 1884 adventure. Indeed, Roosevelt failed to bag a moose on several hunts that targeted them specifically, only eventually killing one in the Bitterroot Mountains of western Montana.

Wyoming residents are quick to assert that the moose population remains healthy in the Big Horns because the gray wolf, introduced to the Yellowstone ecosystem in 1995, has not yet reached the vicinity, at least in significant numbers. They have a point. In Yellowstone Park and the wilderness directly north of it, moose were the first species enjoyed by the northern Canadian wolves, old hands at killing the big moose of that region. The smaller Shiras moose of Montana and Wyoming, relatively free of predation for generations, have proven to be innocent and easy prey.

Apparently, the wolf's preference for moose meat was well known in TR's time: "The bear occasionally makes a prey of the moose; the cougar is a more dangerous enemy in the few districts where both animals are found at all plentifully; but next to man its most dreaded foe is the big timber wolf, that veritable scourge of all animals of the deer kind."[8]

But the Big Horns did have bears, not only the blacks that inhabit the area today, but grizzlies, big ones. TR and his party killed five in 1884, including a true monster that he and Merrifield estimated at 1,200 pounds! We can doubt that weight, but should remember that the two men were experienced stockmen, familiar with the weights of steers and bulls. Roosevelt asserts that this bear was bigger than any he had seen brought in by hunters before or since, that it was far heavier than any of their horses, and that they skinned it only with extreme difficulty. They did try eating its meat, but found it mediocre.

The actual kill was dramatic only in that it happened at extremely close quarters. Anyone who has studied grizzly encounters realizes how easily the situation might have turned south, how the big bear could have changed history. Merrifield and Roosevelt were tracking the bear, Merrifield in the lead when he dropped to one knee, his face "fairly aflame with excitement" and signaled to TR, who "strode past him."

> There, not ten steps off, was the great bear, slowly rising from his bed among the young spruces. He had heard us, but apparently hardly knew exactly where or what we were, for he reared up on his haunches sideways to us. Then he saw us and dropped again on all fours, the shaggy hair on his neck seeming to bristle as he turned toward us. As he sank down to his forefeet I had raised the rifle; his head was bent slightly down, and when I saw the top of the white bead fairly between his small glittering, evil eyes, I pulled the trigger.
>
> Half-rising up, the huge beast fell over on his side in the death throes, the ball having gone into his brain, striking as fairly between the eyes as if the distance had been measured by a carpenter's rule. The whole thing was over in twenty seconds from the time I caught sight of the game; indeed it was over so quickly that the grizzly did not have time to show fight at all or come a step toward us. It was the first I had ever seen, and I felt not a little proud, as I stood over the great brindled bulk, which lay stretched out at length in the cool shade of the evergreens.[9]

Oh, the things that could have gone wrong. First, the grizzly did "show fight" by dropping back down to all fours as the hair on his back bristled. Grizzlies charge like large dogs, bounding with blinding speed, not standing on their hind legs as is often depicted. Secondly, the brain of a grizzly is relatively small, and it is extremely well protected by a massive skull. Roosevelt's .45-75, though modest in power compared to a modern "heavy" rifle, launched a 350-grain bullet, and was certainly potent at such close range. But missing by an inch or two in any direction could well have meant a mauling for one or both men, and maybe worse.

Roosevelt's analysis reflects a hunter who is young and perhaps lucky:

> A bear's brain is about the size of a pint bottle; and any one can hit a pint bottle off-hand at thirty or forty feet. I have had two shots at bears at close quarters, and each time I fired into the brain, the bullet in one case striking fairly between the eyes, as told above, and in the other going in between the eye and the ear. A novice at this kind of sport will find it best and safest to keep in mind the old Norse Viking's advice in reference to the long sword: "If you go in close enough your sword will be long enough." If a poor shot goes in close enough he will find that he shoots straight enough.[10]

Roosevelt goes on to say that he killed five grizzlies with seven bullets on this sojourn to the Big Horns. But I suspect his narrative would make the average Alaskan guide, seasoned at accompanying dudes in quests for grizzlies and brown bears, reach for a tin cup of camp whiskey. Yes, most shooters *should* be able to hit a pint bottle offhand at thirty or forty feet (though I'm betting some can't), but only if the target is stationary and they're not panting from both exertion and abject fear at being that close to an animal perfectly happy to pounce on the hunter and shake him in its teeth like a rag doll.

Few who know the great bears recommend aiming for the head, except in dire circumstances when the critter has charged and is nearly upon you. Better to put a heavy bullet through both shoulders, disabling the bear, and then use whatever finishing shots are necessary to kill it. And as to range, though no one approves of long-range shooting at these formidable but beautiful animals, few would recommend getting yourself within spitting distance. Here again, as with Manitou and the flooded, ice-choked river, we see that charmed life or, if you prefer, the guardian angel.

• • •

I've never hunted grizzly. In the Yellowstone ecosystem where I live, and indeed, in all of the lower forty-eight states, the animals have been listed for many years under federal law as "threatened," thus prohibiting state management of the species. As I write this, grizzlies in Montana, Wyoming, and Idaho, have been on the increase, so documented by careful study for many years, and have now been delisted. States, thus, could carefully reinstitute very limited hunting quotas on them, but always under jeopardy of lawsuit from groups that refuse to believe, notwithstanding all of TR's efforts and most of American wildlife history, that hunting is the backbone of successful wildlife conservation.

An argument for some limited hunting is the changing nature of the big bear's behavior. King of the mountain for many years, grizzlies have lost much of their fear of humans. Indeed, around the Cody, Wyoming, area (which Roosevelt later frequented), the sound of a rifle shot during elk season is a signal to bears that a steaming, delectable gut pile from a downed elk might just await their efforts. So the bears gravitate toward the shot, not away from it.

Tales abound of hunters killing an elk, dressing it out, then returning with horses or companions to pack out the animal, only to find that a grizzly has commandeered the carcass and is ready to defend it. Pity the poor hunter who stumbles carelessly into this situation. If he's smart he has dragged the elk quarters into any open clearing available, a clearing he can watch from some distance so that he does not blunder into a ticklish situation. If a grizzly has taken over, all advice is to abandon the carcass to this far bigger, stronger, and fiercer creature and attempt to convince the fish and game department that you should be issued another elk tag.

The situation has grown very serious. A Cody, Wyoming, couple I know well, lifetime elk hunters, have actually abandoned their annual hunts because of the "bear problem." To them it is not worth the risk of an encounter, either with a bear or with the legal repercussions of taking lethal action against the bear. The self-defense plea can be difficult to prove.

A limited hunting season with a strict quota would tend to eliminate a few of the most aggressive and fearless bears because they would also be most vulnerable (and most easily located) by the lucky hunter with a tag. Like all big predators, grizzlies are smart. It is likely that, in time, the sound of a shot would cease being synonymous with a dinner bell to the powerful creatures.

Bow hunters during elk season are even more vulnerable than rifle hunters. They tend to hunt silently, they camouflage themselves, and, to mask their human scent, they use more secret potions than a prom queen. The result is all too effective. With mediocre eyesight, the grizzly walking upwind of the hunter stumbles onto him, and there is a sudden close encounter of the most frightening kind. Two separate bow hunters in the Gardiner, Montana, region were mauled during one hunting season recently. Both survived, but one just barely.

One of the most dramatic events of this sort happened a month before this writing, when a Wyoming man took his sixty-five-year-old father on his very first bow hunt for elk. The son was attacked by a grizzly, and the father came to his assistance, launching an arrow that cleared his son by a mere two feet and struck the bear in what turned out to be perhaps the luckiest bow shot since William Tell. It is unheard of to stop a grizzly with a bow, yet it happened, the arrow neatly severing the aorta. The grizzly continued to attack, but not for long with such a wound.

Once, during my childhood, I was as close to a grizzly as I ever care to be. In those innocent days Yellowstone Park was overrun with black bears and a significant number of grizzlies. Garbage dumps still existed near most of the park villages, and these drew scavenger bears of both species. By the time my father took his brood on their annual vacation to Yellowstone, park officials had begun improving garbage control, and it is said they did some unpublicized off-season bear control with rifles. But black bears, particularly, still overran the place, and it was hard to progress down any of the park's highways without constant stops where traffic choked while tourists photographed, and, too often, fed the bears.

In retrospect, after raising three boys of my own, I'm staggered by my father's level of dedication in exposing his many children to nature and wildlife. He would work all year for these annual jaunts, his pastor's salary furnishing no extra money for the effort. But that did not deter him. He found a way to carry a fairly large boat on top of our Chevy station wagon, and he built a camping trailer of plywood that furnished sleeping quarters for Mom and him, my older sister, and the smallest children. My brothers, Andy, Steve, Art, and Luther, joined me in a canvas umbrella tent.

We were camped, I believe, at Canyon, and we had been warned by park rangers that a grizzly was in the vicinity. (Today, the officials would close the campground under similar circumstances.) We were too innocent to be particularly concerned. But I do remember a sign from nature we should have noted. As we set up our tent and leveled the trailer, we had noticed three or four black bears were visiting the campground, this being such a common occurrence, that we paid little attention. These begging bears were making their rounds from campsite to campsite, checking the vulnerability of the garbage cans, trying to convince people to throw them some sort of morsel.

But as dusk came, the black bears vacated the area. A couple of them actually loped toward the woods, while the others simply hurried away. We took little notice. Then the long summer evening turned dark, and we snuggled into our sleeping bags. I'm not sure how long we slept, but I was awakened by the sound of my father's assertive voice shouting something like, "Get away, bear!"

I remember even more clearly the way he told it to parishioners upon our return—I heard the story many times: "My usual way of handling a bear in camp was to step out of the trailer with my big flashlight and my toolbox. I'd shake the toolbox and shine the flashlight in their eyes and take a step toward them, and they would always run away. But something was different with this bear. She took a step toward me! I could tell it was a grizzly." Dad freely admitted to retreating into the trailer.

There was more to it than that, and had he been fully aware of it, the alarm he sounded would have been considerably more decisive, though it's hard to imagine exactly what he could have done. This was a grizzly sow with cubs. As I awakened, my brothers and I were aware of a low murmuring, a sound vaguely like a mother dog talking to her pups, and also of sounds in reply. Then we boys became aware that one wall of the tent was pressed in toward us in two round spots a foot or so wide. The sow had planted her cubs squarely against the wall of the tent while she meandered around the campsite looking for tidbits.

Sometimes innocence is a saving grace. I remember being afraid, but not terrified. I do recall being aware that we were in an awfully tight spot, that making noise could be interpreted by the sow as an attack on her cubs, that it was better to just wait it out. I don't know how long it lasted, this fright at the bodies of young grizzlies a foot or two away with only seven-ounce canvas duck separating us from them and from a mother bear that could walk through the tent and rip us to pieces if she saw reason to do so. I only remember that strange and wild communication we heard between the cubs and the mother, and being fascinated by this frightening glimpse into their world, the world of the wild. Then, whatever "words" she was saying to them must have meant "move on," and they did so, silently, the shapes through the canvas stirring, then departing. Scared as I was, I remember a strong temptation to reach out and touch one of those shapes that bulged through the canvas, to be able to say I touched the warm skin of a live grizzly bear through thin cloth, and I almost wish I had done so. But who knows what may have resulted.

I recall, too, lying there thinking about the live mounts of a cub and two sows we had seen in one of the park museums. Grizzly cubs, when viewed closely, are not cute. Black bear cubs, wolf pups, deer fawns, and the young of virtually all domestic animals qualify as "cute." Grizzly cubs do not, and that is because of their eyes. Look closely, if you ever have a chance. You will be viewing nature at its most powerful, at its most indifferent toward Man and all other weak and inferior creatures.

• • •

I do not know just when the nickname Old Ephraim was first applied to a lone grizzly. I do know that the epithet was in use long before being applied in the early twentieth century to a massive, stock-killing grizzly in Utah, or to an earlier, similar one in California. Certainly, the nickname was in wide popular use by the time Theodore Roosevelt so titled his chapter on grizzlies in *Hunting Trips of a Ranchman*, published in 1885. Some assert that it was the mountain men who gave the grizzly this interesting nickname, but it's unlikely to have emanated from an *average* mountain man. The biblical origin is likely too complex to have been known and applied by the typical fur trapper, even one with a childhood Sunday School background.

The biblical Ephraim was the younger son of Joseph and received his father's birthright, an honor that would normally have been granted to Mannaseh, the older brother. Ephraim founded one of the tribes of Israel, and eventually his name became synonymous with the entire nation of Israel. Application of his name to the great, fierce bear of the West implies some interpretation of this biblical figure's life, an interpretation that varies considerably within the Judeo-Christian tradition. But a quick look at some of the interpretations reveals words for Ephraim's character such as "domineering," "haughty," "discontented," and "jealous."

William Faulkner, in writing "The Bear," went a different direction in characterizing the anachronistic animal inhabiting the last of a dwindling wilderness in the South. The mid-nineteenth-century timeframe of Faulkner's story certainly allows the possibility that this bear was a grizzly, the last of his species marooned alone in a shrinking habitat. For this bear Faulkner tapped a figure more prominent in Greek mythology than in the Bible: "the old bear, solitary, indomitable, and alone; widowered, childless and absolved of mortality—old Priam reft of his old wife and outlived by all his sons."[11]

The reaching out to epic figures of the past to describe this big bear that shrugged off the puny firearms of the first western explorers, the creature that Lewis and Clark could handle only with the gang efforts of their band, is understandable. The grizzly was a new dimension. But my own suspicion is that "Old Ephraim" may have been first applied by Jedediah Smith, the Methodist mountain man famous for his quiet competency and for the fact that a Bible accompanied him through thick and thin. And, if so, as a minister friend suggests, Smith may have been assigning respect to this great and powerful creature of the wild, this apparent leader of all the tribes of the wild.

Jedediah Strong Smith, born in 1799, is said to have read an early account of the Lewis and Clark expedition while still a boy. His storied career before being killed in a fight with Comanches at age thirty-two, was the stuff of legend. He knew grizzlies well. Hugh Glass, the mountain man immortalized by his unlikely survival after being severely mauled by a grizzly and left for dead by his expedition, was a companion of Smith's on General Ashley's famous fur expedition. (Glass recounted Smith giving a eulogy and prayer at the burial of an expedition member who had died.) Even more pertinent, Jedediah Smith was himself severely mauled by a grizzly, his scalp torn nearly off and hanging, and an ear severed. He convinced another mountain man, Joe Clyman, to sew the scalp back on and to tackle, even, the ear, a crude surgery that was apparently successful. In two weeks Smith was off again, sufficiently recovered to assume leadership of his party.

It is easy to admire this mountain man so revered by those around him, so serenely individualistic as a religious man, in company seemingly so at odds with the rough humanity around him. But to me he is an illustration of a principle well known, too, by Theodore Roosevelt. Comfortable in their own skins, sticking to their moral principles, both men while very young were sought as leaders by the less capable men around them.

And so, I once did my part in honoring the legacy of the mountain man by naming a promising sorrel colt Jedediah Smith. Alas, the immortalization was brief, and perhaps not that appropriate. My colt was a bit of a clown, easy to like, but not particularly distinctive in stature or dignity, though he had promise. On a pack-in elk hunt with my friend Billy, "Jed" did just fine carrying his load to camp, the first real work he had done, save the several short training rides I had put on him. But he showed a tendency quite the opposite of Roosevelt's Manitou. He liked to wander, and he was quite good at it. Hobbles were a bit of a joke, and I have the image of this lanky sorrel, bracelets around his front pasterns, loping effortlessly toward the most inviting tidbits of grass.

So it should not have surprised Billy and me when Jed vacated our camp at a dead run up the steep side of a small basin, hobbles notwithstanding, leading two others of our string with him. Little Mack, luckily, was tied to a highline, ready for such a contingency. I threw on a saddle and galloped off in pursuit, up the muddy trail and over the ridge, fearing the horses would make it all the way to the trailhead and beyond. But I caught up with the band on the flat right above camp, where they were grazing quietly but looking a little lost and foolish.

Jed did share one thing with his namesake: he died young, victim of a huge cottonwood branch dislodged from a hundred feet above him by a terrible windstorm. It was a harsh but sudden fate for the friendly colt, but certainly better than losing a fight with Comanches or with Old Ephraim.

• • •

Before I left them completely, before I lived with my decision to hunt no more in the Big Horns, I wanted Emily to see more of them than she knew from highway vacations. I wanted her to see the campsites I had shared with our sons, and maybe hear an elk bugle, though our late-August window of available time was a bit early for that. So, horses in tow, we headed south from our Montana ranch, then west through the Wyoming towns of Powell and Lovell, and finally up the infamous Highway 14A. We found the junction of our graveled county road, checked out the campsite I had used with our sons, and then settled into a lovely clearing higher up, with forest to our backs and nothing to our west but a ridge of open sagebrush and the promise of a spectacular sky as the afternoon ran out.

Four years earlier, during bow season, when David and I scouted this area, there had been a huge camp near the quiet spot Emily and I now occupied. Made up of several camping trailers and a wall tent perhaps fifty feet long (actually, several tents joined), the camp's most memorable feature was, of all things, a satellite dish. A visitor from another camp dropped by our fire that evening, entertaining David and me for a couple of hours while we ate peanuts and drank the beer he had brought with him. (Later, in his absence, recalling A. B. Guthrie's *Big Sky*, we nicknamed the young man "Poordevil," in memory of the impoverished Blackfeet Indian who stumbled into the camp of Boone, Jim, and Summers, making immediate friends because he carried an antelope over his shoulders, which he dropped by the fire as an offering.) The young visitor to David's and my camp that night reported that hunters in the huge group camp boasted that their satellite dish allowed them to watch five porn channels. Intrinsic values, indeed!

But Emily and I, luckily, had no teeming camps to avoid, no distractions, nothing save a pleasant evening with steaks on the grill and anticipation of the promised sunset. There was no creek nearby, so to water the horses we rode down a ravine that I knew held a spring, marked now by a harlequin herd of cattle, all colors, all breeds, bedded in the tall grass where water emerged from spongy ground, collected itself, and grew into a tiny creek. I told Emily about the line shack farther down the ravine that David and I had explored on that earlier trip, about the hard winters cowboys in such shacks endured, about their daily rides in opposite directions to meet up with their counterparts in similar shacks, keeping the cattle on the fringes of the range. We considered a ride down to it, but with darkness near, settled with riding through the cattle that reluctantly gave up their beds and let us pass. The horses drank deeply from tiny pools of clear, icy water, throwing their heads into the air frequently, with snorts in the direction of the colorful cows.

The Big Horns this year had enjoyed ample moisture, big spring snowstorms followed by good rains in June, so the Forest Service had not imposed a campfire ban of the sort that has become nearly routine in our dry western forests. I tried out my new cruiser axe, tackling the smaller branches of a nearby fallen tree, and long before dark we had pine crackling and smoke rising straight up into the cloudless sky. Then began the transformation, the green around us adopting a hint of yellow, the sun gone behind the ridge, the day's warm air spiked with the cool core of night, prompting Emily's retrieval from the pickup of a down vest for each of us.

Even during the relatively long days of late August, it happens very quickly, this coming of dusk. We spotted movement to our west below the ridge perhaps two hundred yards in front of us, the light-gathering power of our binoculars confirming that we were watching a small band of mule deer feeding their way through the sage. The sight is a common one for us, since daily on our ranch mule deer come down from the hills into the alfalfa fields while their cousins the whitetails emerge from the brush at the river bottom with the same destination in mind. The two species mingle while feeding, but when spooked, flee their separate ways.

But we will never be so jaded by the overpopulation of deer near our home that we will fail to enjoy the touch of the wild they always provide. So we watched this band with pleasure, squinting against the failing light. And then, on the skyline, four hundred yards away, brightly silhouetted by the remaining daylight behind him, was a mule deer buck of the sort that makes one have to talk himself out of the possibility that he's looking at an elk. Heavy-horned, with an antler spread double the tip-to-tip span of his mule-like ears, the buck, followed by two others nearly as large, made eye contact with me through the lenses of my eight-power binoculars, but only for a second or two. Then, assimilating what he was seeing, the fire, the vehicles, the picketed horses, and the people, he exploded into a sprint that took him out of sight in a flash, pulling his two cohorts along with him. And the lesser mule deer two hundred yards in front of us continued to graze. All critters are not equal. Some are gifted, and among mule deer bucks, those are the ones that grow antlers that make hunters salivate.

A few weeks later we attended the grand opening of a sportsman's super store. One of the attractions was a deer exhibit, a dozen or so trophy mounts of both whitetail and mule deer, typical and non-typical. We stared hard at the largest of the trophy mule deer mounts, one ranking high in the ratings maintained by the Boone and Crockett Club TR founded, and compared him with that never-to-be forgotten mental image of the bighorn buck on skyline. We agreed: "our" buck was the equal of the one exhibited.

And if my experiences in the Big Horn Mountains were to end right there, that would be fair enough. A great day, a fine evening, and a signature and exclamation point from a magnificent wild creature. It could get no better.

In the morning the wind blew hard from the west, and the friendliness of our high-altitude campsite was gone. We had a second destination, west through Cody, Wyoming, and on to true grizzly country near Cooke City. But mixed with our departure was a regret of the sort one has when recognizing the passage of a certain stage of life, in this case both TR's and mine. The Big Horn Mountains for me are the domain of the young TR, the edge of his brash confidence knocked briefly down by a left-right combination dished out by life on that day when double death came to his house. It was here, across the intimate flames of a campfire, under brilliant stars, the bugles of elk reverberating through the pines, that he could unburden himself to others he held subordinate but who were nevertheless friends.

At what point does a historical figure become more than

facts learned in public school, interpretation of those facts learned in college and graduate school, and later, in review, a timeline of an American life readily Googled? At what point does another, long dead, his time having come and gone, become a fellow human being, an acquaintance, even a friend? I suppose this stage is reached when one no longer simply thinks about the person, but begins to feel happiness at his happiness, sorrow at his sorrow. I am there.

There is no hero worship, here. There is admiration for one of the most remarkable men I have known, yes, but there is also awareness of the flaws and weaknesses that mark even the best of us as human. And so, on a camping trip to the Big Horn Mountains, with a warm wife of more than forty years, I can feel almost with guilt what TR missed while he was here, and like Merrifield at the campfire, I can hurt with him, attempt to comfort, and when that does not work, show my respect by leaving him to work it out by himself.

CHAPTER FIVE

The Absaroka

Children of the Large Beaked Bird; Buoyer and Leforge, Huskies and
Indians; Plenty Coups and Cody; return of a warrior; *mi patria chica*

THEY WERE A SMALL TRIBE, perhaps only four thousand or so,
perhaps larger before smallpox struck them during the early
nineteenth century, a generation before the illness decimated the Blackfeet and other tribes. The meaning of their name
in their own language is pure poetry, "Children of the Large
Beaked Bird," a mythological bird, a beautiful, powerful, spiritual bird. Victims of improper and possibly derisive translation, perhaps perpetrated by enemy tribes or by whites, or by
simple misinterpretation of a hand and arm signal given to
indicate their tribal origin, the Absaroka became known in
English as the Crows.

Insofar as Plains Indians could occupy or claim a given region in the era before borders and survey lines were drawn
by white men, the Crows considered their territory to be the
very best of it. Arapooish, their greatest chief, died in 1834
after exhorting his people to be friends with the white man.
His description of the Crow country is justly famous:

The Crow country is a good country. The Great Spirit has
put it in exactly the right place; when you are in it you

fare well; whenever you go out of it, whichever way you travel, you fare worse.

If you go to the south, you have to wander over great barren plains; the water is warm and bad, and you meet fever and ague. To the north it is cold; the winters are long and bitter, with no grass; you cannot keep horses there, but must travel with dogs. What is a country without horses?

On the Columbia they are poor and dirty, paddle about in canoes, and eat fish. Their teeth are worn out; they are always taking fish bones out of their mouths. Fish is poor food.

To the east they dwell in villages; they live well; but they drink the muddy water of the Missouri—that is bad. A Crow's dog would not drink such water.

About the forks of the Missouri is a fine country; good water; good grass; plenty of buffalo. In the summer it is almost as good as the Crow country; but in winter it is cold; the grass is gone; and there is no salt weed for the horses.

The Crow country is exactly in the right place. It has snowy mountains and sunny plains; all kinds of climates, and good things for every season. When the summer heat scorches the prairies, you can draw up under the mountain, where the air is sweet and cool, the grass fresh, and the bright streams come tumbling out of the snow-banks. There you can hunt the elk, the deer, and the antelope, when their skins are fit for dressing; there you will find plenty of white bears and mountain sheep.

In the autumn when your horses are fat and strong from the mountain pastures, you can go down into the plains and hunt the buffalo, or trap beaver on the streams. And when the winter comes on, you can take shelter in the woody bottoms along the rivers; there you will find

buffalo meat for yourselves, and cottonwood bark for
your horses; or you may winter in the Wind River Valley, where there is salt weed in abundance.

The Crow country is exactly in the right place. Everything good is to be found there. There is no country like
the Crow country.[1]

The Crows, for the most part, took their chief's advice and
forged friendships with the whites, though there were periods of uneasiness. Horses, as for all the Plains tribes, were fair
game. Crow warriors were quick to relieve whites of such bounty, just as they took joy in stealing horses from their various
tribal enemies. And they had many horses—their skills at handling them were universally admired—and many enemies.

Pressed by the Blackfeet nation to the northwest and the
Cheyenne and Sioux to the east, Crow survival was often in
doubt. Indeed, an alliance of enemy tribes once actually orches-
trated an attempt to eliminate the tribe completely, a planned
genocide. In an epic battle the Crows, greatly outnumbered,
fought with every man, woman, child, and weapon they could
muster. It was their Agincourt. They prevailed.

The Crow hunting ground, south-central Montana and northern Wyoming, was just as Arapooish described. Early whites
who traveled the length of the Yellowstone River from today's
Livingston to the border of Dakota territory reported being
constantly within one continuous herd of bison, elk, antelope, mule deer, and whitetail deer—this for some five hundred
miles! Tribes migrated even farther than that, from Canada to
the north and desert country to the south, to hunt seasonally in Crow country, and that was fine with the Crows—as long
as the visitors went home when their bag was full. Land ownership was not an Indian concept, but the idea of a home territory, a territory where they belonged and another tribe did
not, was within their lexicon.

Arapooish seems to have seen the signs of a coming white tide. Less visionary chiefs of less visionary tribes held hopes that the earliest explorers and mountain men were a strange all-male tribe. (They were astonished when they first saw white women, wives of missionaries.) Perhaps this tribe would move on. But the gold rush probably made such a hope faint indeed, and the railroad, of course, ended it completely. But before either, Arapooish gave his sage advice.

In 1851 the Crows, along with other tribes, spurred by the leadership of that Jesuit bundle of energy named Father De Smet, forged a loose treaty with the United States under which they did exceedingly well, too well to hold, considering the rush of whites westward and the immigration of another force as well, the Sioux nation. The Sioux were the largest and most powerful Plains tribe (the pre-smallpox Blackfeet may have rivaled them in size and power, but the disease had reduced their population by half). As the Sioux migrated westward away from conflict with the whites, they gradually laid claim to Crow country. In a war lost by the United States, Red Cloud closed the Bozeman Trail and forced the Treaty of 1868, which scandalized senior army officers as well as the Crow and their friends the Shoshone, all of whom considered the Sioux to be invaders from the East, taking by force what was never theirs.

So those who have berated the Crows for their role on the side of the whites, for the fact that they scouted for Custer, for their gallant effort to help General Crook at the Battle of the Rosebud one week before the debacle at the Little Bighorn; those who have accused the Crows of selling out to the whites simply have not read their history. The Battle of the Little Bighorn occurred not only in Crow country but on the Crow Reservation itself, on land deeded to the Crows by treaty in 1871. From the Crow point of view, the Sioux posed a greater threat than the whites. It was a very natural thing to ally themselves with those they must have seen as the lesser of two evils. They could talk, at least, to the whites!

But there was, of course, the mutual admiration for other warriors, even enemy ones. Frank Linderman interviewed the last Crow chief, Plenty Coups, shortly after World War I. The chief described a "Mexican standoff" with a band of Sioux warriors who paraded on the other side of the Bighorn River, flooded in spring, too high to cross. Neither war party would dare try, for to force their horses across the swollen tide would make them swimming ducks, easy prey for the other. So, instead, both the Crows and the Sioux had to be content with shouting and gesturing insults (one can only imagine!). However, Plenty Coups could not help but admire the colorful parade he saw across the river, painted warriors and spirited horses, shields, feathers, and finery. His summary was something like this: "We hated them, but they sure looked good!"

Overall, though, the Crow's political prowess paid off, and they were initially granted a massive reservation, approximately eight million acres, encompassing south-central Montana from the "Great Bend" of the Yellowstone (today's Livingston, Montana), halfway to the Dakota border, from the Yellowstone River south to the Wyoming border. Hopes that a small tribe could hold onto such a prime piece of real estate, given the press of westward migration by miners, railroad men, ranchers, and homesteaders, were dim, and the reservation was twice reduced in size, chunks of Crow land each time being opened to settlement. Some would say the Absaroka came out relatively well, with a reservation remaining today that is larger than that of many tribes, but that depends, of course, on one's point of view.

The first Crow Agency, located on Mission Creek near Livingston, Montana, was one both Indian and white were glad to leave. It was perched where canyon winds blow incessantly. Tales survive of horses, tied for the day to the hitching rail outside the agency, dying of exposure (hypothermia). So there were probably few regrets when the tribe's agency, pressured

by the growth of white settlements in the area, moved eastward to a quiet valley on the East Rosebud River, a tributary
of the Stillwater.

At this point the Absaroka story and my story move toward
a convergence of stone and grass and sage. Two famous scouts,
Mitch Buoyer and Thomas Leforge, married to Crow women,
had been sent to locate a place for the second agency, with exhortations that they find a spot "out of this damn wind" and
far enough south of the Yellowstone River to be relatively unmolested by the whiskey traders prowling the north side of
the river in the area now known as Columbus, Montana. They
found a spot just above the convergence of the East and West
Rosebud Rivers, which joined to flow north to the Stillwater
and then to the Yellowstone. The spot they found is relatively flat, easy to water with irrigation, a pretty place under the
cottonwoods between the East Rosebud and a smaller stream
named Butcher Creek. They built their second agency there
in 1875, first a fort of cottonwood logs that soon burned, then
a more substantial one of adobe bricks, which they manufac-
tured. And that place where they built it is some three hundred yards from my office upstairs in a horse-training arena,
the place where I write. They dug the first irrigation ditch, one
I still use to water my fields.

Barriers of time, here a century and a third, dissolve when
experiences are shared, and when land, especially, links my
boots with their moccasins, my horse's hooves with those of
their ponies. And Buoyer and Leforge cannot be left so soon.
Buoyer was highly sought as a guide and scout by parties of
all sorts. Part Sioux, with a Crow wife, he knew three cultures
intimately. He died with Custer. There is suspicion that he
may have been a sort of double agent, that he visited a Sioux
encampment not long before the battle. Maybe. If there was
treachery, he did not survive it.

Thomas Leforge should have died along with Buoyer, but

fate, in the form of a horse wreck, intervened. Leforge had enlisted as a scout along with Buoyer, but a week or so before the Battle of the Little Bighorn he lost a fight with a baby antelope. The disoriented little critter buzzed straight toward him, his horse blew up, and he landed in the rocks with a broken collarbone. Too hurt to ride with Custer, Leforge went on to a career off and on the Crow Reservation, and had many children both biological and adopted, leaving many descendants with his name.

Emily and I know something about baby antelope. Riding our young horses one day we crested a ridge on our east range and spotted two antelope does with small fawns a quarter mile away. Never having had a good look at young pronghorn fawns, we pulled a stalk, riding on low ground out of sight, then popping over a gentle ridge near where we had seen the two pairs. We spotted the does immediately 150 yards in front of us. But where were the fawns? That question was soon answered by two thirty-pound torpedoes hurtling straight toward us, clipping the top of sagebrush toward two horses that thought their world was about to end. We spun our horses in circles, touch and go, neither quite bucking, finally stopping them to face the antelope, all four now reunited, running straight away, our horses snorting and wide-eyed.

It was years later that I read *Memoirs of a White Crow Indian* and learned of Tom Leforge's exceedingly lucky accident. But I feel I know him in another way, having wrestled physically with one of his descendants.

It is 1961, a crisp fall day tailor made for a homecoming game between the Absarokee Huskies and the Lodge Grass Indians. I was the Husky tackle on the right side of the line, on both defense and offense. Having frustrated my coaches during my earlier high school years by what they perceived as laziness while running, too shy to tell them that every footfall caused excruciating pain from weak and falling arches, I had finally, as a senior, come into my own. My feet were now flat, had nowhere else to go, and had thus quit hurting sometime during the previous year. Stacking hay bales during summer had bulked me up. I was now enjoying football.

A white kid named Bobby Ball was the Indians' quarterback. I knew him from a trip to the state music festival the previous year. The two schools' music directors were friends and had combined expenses to get a singing group and our brass quartet (my trombone, two trumpets, and a baritone, on Vivaldi) to Missoula for the state competition. But this homecoming day the quarterback did not fare well. An injury knocked him out of the game during the first quarter.

The Lodge Grass coach fell back on simplicity as the best approach. He put his biggest, strongest athlete at tailback position and pounded him at the line on nearly every play. That boy's name was Leforge. He looked like a mountain to me, a face serious and businesslike peering from beneath his helmet, hint of a mustache on his lip. I had a chance to see him "up close and personal" because he or their coach must have had something against me. I only know they tried repeatedly to pound a hole through my part of the line, and I know that I stopped him with little or no gain every single time. The collisions were so hard that everything in my vision was black around the edges for a moment each time I picked myself off the turf. It was the one football game in my unstoried high school and one-year college football career on which I look back with unadulterated pride. It drew accolades from coaches normally stingy with praise, along with a little teasing from friends who claimed I played so well to impress a Lodge Grass cheerleader I had met on the music trip. I denied that and still do—there was no time to concentrate on anything but staying low and flinging myself toward this imposing attacker.

At the time, of course, I had no idea I was bumping helmets with a descendant of the well-known scout. Fascination with the Crow was a developing thing. I learned later that Leforge's size was in keeping with a genetic heritage well documented even a century earlier. One of Custer's scouts was six feet six inches tall. A generation earlier a white trader measured Crow men who came into his post: they *averaged* six feet tall.

But there was an intimacy with Leforge's ancestors born for us on the land we frequented as children, in the walls of foothills that sandwiched our little valley town, the sandstone outcroppings, the coulees that held occasional relics found by treasure seekers. Below two intimidating cliffs above which we perched on Saturday afternoons, our .22 rifles at the ready, watching the river below, were two caves called simply "Big Indian Cave" and "Little Indian Cave." They did not penetrate the sandstone for any great distance, so we had no Tom Sawyer–like experiences within them. Once, while watching the brush between the caves and the stream, I heard a crackle and looked in time to see the rear half of a bobcat disappear from view.

We did not mix with Crows contemporary with us, their world on the reservation a couple of hours drive to the east as far away and as sharply divided from ours as if it had existed on Mars. Occasional school trips for sporting events were the exception. But we learned of the Absaroka from teachers at school (information mixed with misinformation, tinged sometimes with prejudice) and the passing down of anecdotes from that day when our town was a few miles from agency headquarters. We learned that the last days of the agency featured a fully integrated school, of a Crow girl who lost her temper while being disciplined by a teacher named Miss Armstrong, who had grasped her shoulders. The girl grabbed the only thing handy, Miss Armstrong's hair, which turned out to be a wig, which promptly came off in the horrified student's hands. Miss Armstrong, bereft and bald, fled in one direction, and the student, screaming, "I have scalped the teacher!" fled as well and could not be persuaded to return.

But we always felt close to Crow culture. We scoured the hills and coulees not only for rabbits and other game, but for artifacts from an earlier, mysterious, and romantic past. Friends up the street found a cavalry sword that they liked to think may have seen service at the Little Bighorn. Many found stone arrowheads, though in our innocence we did not realize that the day of the stone arrowhead in use by the Plains tribes was long gone by the time Custer went down. Metal had replaced such arrowheads once it became available via the Hudson's Bay Company. (An old Crow man said in the late nineteenth century that he could not remember a day when such arrowheads were made, and in Crow legend, the tiny cave-dwelling "Little People" made them.)

Right after high school, when it became clear that the ranch girl I'd met in the third grade would be friend and more for life, Emily showed me the last horizontal stick in a gnarled ponderosa pine in a timbered draw we know as Indian Coulee. Sitting on Brownie, the favorite horse she shared with her dad, she explained that we were looking at a Crow tree burial, more of which had once been visible to her father and, earlier, respected and preserved by her grandfather, who must have seen the shroud and bones. The tree fell, finally, while I was in Vietnam. But it's there in my consciousness, forever, I guess, evidenced by the fact that I don't seem to be able to write a book without mentioning it.

• • •

Plenty Coups, then graduating from Pipe Holder status (similar to a squad leader in the U.S. military) was one of the Crow warriors who arrived at General Crook's encampment in June 1876, shortly before the Battle of the Rosebud (named after a different Rosebud, a river many miles east of the one near the Crow's second agency). Born in approximately 1848, ten years before Theodore Roosevelt and twenty before the Bornholm birth of the immigrant Magnus Johnson, Plenty Coups had already paid his dues, had survived the Crow version of a Marine boot camp. As a small child he had chased the butterfly, egged on by elders, to build speed and endurance. Among other challenges, he was cheered on in the task of grabbing by the tail a bison bull that was trapped in a circle of warriors. He braved cold with minimal clothing on horse-stealing raids, and he had fought well in battles with the many enemies of the Crow. Like Roosevelt, he was an early achiever, a man quickly singled out by his contemporaries for leadership. Now, at age twenty-six, he was edging toward his role as the last Crow chief, eventually to become leader of all three bands of his tribe.

The band that arrived at Crook's camp, near present-day Sheridan, Wyoming, ushered in first by scouts Grourard and Richaud and a "gigantic" Crow chief, made quite a stir. Crook's soldiers were impressed. An observer named Finerty recalled, "a grove of spears and a crowd of ponies upon the northern heights," and recounted, "There broke upon the air a fierce, savage whoop. The Crows had come in sight of our camp. . . . We went down to the creek to meet them, and a picturesque tribe they were. Their horses—nearly every man had an extra pony—were little beauties, and neighed shrilly at their American brethren."[2]

But admiration was equal from the other direction. Plenty Coups was awed at the numbers and uniform appearance of the American troops:

> I shall never forget what I saw there. It was nearly midday and countless little tents were in straight rows in the green grass and there were nearly as many little fires. Blue soldiers were everywhere. I could not count the wagons and horses and mules. They looked like the grass on the plains—beyond counting.
>
> The Wolves [scouts] of Three-Stars [General Crook] had seen us and told him we were coming. Even before we

dismounted to dress up and paint ourselves for war a bugle sang a war-song in the soldiers' village, after which many blue men began running about. Then, under our very eyes, and so quickly we could scarcely believe them, countless blue legs were walking together; fine horses in little bands that were all of one color were dancing to the songs of shining horns and drums. Oh, what a sight I saw there on Goose Creek that day in the sunlight! My heart sang with the shining horns of the blue soldiers in Three-Stars' village.

Our faces painted, we put on our war-bonnets and sprang upon our horses. We gave the Crow war-whoop, and, firing our guns in the air, dashed down the hill. . . . Ho, Suddenly—like that—the soldiers stopped, all in little bands. . . . All were in straight lines, *all*, with Three-Stars and his men on beautiful horses in the lead.

. . . Our guns were cracking and we raised a big dust. We threw our bodies first one way and then another on our horses, just as we do when fighting. Some of us sprang to the ground and back again without even staggering our horses, and all the time our beautiful bonnets were blowing in the wind. Ah, that was a great day![3]

The Battle of the Rosebud was a classic cavalry confrontation, Crook's troops aided by Crow and Shoshone contingents against Crazy Horse, his Sioux, and some Cheyenne. In tactical terms it was a draw. In strategic terms it was a victory for Crazy Horse because Crook had to draw south for resupply, thus dropping out of the loose, three-pronged pincer movement intended to trap the hostile Sioux and force them back onto their reservations. Custer, under Terry, completely out of communication with Crook or with General Gibbon, who was coming from the west, got there first.

Participation at the Battle of the Rosebud may not have been Plenty Coups' San Juan Hill, but it was certainly another in many achievements that pointed toward his rise as leader of the Absaroka during a crucial time, their transition to a reservation way of life. In his youth he had sought his "medicine," his spiritual power, by depriving himself of food and water, and waiting for a dream. Plenty Coups found his medicine atop a cliff in the Crazy Mountains. The creature that would epitomize his power was not a bear or a wolf or a lion but a pretty little bird, the chickadee, known across North America in the lore of many tribes as a wise and quiet bird, a bird that knew how to coexist with other species. And so, to become a leader of a people seeking peace, Plenty Coups proved himself in war. It was not the first time that had happened. Warriors, it seems to me, best understand peace.

So it was at the end of the Indian Wars that Plenty Coups' career really began, but he never realized that. The interviews with Frank Linderman that became *Plenty Coups: Chief of the Crows* stopped abruptly with the end of tribal warfare and the passing of the buffalo. When those things ceased to exist "our hearts fell to the ground," the chief said, and what followed was not important. And yet, though he would not admit it, Plenty Coups took a certain pride in those accomplishments considered so stellar by whites.

By 1879 Plenty Coups had made his first of a dozen or so visits to Washington as an Indian representative advocating for his and other tribes on one defensive issue or another. The trip in 1908 was prompted by a political move to open reservations to white settlement. Under the proposal the tribes would not be paid, at least directly, the United States acting only as a sort of real estate agent. By this time Plenty Coups and his colleagues had learned the ropes, had learned that accomplishments in Washington require lawyers, money, and like-minded individuals. They won the day in the trenches. But while there, Plenty Coups called on President Roosevelt and presented him with a war bonnet. I can only imagine these two men of stout, powerful build, the veteran of San Juan Hill, his knowledge of Plenty Coups' homeland thorough from his days there as a rancher and hunter, the Crow warrior molded with the help of the Chickadee into the statesman his people needed at a time of trial, the handshake, the gaze of each into the eyes of the other. I reach for a word and find it in Spanish: *simpatico*.

• • •

During the 1980s, teaching in the small town of Bridger, Montana, I yearly loaded chattering students onto a yellow bus for a field trip to Pryor, Montana, then across the southern sweep of the Pryor Mountains through St. Xavier, site of the first mission among the Crow, then to Crow Agency and finally across the Little Bighorn River to the battlefield bearing its name. The curriculum of my Montana History class was structured in such a way that this trip usually fell during early October, and the students and I, itching for the beginning of hunting season, combined "on task" discussions with field evaluations of the many antelope and mule deer we saw along the way, particularly along that lonely stretch of highway fringing the northern face of the Pryor Mountains. The air was crisp, the aspen groves golden against the dark-green timber of the mountains. It was a good time to escape the classroom.

When time allowed we began our trip on a gravel county road through Pryor Gap, a natural opening in the west portion of those mountains that we learned had been a crossroads for Indians and whites over the centuries. A narrow-gauge railroad had been built through the gap by Chinese laborers hired by Mormon contractors. A tunnel carved through a hundred yards of rock was partially caved, but allowed passage, and we braved the walk through it. (I understand the tunnel is now completely closed, and the road as well, locked in a right-of-way dispute.)

We saw low mounds of earth where the Chinese had buried their dead during a diphtheria epidemic that took many of them, and we saw rocks below a cliff that had been a favorite dreaming place for Crow boys seeking their medicine. Sometimes it took days of thirst and hunger and sleep deprivation before the dreams came, and the warriors-to-be threw stones off the cliffs to pass the time. And, because of a family connection offered by the mother of a student, we gained permission from a rancher to see the Little People caves. There was a flat-rock formation, almost as level as pavement in some places, on which we walked, looking through fissures to passageways seemingly designed for a race of the tiny people figuring so prominently in Crow mythology. And who am I to say they were not?

The timeframe of our trips, some fifty years after Plenty Coups' death, was early enough in history that we were twice accompanied by individuals who remembered the chief from their childhood. A man who drove the bus for us had been raised by a rancher father who leased pasture for thousands of sheep from the Crow. As a boy our bus driver had lived a life even TR would have envied, had owned fast horses and hounds with which he coursed coyotes, shooting them for the bounty after chases over vast, fenceless, sagebrush flats. He remembered Plenty Coups vaguely as, simply, a nice old Indian man, but he better remembered his father's tales of relations with the chief, with whom lease agreements were discussed. "A straight shooter," the bus driver called Plenty Coups.

The student's mother who gained us access to the Little People caves remembered Plenty Coups from when her parents worked on the reservation as caretakers for the estate Plenty Coups donated to the state of Montana five years before his death. "He gave me a name," she said, stifling a giggle. "Mouse Woman! It was because of the way I scurried around his house."

The house, an imposing wooden structure in which Plenty Coups was never particularly comfortable (he often slept in a teepee pitched nearby) is the centerpiece of a Montana state park within the reservation boundaries. The chief had visited Mount Vernon during one of his trips east and was impressed by the Great White Chief's dedication of his home to all people of all races to visit and enjoy. Following Washington's example, Plenty Coups deeded a central plot of his own land, a pretty spot on Pryor Creek where flows a sacred spring, to all people, so ownership and management have settled into the hands of Montana Fish, Wildlife and Parks. And, just as Plenty Coups wished, Crows and non-Indians alike can walk the path under the tall cottonwoods and fish in the waters of Pryor Creek.

There is a small museum nearby, open seasonally but accessible off season by prior arrangement. Alerted by the arrival of the yellow bus, the caretakers always met us there with the key, admitting my students to a quick panorama of the chief's life. In a section of memoranda, photographs, and notes from famous people, there is the autographed photo of Theodore Roosevelt, kept in the days before the museum, we learned, in a special corner of the frame house, where Plenty Coups stored those things most precious to him.

• • •

Logan International Airport, Billings, Montana:

The lobby is bustling with the usual scene of humanity, cowboys returning from rodeos, fly fishermen dressed in the best from Abercrombie and Fitch, business travelers coming and going, rumpled college students yawning as they scan the luggage carousels. Then, through the doors from the parking area, a parade begins, Crow or Cheyenne, children with American flags, old laughing women, high school boys whose dress owes more to music videos and hip-hop than to Plains

Indian culture, Indian ranchers wearing Stetsons. A contingent with drums pushes through the revolving doors, the men who are carrying the equipment scanning the lobby for the best location.

Soon several hundred twenty-first-century American Indians form a joyful semicircle at the base of the escalator and stairs, and everyone else in the lobby, all the "civilians," are awed out of their hurry and fix their eyes on the scene. Never mind that dinner with a client, that business appointment, even that rush to the rental-car desk, for this is something they are not likely to see again. The non-Indians are compelled to watch, magnetically drawn. Caught in the tide, they expand the semicircle, careful to stay toward the rear. And then the drums begin, and an old man shakily picks up a war chant and is joined by a few younger, stronger voices.

Passengers descend the stairs, blinking at the scene, slightly embarrassed but smiling, too, because they have an inkling of what is to come. They have seen the celebrity on the airplane. The people in the crowd below watch each passenger push through the door at the top of the stairs, with a momentary suspension of breath, and a disappointment they try not to show. And then it happens, the arrival of the promised one.

The young man or woman who walks through the door and receives a deafening cheer is not a senator or a general or a chief or a president. The young Marine or soldier is more likely a lance corporal or a sergeant. It does not matter. He (or she) is the very best anyone can be in the eyes of that welcoming crowd below, a warrior, a warrior returning from the battlefield alive and well and proud. The drums beat, the band plays, the family of the warrior smothers him with kisses, and a child is thrust into his arms. An elder places a headdress on the warrior's head. It is good, it is right, it is beautiful. It is just as it should be.

The above scene has not happened just once. It has been

repeated dozens of times through the long wars in the Middle East. As in all wars, Montana Indians serve in percentages all out of proportion to their population, even when compared with the white residents of Montana and Wyoming, who enlist at a higher rate than in any other state. The warrior tradition has never died among the Plains tribes, and they transferred it readily from focus on tribal enemies to zeal for fighting the foreign enemies of the United States.

Joe Medicine Crow, one of my personal heroes, still alive and sharp at this writing, had earned his master's in anthropology at the University of Southern California and was working on his doctorate when the United States entered World War II. He dropped everything and enlisted. Turning down a commission (he jokes today about the wisdom of that), he entered the army as a common private, believing, like all Crows, that leadership is earned by deeds, not by appointment or political connections. In Germany he counted coups, defeating an enemy soldier in hand-to-hand combat (he declined to kill him when the desperate soldier called to his mother—killing an enemy was not necessary to count coup), and stealing the horses of German officers. (Yes, horses were still used during World War II in mechanized Germany; half the artillery of the German army was still horse-drawn at the beginning of the war.) Medicine Crow wore an eagle feather under his helmet, and donned war paint under his uniform. He sang a war song as he stampeded the Germans' horses triumphantly from their camp.

And during the previous world war, Plenty Coups was chosen as the American Indian representative to lay the wreath on the tomb of the Unknown Soldier at Arlington in 1921. It's a pity Theodore Roosevelt missed it. He had died two years earlier, his son Quenten having given his life as a fighter pilot in what the Europeans still call "The Great War." Certainly the two old warriors, both of whom, in their respective but overlapping cultures had challenged themselves to learn from the ground up, to build their bodies, to fight, to lead their people in both war and peace, would have reunited on that day.

• • •

Again I borrow from the Spanish, this time their pretty term for the region of one's homeland, the tract of land, not the country, to which he or she is native: *patria chica*. The most patriotic citizen cannot have quite the same emotional feelings for an entire nation that he has for a region with which he is truly intimate. One's patria chica is a homeland within a homeland, a tract of country with which one is as intimate as with the living room in his home. My patria chica is that of the Crows. I say with Arapooish, the Crow country is the good country.

In my patria chica there are two federally designated wilderness areas named after the Crow, the Absaroka-Beartooth in south-central Montana and the North Absaroka Wilderness Area in northwest Wyoming. Both border Yellowstone Park, the Absaroka-Beartooth on the north, the North Absaroka to the east of the Park. Both use the earliest commonly accepted translation of the Crow name, *Absaroka*, but it's important to note that modern scholars, Crow and white, refer to the tribe instead with several similar but probably more correct phonetic labels, *Absarake*, *Absalooke*, *Apsa'alooke*.

And it's in this general area, northwest Wyoming and south-central Montana, that I've done most of my wilderness hunting. Western Wyoming, particularly, became an important region for Theodore Roosevelt, for he did much of his later western hunting there. He was no stranger to the Cody, Wyoming, area, and knew (as nearly everyone did) the town's famous namesake, William Cody, Buffalo Bill, the young scout who emerged with Crook and Terry in the aftermath of the Custer battle. Victory by the Sioux and Cheyenne had signaled their final demise. A nation whose eastern politicians had not quite believed that the Plains Indians formed any serious threat saw during its centennial year a famous Civil War officer and his unit annihilated. The Custer battle became a sort of Pearl Harbor, solidifying support for a western war effort. In the year following June 25, 1876, it was pretty much over. Crazy Horse came in from the cold that was killing his people; Sitting Bull fled to Canada.

The young scout Cody went on to more lucrative things. Enlisting old friends and even hostiles such as Sitting Bull, who joined him for a stretch in old age, the flamboyant showman put together the famous Wild West Show that toured the world. And, like everyone in the region, he knew and admired Plenty Coups, who joined him in parades and accepted from him and the Prince of Monaco a presentation rifle in 1913. The Crow country seems to have been central to many.

All of these people are gone, but the land remains. The jackpine, the spruce, and the fir still hold deer and elk and bighorn sheep. The mountains surrounding proud Granite Peak still fringe my world to the south—sometimes, depending on time and season and weather, purple and so defined I think I can reach out and touch them from twenty miles away; other times, blue-green and velvet, never quite the same from day to day but always there. I have backpacked across these mountains, skied into them with a pack on my back, patrolled them with reserve Marines, and mushed into them behind a team of malamutes I raised and trained. I have ridden good horses many, many miles in this patria chica, my knee on the lead rope of the packhorse behind me. And I have hunted in them for deer and elk and mountain goat.

And through this region my connection with Theodore Roosevelt does not come from tracing his very steps, as I have done near Medora and in the Powder River country. It is his legacy, here, that I trace, the stones on the trail under my horses' hooves solid evidence of his vision. Roosevelt was convinced that modern civilization and the character of its people lose something precious when their environment can no longer sustain the natural prey of the human hunter. And he did something about it. He was never a conservationist who also happened to be a hunter. He was a conservationist *because* he was a hunter. A good hunter looks to the well-being of the animals he hunts, and that well-being is totally dependent on the quality of its habitat.

CHAPTER SIX

Slough Creek

Fire and wolves; a solo adventure; Xanadu; Little Mack and a flying mule; lady rangers; Bubba the gaited jack; "dinner bell grizzlies"; compatible companions; Orion; a Cheyenne friend; "I am Dutch Reformed"; Stewards of the Garden

THERE IS, IN THE MOUNTAINS of south-central Montana, a clear stream born in the high mountain snow of the Absaroka Mountains at the head of a valley that looks south toward Yellowstone Park. The little stream gathers reinforcements from the many rivulets of melting snow and from bubbling springs, gradually swelling in size as it tumbles down granite slopes, then slows as the valley widens into meadows fringed by timber. Eventually Slough Creek, as it is known, enters Yellowstone Park, joins the Clarks Fork of the Yellowstone, and heads east out of the Park, then north to join the Yellowstone River and eventually the Missouri and Mississippi.

The name Slough Creek and what it invokes to hunters of my region is a classic lesson in denotation/connotation, for there is nothing about the word "slough" that suggests beauty to most westerners. Isn't a slough a sort of swamp, considered a rather alien environment in the arid West? But this clear stream, the beautiful valley it inhabits, the hunting traditions central to it, connoted to the older hunters with whom

I grew up a near paradise. There was (and still is) reverence, a worshipful tone when its name is spoken. A man who out-fitted there for many years can scarcely pronounce its name without mist in his eyes. Another, when I was a boy stacking hay, would, at the most frustrating moments, when the equipment broke down and sweat poured off his face as he juggled a wrench into place, stop everything and say simply, "I wish I was up in Slough Creek right now."

A characteristic of speech in this region is pronunciation of "creek" as "crick," though the former has now become common enough that it doesn't necessarily mark one as a "dude." Additionally, two-word place names consisting of an adjective and a noun receive emphasis on the first word, the adjective. *Trout* Crick, *Red* Lodge, *Big* Timber, and *Slough* Crick; opposite emphasis marks one as an outsider.

Throughout my boyhood these two words, Slough Creek, pronounced as above, suggested a mecca to the hunters and packers I knew. Men with packing experience invoked the name of the stream and its famous valley as central to their résumés. A sentence I heard more than once was, "I learned my packing in Slough Creek working for Ray Guthrie." Guthrie was a packing guru. To have apprenticed for him along the fabled creek was an ultimate qualification. One could assume that a man who had done so could tie a diamond hitch in the dark.

But changes, some natural, some man-made, have somewhat tarnished the area's reputation. The same outfitter who used to stop his hay-stacking operation to wax poetic about the area turned to me recently, forty-five years later, when he heard I was planning a trip to Slough Creek. We were at the funeral of another outfitter, an extremely popular man, so popular that the throngs in attendance jammed the parish hall that adjoined the church with overflow seating, and we were waiting for the proceedings to begin. Morris, sitting in front of me, turned to remind me that he outfitted in Slough Creek for thirty years. Then, he said rather solemnly, "It's not like it used to be." He turned to face forward, sighed, then turned back toward me again. "But it's still good."

The natural transformation of the area was caused by the great fires of 1988, fires that raged through much of Yellowstone Park and the surrounding ecosystem. Few dispute the ultimate good, the opening up of the jackpine seeds, the eventual second growth superior in sustaining wildlife. Few who know the area also fail to feel sorrow at the loss of a beauty that will not return during their lifetimes.

The second change, mostly resented by the old hunters and outfitters, was the importation of northern Canadian wolves into the region, beginning in 1995. The move has been adored by tourists in Yellowstone Park, who, I'm told, frequently jump out of their cars to photograph coyotes, thinking they are viewing wolves. The romance surrounding the animal, the hype preceding its introduction (wolves are timid, loving creatures that never harm humans and mainly eat mice and other small game) and its converse (wolves will help control the overpopulated bison herd in Yellowstone Park) was politically overwhelming. So was the power of the federal government under the Endangered Species Act, which prohibited management of wolves by Montana, Wyoming, and Idaho, the three states involved.

The wolves' reintroduction was motivated by two general lines of thinking. Some believed it to be healthy ecologically, that this big predator, missing from the area for decades, would restore the ecosystem, would recreate a natural order of things, would reestablish balance between predator and prey. Others were motivated by a sense of justice. The catchphrase was that wolves had been "hunted to extinction in the Lower 48" by the federal government and by cattlemen (Theodore Roosevelt among them) and that their restoration would redress a past wrong. This line of thinking viewed wolves similarly to a human minority that had been once abused and now deserved a different sort of treatment.

All arguments aside (and there are dozens of them), the reintroduction has been either wildly successful (if you are a wolf proponent) or a plague and a scourge (if you are not). Total numbers today are triple those targeted, thus exceeding by far the quantity that had been pledged to trigger delisting of the animals and return management of them to the states. This happened, briefly, until the delisting was shut down by lawsuits from pro-wolf groups not yet satisfied.

And, in a twist of which the public has little awareness, hundreds of wolves have been killed from the air by federal authorities bound by an agreement to control animals that prey on livestock within this "experimental" population. As with any predator, one taste of beefsteak or lamb chops or llama loin seems enough to convert wolves to domestic tastes.

The *Billings Gazette* on December 15, 2008, reported one of the largest wolf kills in recent memory, all twenty-seven members of the "Hog Heaven" pack being taken out by federal wildlife officials after earlier attempts that killed only the dominant animals failed to control the wolves' affection for domestic meat. The pack was responsible for at least five cows, five llamas, and a bull. The wolf coordinator for Montana Fish, Wildlife and Parks, Carolyn Sime, told reporters, "In the course of conserving wolves, some will die." She went on to point out that removing problem wolves is necessary for the animals to coexist with humans. "It's not a national park. We live here," she said. But wildlife activists protest.

Most of the burgeoning wolf population still feeds on wild game. As mentioned earlier, the moose population suffered first, the Canadian wolves being professionals at killing that sort of prey, and our smaller Shiras moose proving relatively innocent pickings. The bulk of the wolves' diet, however, consists of elk.

The northern Yellowstone elk herd is but a fraction of its former self, and wolves are the primary reason, though grizzlies, also on the increase, enjoy dining on newborn elk and seek out calving grounds for easy meals. Wolves, contrary to all predictions that they would prey primarily on the old and sick, take a good number of mature bulls after the rutting season when the males have exhausted their physical resources in search of cows and in combat with each other, when food has taken a backseat to reproduction. In this depleted condition they must fight deep snow for sustenance and, thus weakened, are no match for a pack of wolves.

No one can deny the appeal of wolves, their beauty and intelligence. I've seen them but once, on a large private ranch in bitter cold and deep snow. Another rider and I crested a ridge and watched through binoculars a cow moose lope out of a patch of willows nearly a mile away. Then, a few minutes later, what appeared to be two dots in the snow revealed themselves as wolves, and they were streaking. They did not appear to be chasing the moose, but we suspected she had winded them and was getting out of their way.

It was clear the wolves were running from us, spooked at even this substantial distance. I had been told the rancher had a shooting permit for two wolves that had been harassing his livestock, and I remember thinking, "Well, good luck. You'd better have a laser gun that can hit running targets a mile away." Yes, they are beautiful, exciting creatures. They are also killing machines requiring immense quantities of fresh red meat to keep them going—and they are just so damned efficient at getting it.

The epicenter of wolf predation on elk is the very valley about which I heard so much as a boy, the Slough Creek Valley joining Yellowstone Park on the north. Its combination of wide green meadows bordering deep timber constitutes some of the best elk habitat imaginable. A disgusted outfitter who had moved his operation to backcountry in another region referred to the area as a "predator pit," but that is far too harsh for me. The magnet is still there. Hunters and packers plan all year, anticipate all year a wilderness adventure in this wild region north of Yellowstone Park. Montana Fish, Wildlife and Parks still maintains the early rifle season for bugling elk in this region, one of just a few such seasons in the state. It is still a beautiful place.

But you no longer go there with high expectations for trophy elk. You go there because it is there, a tradition of wilderness adventure where odds of meeting a grizzly are as good as they are for seeing a trophy elk. You go there in mid-September, when golden aspen groves garnish the black timber, when, with luck, you'll hear the whistle of a big bull, when weather can alternate from summer to winter and back. You go there for the fun, for the smell of crackling pine in the sheet-metal tent stove, for camp food and friends and booze. And maybe for elk.

So it was not with any illusions that Billy and I powered our way to the high trailhead at Daisy Pass above the town of Cooke City. Had elk meat in the freezer or antlers on the wall been our only motivators, we would probably have been unloading elsewhere. But the wind on the mountaintop blew from the west, and the trailhead enticed, though I felt the usual uneasiness I experience at high altitude in wind, with horses tied to the trailer, snorty and pawing, their manes and tails lifting with each gust.

We were far from alone. Dusty pickups hooked to gooseneck trailers were jammed everywhere astraddle the wide spot in the road, some long deserted by early birds who had packed in their camps well in advance of the September 15 opener. Other outfits were still surrounded by tied horses and mules, packs in the making, manties and panniers scattered on the ground, the men bustling and happy. Next to us was a young mule man preparing to pack supplies alone to an already established camp. He turned out to be the son of a man I'd known in boyhood, who, in turn, was the son of one of my father's friends and parishioners at the country church in the dryland foothills I knew so well as a kid. After a brief exchange of information, he was a stranger no more. I watched him deftly prepare his packs and ready himself to set off alone with a pack string, noticed his hard-muscled confidence, suspected that in a tight spot he'd stack up very well against the Abercrombie and Fitch–equipped urban adventurers who turn wilderness tripping into a competitive sport.

So Billy and I combed our five geldings, all Tennessee Walking Horses bred on my ranch, Billy's grays named Smokey and Blaze, my high-energy, old reliable Little Mack, the tall young black Skywalker, and Emily's gelding Redstar, a smooth sorrel, one of our best cow horses and an old hand at the wilderness. Billy's young horse, Blaze, would pack the bear-resistant panniers Billy had recently purchased. These fiberglass boxes, with finger-pinching recessed thumbscrews on the lids, had apparently passed the grizzly torture test required for certification and thus met the Forest Service's requirement for food storage in grizzly country, where you have three legal options: someone can stay in camp at all times; you can hang all food high in a tree, a given distance from the trunk (an onerous task when done in the dark at 4 a.m. before hunting); or you can keep everything edible stored in these bear-resistant boxes.

Little Mack, for many years my pack string leader, would not carry me on this trip. He and Redstar would carry manties on Decker packsaddles, the packing combination we've come to prefer. Manty, from the Spanish for blanket, refers to a small canvas tarp, but also to the finished pack for which it is used. Simply put, all cargo is placed carefully on the tarp diagonally, the bundle is made with several tight half hitches, and the load is basket-hitched onto the Decker. There's no diamond hitch to tie, no top pack, simply two vertical packs on each side of the animal, free to swing when they hit a tree, and easy to adjust should one prove slightly heavier. (The heavier manty is slung a little higher.)

Roosevelt spoke with some envy of those who had mastered the diamond hitch, the rather intricate lacing of line typically used to hold a top pack in place. On his first trip to the Big Horns he readily admitted that neither he nor his ranch-oriented companions were, at that time, accomplished packers. The penalty was broken packs and scattered cargo as they drove their pack animals through the timber up the side of a mountain. The Decker was yet to be invented, though TR could have encountered it late in life in Idaho and western Montana. Originating in mining areas for carrying ore, the Decker is stronger than the more traditional sawbuck (crossbuck) and, with the manty method, simpler to use. Billy and I had jumpstarted the effort for a quick exit from the trailhead by assembling our manties at home, so it was a matter of saddling our horses, slinging our loads, and pointing the eager animals toward the trailhead sign, where the trail plunged steeply down toward our anticipated adventure.

• • •

Thirteen years earlier Emily and I and our two younger sons had parked at this same trailhead on a July day that looked more like November. A light snow fell. Higher, on the Beartooth Highway, we had pulled over to wait for a snowplow during a storm that had briefly closed the pass. Now, at this high-altitude trailhead, my planned solo adventure, to go with two horses from the Slough Creek drainage across a pass to the Stillwater River Valley, then home, seemed more foolhardy than brave.

Traditionally high-altitude trails in this area do not open until after Independence Day, and even then one must expect snowdrifts on the passes. This particular year, though, storms and cool weather lingered. It was past the middle of July before things cleared somewhat and I had reason to believe the trails would be passable. (I discovered later that I was the first horseman of the summer to traverse several of them.)

It was an odd, cold summer, sandwiched between two hot, dry ones, and it was, too, a "damp, drizzly November in my soul." I'd suffered the usual midlife losses, the death of my mother prominent among them, and had butted up against the cold, hard wall of middle age. Melville's Ishmael handled his ailing psyche by going to sea. Roosevelt treated his by heading west. I intended to soothe mine, maybe restore it, by going to the mountains. But as I looked at the Wolverine Creek Trail, ledged into the side of the mountain, snaking down, shrouded by fog and falling snow until it disappeared from view, I felt far more like Hemingway's Nick Adams than Melville's Ishmael. Nick, tender physically and mentally from wounds suffered in war, tempted as he is by giant trout, deigns to fish the swamp. Another day, perhaps, but not today.

I was after an adventure, not an ordeal. To head down a trail I did not know with two green horses, a trail that did not appear to have been used since hunters packed up their camps the previous fall; to drop down the mountain into a cloud of snow and fog on a trail that may be blocked, for all I knew, at a treacherous spot; to ask Emily and my sons to watch me disappear into the fog on a mountainside; these things crossed the line. Besides, there was another possible avenue.

In Yellowstone Park the Slough Creek trailhead, at relatively low elevation, is open to horses. An added bonus of launching out there would be seeing the fabled Silvertip Ranch, located north of the Park border, a guest ranch on a piece of private land legally grandfathered when the wilderness area was established. With national park to the south and federally designated wilderness to the north, the Silvertip is supplied completely by horse and wagon traveling a two-track south to the Slough Creek trailhead. This route cannot be used to exit the Slough Creek drainage during hunting season, however, because packing meat—elk or deer quarters—is prohibited in the Park. Firearms are "allowed" on a basis similar to the military's "don't ask, don't tell" policy. Technically, they're prohibited. Realistically, they are to be encased and inaccessible, I suppose to prevent in theory a trigger-happy and unstable individual from being tempted to kill a trophy animal.

So, making the decision to descend the rough road down to Cooke City and travel into the Park, I first opened a manty and packed away my Ruger Bisley .44 magnum and its ammunition. I had loaded 300-grain hard-cast bullets to all the velocity and recoil the gun and I could handle—grizzly loads if such exist for any handgun. (Were I making the trip today I would also take a can of bear pepper spray.) I planned to extract the handgun from the pack the instant it was legal.

The Slough Creek trailhead in Yellowstone Park was teeming with the most varied conceivable set of humanity. Muddy horse trailers sat next to luxury motor homes. Grizzled packers, assembling loads of clients' gear for fishing excursions into the wild, rubbed elbows with urban tourists, who dodged horse droppings as if they were landmines. Most were headed up the Slough Creek Trail, but I suspected that only the packers would go very far. Some would day-hike or fish for only a few hundred yards; others, more adventurous, might make it several miles. But I suspected that I would be alone on the two-track trail by the time I reached the park boundary and the Silvertip Ranch eleven miles to the north.

The weather was briefly better at this lower-elevation trailhead, though clouds occasionally blocked the sun and spit rain. It was after I said my good-byes to the family, though, after I mounted Major and picked up Sugar's lead rope, reined past the trailhead signs, and threw Emily and the boys one last wave, that the weather closed in on me in a way my psyche did not particularly need. I rode in hard rain for ten miles. My layered clothing topped by a Gore-Tex jacket kept my torso relatively warm, but from the thighs down I was soon soaked, and I stayed that way. As fatigue set in, I wondered why my left hand had grown so numb, only to discover that my broad-brimmed hat formed a rain gutter that neatly dropped its icy stream squarely on top of the hand where it rested on the saddle horn holding the reins. I simply had not noticed.

But even in this there was beauty. The sun teased us with cameo appearances that lit up the grass bordering Slough Creek with fluorescent green. A huge bull moose fed in a deep, slow pool in the creek, rearing its head and antlers from the water in a cascade that drew snorts from my horses, who warily quick-stepped with sidelong glances at a creature that looked strange and dangerous to them. There was the trip through the Silvertip Ranch, a strange oasis of private land, with well-kept stables and barns and a wary cowhand who nodded as I passed.

And finally there were, when I was tired and cold and probably into the earlier stages of hypothermia, the famous meadows and parks of the Slough Creek Valley, partial sun now, a bit of drying, the steam from my sweaty horses' coats rising as their wet hides warmed. I made a camp, got a smoky fire going, perked coffee, and tried to catch some uncooperative fish. I wrote to Emily in my journal an entry that reflects, as I read it today, the disparate sides of the experience: *"Frankly, I'm having a little trouble keeping my morale up, with the wet weather, nervous start, etc. I just saw a hummingbird. He came up to the cooking area, hovered looking it over, then left!"*

I once gave a class of high school seniors a pop quiz on *The Adventures of Huckleberry Finn*. They had read the book in my class exactly one year earlier. The students did extremely well on the quiz, proving a point I had tried to make to them. A really good book sticks. They admitted, the more avid readers among them, that other books, adventure and romance stuff they had read in the interim, had faded completely from memory. But Huck and Jim had stuck with them.

I suppose the solo experience up the Slough Creek Valley stands a similar test. I've done many other things during the last fifteen years that I remember little if at all. But certain details of those three days alone with two plucky young horses, testing myself for who knows why, are still bold-typed in my memory.

The first morning, Major and Sugar, far from being fatigued by the previous day's ride, were snorty and ready, perhaps energized by the visit during the night of an entire pack string of outfitter's mules following their bell mare, grazing until their morning wrangler rounded them up. I broke camp and mounted Major, who quivered with excitement. We hit a running walk through famous Frenchy's Meadow, watched by a yellow-slickered outfitter who sat his horse, enjoying a patch of morning sun (and perhaps a respite from the demands of his clients). He and I exchanged a quick "good morning." I answered his question about where we were headed—over to the Stillwater—and he smiled, having seen my horses cruise toward him, and just said, "Well, it won't take you long to get there."

But I had trouble sharing his confidence. There was no low-altitude route home. Via one trail or another we would have to cross at least one high pass, and the mountaintops were shrouded in fog, the wet cold front hanging on. Fog up high translates into snow, but this day, too, there were occasional sun breaks, enough to keep me hoping. Major and Sugar eased back into a ground-eating flat walk as we left the expansive meadows for a narrower, more timbered part of the valley. In a green glade under tall spruce, unburned by the conflagration of 1988, I rode right into a herd of elk, cows and calves rising from their beds, taking time to stretch before they trotted away. I was thrilled to see them but regretted my intrusion.

We found the trail junction to begin our ascent on the chosen route, only to see a weathered Forest Service sign that read "Trail not maintained." Seconding this notice was the trail itself, overgrown with a foot of grass, deadfall strewn across it. Ah, the limitations of maps. Plan B involved backtracking a mile, spotting the ford across Slough Creek, now a shallow rocky stream with none of the deep meandering pools we had seen farther down the valley, and plunging across to a discernable trail heading east up the mountain through the timber. It was quite obvious that no one had traveled these trails since the previous hunting season, a disquieting bit of knowledge to ponder.

Long before this area had been designated wilderness, there had been mining exploration, primarily for gold. I once heard that the last remaining bulldozer involved in such exploration was piloted out of the region on the very last day before mechanized travel became illegal. The trail on the east side of the valley, which I now ascended, showed that mechanized past by remnants of bulldozer roads, long ago grown over, occasionally merging with the trail, sometimes becoming the trail. Covered with the green of a very wet spring, the crisscrossing roads and trails became a maze.

So, while I did not become lost, I did become, as the saying goes, confused for a while. I continued to ascend the mountainside, always on one sort of trail or another, but continually uncertain as to whether it was the right one. A GPS unit was still several years in my future, as was the government's perfection of the system that has now become mundane. My map and compass skills, though, born in boyhood and polished in the Marine Corps, shed their rust as I shot resections from the valley to the south and prominent peaks on several sides of me. I was exactly where I should have been—but the trail wasn't!

Finally, nearing the top of the mountain and seeking

confirmation of a trail I had spotted bending left, to the north, I somewhat rashly dismounted and loosely slip-knotted Sugar's lead rope to the saddle horn on Major, then, leading the horses up a slope too steep to ride, climbed straight up the ridge. We scrambled over tundra and around truck-sized boulders all the way to the top and looked over a cliff. Horseshoe Lake lay just where it ought to be, a thousand feet below, a blue gem surrounded by scrub pine. Now I could rejoin the overgrown trail with confidence.

On the bend around the mountain, before final descent to the lake, I encountered a snowfield covering the trail for several hundred yards on a steep sidehill. I could see the trail emerge from the far end of the snow. To my left was a slide that simply grew steeper, then dropped off the mountain. Losing traction would be fatal. Floundering in deep snow on such a slope would be only slightly more preferable. Major took two tentative steps into the bank, and I breathed a sigh of relief as his feet sunk just six inches into the compacted snow, good for traction. Across we went.

The three of us rested, though nervously, at Horseshoe Lake. I ate a sandwich and drank some water (but not, it turned out, enough). Tired as they should have been, the horses fidgeted, anxious to be off. Though the sun was out, a chilly breeze tossed the stunted pines. I remember thinking about grizzlies and reaching up on Major where the big Ruger revolver rode in its holster tightly lashed with the saddle strings to the front of the horn. I patted its walnut grips. Had I been able to see into the future for a couple of years, I would have been considerably more nervous. It was close to Horseshoe Lake that a teenager from eastern Montana, hunting elk, was attacked by a grizzly sow without warning, knocked flat from behind, and mauled so severely he barely survived. Other hunters got him down into Slough Creek where a surgeon, camped for the early hunt, saved the young man's life.

There are other poignant memories from this trip so long

ago. I took a foolish shortcut through the timber on the east side of Horseshoe Lake, rejoining the trail but below a junction, and went a mile out of my way until it dawned on me that I was losing elevation, rather than gaining. Strange things happen when you're alone. I backtracked, found the junction and began still another ascent, this time to a high plateau that would eventually drop me into the Stillwater Valley. There were other challenges ahead. At my camp by the rushing Stillwater River, I was flattened briefly by a strange and violent sickness in the middle of the night, probably acute mountain sickness brought on by dehydration. I rushed to the tent door to gulp fresh air, then lay dizzy and worried about whether I'd be strong enough to pack up in the morning. Then there was the ride out the last day, my condition shaky but better, saddle time spent again in unrelenting rain, the now-familiar landmarks of a trail I knew well appearing surrealistically out of the fog, friendly, but reminding me of the distance yet to go.

But it was earlier, on the plateau above Horseshoe Lake, that I saw something justifying the entire trip, a sight that has remained indelible in my mind's eye. It was not a grizzly bear or a royal bull elk, but a massive mountain so solitary, so powerful, that it seemed to possess its own indomitable spirit. Very tired and with miles yet to go, I was high above the timberline where the trail was marked only by rock cairns every couple hundred yards. The late-afternoon sun came out. I turned to the east and saw a square mountain, not a peak exactly, but more a massive, fortress-like block, fringed by cliffs on its flanks and velvety green timber around its foot, which now shone brightly in the sun. There was no other peak like it or near it. It stood apart, its own thing, a castle for an unknown king.

Hurried as I was to find a campsite before darkness, I could only stop and stare. Words from the beginning of a poem I'd memorized in high school came to me:

In Xanadu did Kubla Khan
A stately pleasure-dome decree:
Where Alph, the sacred river ran
Through caverns measureless to man
Down to a sunless sea.

Samuel Taylor Coleridge claimed he wrote *Kubla Khan* after awaking from an opium-induced trance (the stuff was legal and socially acceptable for a time), that midway through the vision he was trying to impart of a great king building his enchanted palace, a visitor interrupted him. He never finished the poem.

No matter. The mountain I stared at that day, that made me hold my restive horses from their plunge down into the next valley, finished it for me. Surrounded by other mountains, some higher, some steeper, it spoke of strength solitary and serene.

• • •

Major and Sugar, the two horses who at the tender age of three had carried me with such spirit and enthusiasm over two mountain passes on that trip home from Slough Creek, were not with Billy and me as we made final preparations for our adventure. Both geldings, alive and well at age sixteen, were enjoying semi-retirement on the ranch, still healthy, still useful. Today I wouldn't choose horses as young as they had been for my trip alone across the passes, but Major had matured early, was big and strong and heavy-boned, and Sugar, smaller, was asked to carry only the relatively light packs necessary for a solo trip. As Billy and I scoured truck and trailer for items we may have forgotten, I found myself missing the two sorrels who first knew this country with me. In his lifetime a horseman knows many, raises them, then sees them get old.

The elder statesman on this later trip was the oft-mentioned bundle of enthusiasm and energy named Little Mack. My best cowhorse, Little Mack is not particularly little, but rather middle-sized, his name dating from his days as a gangling colt, offspring of a stallion named Mack, the "stud colt" of my book *Sketches from the Ranch: A Montana Memoir*. Little Mack and I have been down many trails together. I held off riding him until Christmas, when he was $2^1/_2$, and even then with some concern that his wiry, adolescent build would be stressed by my weight. It took only a ride or two to settle that issue. He carried me as if he had been born to do it, as if born to head up mountain trails for the sheer joy of traveling toward the top of the next ridge, toward the patch of blue sky visible at the top through the timber.

In many respects I did not really train Little Mack. I simply *used* him. Yes, I could argue that such an approach is really the best training of all. I constantly hear Elmer's exclamation in my ear from many years ago while he watched a horse doing something absolutely goofy and a rider unable to cope: "The trouble with most horses nowadays is that they're just not *used* enough." Very true. But I'll admit that I left some holes in Little Mack's training by shorting the groundwork and taking him straight to the cowherd and to the mountains.

I rode him that winter just a few times in the round pen before frigid weather set in. In March when the snow melted and the chinook winds cut the frost and made it mud, I got on Little Mack again several times in the round pen, then took him on a single ride into the hills by myself. Still light in build (but with ample bone), he took me to the top of the valley wall behind our house, and as we topped out and looked across the sagebrush toward the far Pryor Mountains, he radiated willingness to climb anything I pointed him toward. Spring work on the ranch then descended on me, but a hint of green in the cottonwoods during early April pulled me toward the mountains, toward a spring bear hunt that had become tradition with a small circle of friends. We never got a bear, and we never really cared. The hunt was an excuse to get green horses out onto the trail, to listen to lies around the campfire while sipping the drink we knew as Mackenzie Gold. (To brew one, put snow into a Sierra cup halfway to the top; add Yukon Jack and unsweetened grapefruit juice in equal proportions.)

Little Mack was slated to pack a load of horse pellets on his first excursion to the mountains, feed required to supplement for our string the meager grass they'd likely to be able to paw from under the snow at the campsite we had in mind. But it was not to be. At the trailhead, Major came down with a case of heaves. Since the ride to camp was a short one, and since I had seen these attacks leave as quickly as they came, much like asthma does in some humans, I believed Major could still go with us. But certainly carrying a light sawbuck saddle and two cloth panniers containing sacks of pellets, a little over 100 pounds total, would be much easier on him than carrying a 225-pound Norwegian, plus his saddle and gear. I looked Little Mack in the eye and said, "Okay, Sport, you're up."

Inwardly, I was not so jocular. It was a little insane to lead a pack string for even a short jaunt into the mountains on a spirited colt that had been ridden exactly once outside the round pen, whose neck rein (necessary so that you have a free hand for the pack horse's lead rope) was still far from established. But I was buoyed by the peer support of my friends Roger and Cliff. I mounted up, took Major's lead rope (Sugar was tied to the "pigtail" on the back of Major's packsaddle), said "Geronimo!" and plunged down the trail. Roger followed on Emily's big black named Marauder, then Cliff on his Quarter Horse mare, leading Opie, his mule.

All went well, which is to say we had no wreck. It was one of the faster trips I've taken with a pack string. If I could read between his ears I believed Little Mack was thinking, "Wow! All this space in front of me and no fences in sight. Cool!" But

16. The author and Little Mack in the Slough Creek drainage.
Courtesy of Dan and Emily Aadland.

I managed to hold him in check, steering mainly with my legs while improving his neck rein as best I could.

After two days in camp, when a wet snow fell without dampening our spirits in the least, after hiking and riding and finding some fresh bear sign but not the bear that made it, we packed up for home. Major, as I'd expected, was well over his asthmatic siege, and I planned to ride him, packing Little

Mack as first intended. But I found myself tempted to ride the colt again. "What do you think, Cliff? Should I switch or ride the colt?"

Of course, I could have guessed the answer that would come from a guy who rides bareback in endurance races, who selects Opie the mule to ride without saddle when he pursues game through the deadfall ("I can just jump better that way," he says). "Well, the colt did really well coming in. I think you should just stick with him."

So I did, climbing the steep, muddy ridge at the beginning of the trail, Roger riding behind and looking out for the balance of my packs. Just as we reached the top, I heard a grunt and an exclamation from Roger, and I glanced back only to see Opie, the mule, tumbling down the slope like a big off-balance bowling ball, first legs, then packs, then legs, then packs. Cliff was back down to her in a flash. "She's alright," he hollered. "She's a mule!" And the packs, too, were all right, Cliff's pannier—diamond hitch combination, skillfully wrought, still intact and requiring only slight adjustment.

So many years later, when Billy and I prepared our string at the Lake Abundance trailhead for descent down Wolverine Creek toward Slough Creek, I reflected that Little Mack had missed a stage of his training I normally require of all my horses. He had never been packed. For me that's essential training for the backcountry horse. True, the world is full of horse training gurus who, if their lives depended on it, could not manty up a load and basket-hitch it to a Decker packsaddle, much less tie a diamond hitch. But with all due respect to their fine work, I've been places and done things that "are not dreamt of in their philosophy." For a horse, one week of carrying an honest load in the mountains, of banging his packs against trees, of feeling the breeching under his tail, of meeting elk and moose on the trail, of crossing rocky streams large and small, of keeping his lead rope slack, no matter the speed of the animal to which he's attached—these things are worth, in my mind, months of arena training and Parelli games.

Not that I was worried about Little Mack. He had reached elder statesman status, was used to everything imaginable, had moved cattle on highways while harassed by the thunder of Harley Davidsons, had carried inexperienced students, had felt everything imaginable bump against him at one time or another. And, as I expected, the two big manties hitched to his packsaddle bothered him not the least. What *did* bother him, what completely perplexed him, was the fact that I was on another horse, that he had no rider, that he was expected to walk second in line. Yes, he had been on trail rides when I had ridden another horse, when he had been expected to walk in line behind me, but with bit in mouth and reins in the hands of a rider, he understood what was expected.

Being ponied behind another horse was descent into a plebian existence for Little Mack, and while he did not look hurt—his perked ears and open-faced eagerness for whatever lay around the next bend in the trail were the same as usual—he refused to accept that he should not be up front, beside the man who had trained him and had been his friend from day one. So from the minute Billy and I mounted up and headed toward Slough Creek, Little Mack tried his best to walk beside Skywalker and me. On narrow ledge trails or on sections threading tightly through timber, he moved back onto the trail. Otherwise, defying the perils caused by steep banks, sagebrush, or treacherous footing on the side of the trail, he did his best to walk alongside me, and none of the usual yanks on the lead rope with admonitions to get back did much good for long.

We had gone only a mile or two when we passed the young packer we'd visited with at the trailhead, his horse and mules tied off to the side of the trail to nearby trees. He had left a half hour before we had, and I was a little curious about his making a rest stop so soon, but some of the codes of the West are still intact, so I didn't stop to ask. Then, after another quarter mile I heard Billy exclaim, "Oh, Oh!" the words followed by a series of metallic clangs. Our frying pan had managed to worm its way through the folds in a manty tarp, drop out of the pack, and clatter along the rocks of the trail for a couple of yards.

I had confined many loose items into this particular manty, trying to give it shape by enclosing a tent pole on each side, but I had been too greedy, had included too many small pieces of gear, which left too little overlap in the folds of the tarp. Oh, well, it was not a major wreck. We tied up to pines by the trail and commenced repacking. As I was tying the half hitches in the rebuilt manty, the young packer rode up. "Kinda embarrassing having to rebuild a pack only a mile down the trail," I told him, "especially when it's the frying pan you've lost."

"Nope," he said. "That's what I was doing back there where I was tied up. Had to rebuild one myself!" He rode on. Real packers don't laugh at other people's wrecks. We've all been there a time or two.

It comes to my mind on all trips like this one, the saying from a character in *Lonesome Dove* about how fine it is to ride a good horse in new country. This was a trail neither Billy nor I nor even Little Mack had ever seen, though the horse, in his usual manner, pointed his ears toward attractive clearings, telling me they would be suitable places to camp. The gelding never forgets a campsite we've actually used. I've several times traveled drainages he has seen just once and had him attempt to turn into the campsite we used a decade earlier.

We descended into healthy, unburned timber, then toward a ridge that had been spared during the fires of '88, its spruce a deep green flanked on the left by a granite wall. Once over it, the trail was a steady descent along Wolverine Creek into the Slough Creek drainage. We took our time, soaking it in, stopping occasionally to look for elk and bear sign. And once, while we were stopped to "let out some coffee," a man passed us heading down the trail on a lanky, fast-walking horse, an equally lanky, fast-walking mule behind him. We had no idea where he'd come from, but he gave us a cheerful wave. The mule was lightly packed with a long, slim bundle right on top of the packsaddle, probably tent poles. One of the man's hands held the reins and lead rope while the other maintained an affectionate grip on an outsized can of beer. He hummed a tune as he rode along. That guy, we agreed, knew how to enjoy himself.

Our proposed campsite was partway down this tributary to Slough Creek. We would not camp on the creek itself, on fabled Frenchy's Meadow, because beautiful as the main valley is, it would also be loaded with camps and people, horses and mules, and noise. Better to camp along this tributary and hunt the ridges above us and the main valley, if time permitted.

We found a clearing recommended by a friend, and soon, with a little work, the campsite became home. On a rocky place where the horses would do little damage, we strung a highline, tying several of them to it and picketing a couple out to graze. The spike tent went into a neat little alcove among the trees, close to the creek. A couple of hundred feet away from it, near the trail, we cobbled together a crude shelter for cooking and eating, nothing more than a tarp winged out from a pine tree, two poles ripped from deadfall holding up the corners. We would keep all food here, none in the tent. We were at ground zero for grizzly bears.

A pack string passed camp, and we quickly realized the limitations of the wooden picket stakes we had found already driven into the ground. Our horses simply removed them and waltzed up to the pack string to say hello. They were easily caught and soundly admonished (but did not seem to notice). Then three young ladies came walking down the trail looking as casual and comfortable as if they were on a summer stroll through the mall. Their garb identified them as Forest Service employees, and they quickly did their duty, chatting with us about the fire restrictions still in effect. I offered to make them coffee, but they declined. They had a long way to walk yet to a Forest Service cabin on Slough Creek, and I suspected their marching orders contained restrictions on stopping in camps for coffee with strange men.

After they left, Billy and I had a not-too-politically-correct discussion. What was wrong with this picture? Slough Creek would be awash with hunting camps occupied primarily by mounted men with guns. True, hunters as a group are said to be statistically more law-abiding than citizens as a whole. Still, you have men with horses and guns and whiskey, and who do you send down to Slough Creek to remind each camp that they are not to have campfires, this in weather now becoming drizzly, where such a rule is bound to be taken only semi-seriously? Who do you designate as law-enforcement officers in the middle of a wilderness where any sort of help is far away? A grizzled old ranger, horseback, with a 9mm on his hip? Nope. Rather, three young, nice-looking ladies, afoot, with nothing more on their hips than bear spray.

Not that female law enforcement isn't effective on men (often women can defuse situations where a male cop might inflame them). And bear spray is usually effective on bears and would no doubt be doubly so used on a drunk out of line. Still (and maybe this is the father/grandfather coming out in me), if these women were my employees I'd want them horseback and a bit better armed. Horses would give them the mobility necessary to respond to certain situations, to get help more quickly, if necessary. And, there's a psychological component. A person on foot is at a disadvantage talking with a mounted man, the reason horsemen with traditional good manners dismount for any extended interaction with someone on the ground. It's the reason, too, that mounted policemen in urban situations are so effective on crowds that are afoot.

17. Cooking on Slough Creek. Courtesy of Dan and Emily Aadland.

I can't remember what I cooked that evening, but I know there was lots of it, that Billy, thin as a rail and perhaps eighty pounds lighter than me, matched me forkful for forkful. He's an MD, half my age, in terrific shape, and infinitely patient with an aging friend who needs twice the time he does to climb each ridge.

Billy showed me the device known as a personal locator beacon he had brought at the insistence of his medical office. It was only right that we both knew how to use it. As it is, we frequently joke that though logic would suggest a hunter in his sixties would be most likely to have a health or accident mishap requiring the assistance of a doctor in his thirties, irony could create the opposite scenario. I've told him I don't wish to perform any surgeries by following instructions.

The PLB (as they're called) required the very deliberate movement of two spring-loaded levers toward each other for activation. At that point, as Billy put it, the helicopters are in the air. And they know where you are. But such power to summon help is not to be taken lightly. Assisting search and rescue teams, Billy has seen the results of too quickly relying on devices such as this one, and on cell phones to call for help, possibly diverting emergency resources from those who truly need it, this done for relatively minor injuries that in the old days would have been toughed out. He told me, "It would take a lot to make me pull the trigger on this thing. I wouldn't do it for just a broken leg." And knowing him, I completely believe him.

The drizzle settled in. We periodically rotated the horses from highline to hobbles to picket ropes, never hobbling more than one or two, and never Little Mack, who as senior equine had the power to lead others astray. There was ample grass in the meadow, though I soon regretted our decision not to pack in additional feed. Pellets in any substantial quantity may have required another pack animal, but they would have cut down on this necessary rotation because horses on the highline could have nibbled away at feed in nosebags.

The drizzle became rain. We were very law abiding. Instead of building a campfire we parked our stools under the tarp, the mantle of a small propane lantern an inadequate substitute for crackling pine and aromatic smoke. Still, it was pleasant. The bourbon soon appeared, along with Coke as mixer; then as our supper digested, the peanuts, and it was clear we were having a grand time rain or not, campfire or not. We plotted a strategy for morning. A quick reconnaissance ride in late afternoon had shown a possible horseback route up the ridge to our north, which, like all the mountainsides around us, was a jumbled mass of deadfall, huge trunks of old-growth trees terminated by the fires of 1988, tumbling to the ground five years later when their roots gave way. In the morning we would thread our way horseback through the stuff as best we

18. Billy. Courtesy of Dan and Emily Aadland.

could, and when we could go no farther, tie up and hike to the top of the ridge.

It was sometime after the second bourbon that we started talking about mules. The outfitter friend who had recommended this campsite had suggested one particular off-trail route and had pointedly asked whether we had mules. "I know you have good horses. But do you have any mules?" Like many, when the going gets really torturous, our friend gravitates toward those long ears, horse capability supplemented through cross breeding with the savvy provided by one of man's very most useful creatures, the donkey.

We had each been privately edging toward a decision, and it did not take a terribly long conversation for us to converge on an idea. Billy and I talked about the sort of mules we would get from my string of walking horse mares, all ranch bred for bone, good minds, and natural gaits, mares proven by the rigors of ranch life, hard winters, and mountain trips like this one. A running walk or other intermediate four-beat gait is an added plus in a mule just as it is in a horse, and gaited mules have become very popular. So what had held me back all these years from raising mules? Well, the love of good walking horse colts, my firsthand knowledge of my horses' capabilities, and the fact that the market for our stock has always been strong. I had seen nothing to gain.

Except, maybe, some fun. A friend with much experience raising gaited mules had told me that for a sure thing, it is not enough to have gaited mares. The jack that sires the mules must be gaited as well. I don't know whether all creative ideas are born under the patter of raindrops on a tarp in the mountains, from bourbon-Cokes mixed in paper cups, but this one was. Somewhere during the evening I said, "Billy, we ought to go in together and buy a gaited jack."

He didn't even blink. "Let's do it!" And so, Bubba was born, at least in our minds. When we returned, Internet research, a few phone calls, and a videotape sent for our approval soon had Bubba on his way from Tennessee. A sorrel roan with a natural ambling gait, Bubba's trumpet rivals that of any bull elk and fills the valley around our ranch whenever he thinks it's feeding time. As I write this, my first mule weanling, a delightful Molly named Ruthie (after Festus's mule in *Gunsmoke*) occupies the corral near our house. Billy's sorrel John mule, Henrius, born to the same mare that gave me Little Mack, hangs out with Billy's three gray geldings.

But it is characteristic of good trips to the mountains that we didn't even wait until our return home to plan the future, to plan trips we've contemplated, and in this case to plan to breed animals to accompany us. Real outdoorsmen are incorrigible. There's always another possibility for a pack trip, a bear hunt, a jaunt with good horses into new country. Planning the next trip even before expiration of the current one is the bridge that keeps us going. Billy and I are both passionate hoarders of maps, maps with trails, with contour lines, with green for forest, white for clearings tucked where they might hold elk, maps with UTM grid marks and north arrows. Maps are blueprints for the adventures without which life would be unthinkable.

• • •

For three days we hunted. We did not leave camp in darkness for locations previously scouted, because we did not know the country well enough for that. But we were out at the first hint of light over the mountain. We hunted the steep deadfall-laden mountainsides, sometimes on foot, sometimes asking much of our horses and getting into places that required us to lead them down, weaving around the massive tree trunks of forest ruins. One time we rode to an overlook and watched the Slough Creek Valley, debating whether we should commit the time to ride down into it, then up the creek to an area that looked tempting on the map.

I had once seen the very upper reaches of Slough Creek on a pack trip with Emily that started on the west side, up the East Boulder River. We had camped on the divide between the Boulder and Slough Creek drainages, hosting for the first evening David and his friend Justin who were backpacking their way back to the Stillwater. I had packed a mare named Star for her first such adventure, having ridden her a dozen times but only in the arena. On the second day Emily and I left our camp and I, perhaps foolishly, saddled up Star for her first ride outside the arena, this in wilderness, in grizzly country. But she did just fine. I remember a warm day, too many horse and deer flies, but a good trip down to where Slough Creek began to build into a decent-sized stream. It looked like terrific elk country. But for Billy and me a circle to that part of the valley, to the upper reaches of Slough Creek, would be difficult to accomplish in a day, and we didn't wish to move camp.

We discovered a reasonable amount of fresh elk sign, not enough to suggest a real concentration of the animals, but tracks and droppings common enough to indicate occasional movement of a small bunch of elk through the area. We suspected that such was life for the elk left in this wilderness, a constantly moving lifestyle, animals ever alert, particularly for the howl of a wolf.

And, there was bear sign, though nothing close enough nor fresh enough to be alarming. Still, we were ever watchful. The food all went into Billy's new bear-resistant panniers at night and during the day while we were gone. We soon discovered the hard plastic panniers were also human-resistant, the lids held on by many recessed thumbscrews, tight, nasty things that tended to bark the skin on our fingers and probe the limits of our backcountry vocabulary. During rest periods in camp I read Roosevelt's *Hunting the Grisly and Other Sketches.* Further fuel for watchfulness could have been provided, had I brought it along, by Scott McMillion's *Mark of the Grizzly: True Stories of Recent Bear Attacks and the Hard Lessons Learned.*

A compendium of graphic blow-by-blow accounts of fights between humans and grizzly bears, *Mark of the Grizzly* features accounts of several events that occurred within a couple hours' ride of our camp. Written a century earlier, Roosevelt's book confirms that while literary styles have changed in a century, nothing about the bear has changed. Roosevelt's accounts could dovetail nicely into McMillion's book.

> Very often, however, a bear does not kill a man by one bite, but after throwing him lies on him, biting him to death. Usually, if no assistance is at hand, such a man is doomed; although if he pretends to be dead, and has the nerve to lie quiet under very rough treatment, it is just possible that the bear may leave him alive, perhaps after half burying what it believes to be the body.
>
> . . . it is common to see men who have escaped the

clutches of a grizzly, but only at the cost of features marred beyond recognition, or a body rendered almost helpless of life. Almost every old resident of western Montana or northern Idaho has known two or three unfortunates who have suffered in this manner. I myself have met one such man in Helena, and another in Missoula; both were living at least as late as 1889, the date at which I last saw them. One had been partially scalped by a bear's teeth; the animal was very old and so the fangs did not enter the skull. The other had been bitten across the face, and the wounds never entirely healed, so that his disfigured visage was hideous to behold.[1]

Scalping is common in grizzly attacks, because the bears tend to go for the human face. What has changed since TR's time is the advancement of medicine, particularly plastic surgery. Most of McMillion's victims recover with facial features well reconstructed.

McMillion thoroughly discusses what have been called "dinner bell grizzlies." In the scenario, described earlier in this book, the sound of a shot draws a grizzly to what he hopes is a quick and easy meal on the gut pile left by the hunter, and for that matter, on the elk itself while the hunter goes back for his helpers and horses. One thing that is clear throughout McMillion's book is that a grizzly defending his food is one of the most ill-tempered, dangerous beasts you could find anywhere. He repeats the familiar advice that hunters should get the elk quarters away from the gut pile, if possible locating the meat in the middle of a clearing that can be watched from some distance away, then approached with extreme care.

A well-known "dinner bell grizzly" had occupied the area near Billy's and my camp. McMillion heard of him from a bear-management specialist named Kevin Frey, who "knows of at least one bear that keys in to gunfire on a regular basis":

19. TR heading out for a bear hunt in 1905.
Courtesy of the Boone and Crockett Club.

That bear, an old male, lives in the Slough Creek drain-age north of Yellowstone. When he hears a gunshot, he moves toward it, keeping his distance and waiting for his share of the kill.

"He's learned," Frey says, "He gets a little bolder and a little bolder, circling the people while they're gutting elk. As soon as they start dragging quarters away, he's in there. Zoom."

Bears are born scavengers with keen noses, Frey says. "You can't blame them for being able to smell blood and guts several miles away," he notes. But he worries for that bear's future. Not every hunter with a gun can keep his finger off the trigger when there's a bear in the bushes.

"Someone's going to panic and drill him one of these years," he predicts.[2]

If Billy and I had been inclined to fret, the fact that we were smack in the middle of the area possibly holding the highest concentration of grizzly bears in the lower forty-eight states would have given us reason. McMillion's book features several "close encounters of the fatal or nearly fatal kind" that had recently occurred in the very area we were hunting. We tended, though, in the opposite direction, hoping we might see a grizzly, but at a workable distance, perhaps uprooting one of the many stumps we saw recently displaced or turning over one of the big boulders on the hillside in a search for grubs. There were plenty of the boulders, recently inverted, along with the occasional pile of bear scat. But we saw no bears.

The dearth of fresh elk sign and the lack of good tracking snow pointed, by our third day, toward an obvious conclusion. Completely silent, except for the wind, was the night air in which we hoped to hear that echoing whistle, that bugle of bulls that tantalizes and spices a mid-September hunt, that tells you the bulls are indeed out there if only you can find them. The available options all required more time than we had allowed. We knew the main Slough Creek drainage, lined with hunting camps, would have been hit hard now that we were several days into the season, so we weren't inclined to pull up stakes and move down there.

Our outfitter friend had let us in on several of his secret areas. We knew how serious he was about keeping these pet areas private when he gently asked us not to mark them on our maps, lest we loan the maps to others. He merely pointed to each of the areas, slid his finger along the map, tracing a route he had frequently used, and asked us to commit it to memory. I know him too well to have doubted his sincerity. But the options he spelled out involved bushwhacking, progressing off trail through deadfall, and that, again, would involve more time than we had.

So after an early-morning hunt, we discussed our available options and the limitations of our schedules, and came to the conclusion that we would pull out the next morning. It was drizzling again, and in that drizzly air there was, to my mind, something new, a hint of a bite that suggested something more than rain, and I said to Billy, "Actually, if we got right to work we could still pull out today."

"You think so?" There was just enough eagerness in his answer to tell me that the idea appealed to him. He is a good friend, and I cannot imagine a better companion in the mountains. And in the mountains, as on a small boat or when tackling the rigors of a polar expedition, your companions *better* be compatible ones. I cannot imagine how miserable the alternatives could be. I have heard of hunting trips completely ruined because people had not chosen their companions carefully. On some guided hunts, where paying clients may have no part in choosing others booked by the outfitter, some real disasters occur. And it only takes one person. One who is greedy or inconsiderate or whiny; one who makes hunting into a seriously competitive game; one who refuses to do his share of camp chores; one who invites a friend at the last moment or brings a dog without consulting others.

I have been very lucky, but then, I have also been very careful. To be avoided at all costs are those who spontaneously invite others to join the party, hunters unknown to you. The process can compound, and soon the group has grown unreasonably and all planning is out the window. A good rule is that no one is added without a thorough discussion with existing members *before* any invitations are extended.

Even TR, who had the luxury of leading his own expeditions, of hiring help, of being the sole person who invited others, got stuck once with an obnoxious old reprobate who refused to work, who complained bitterly, and who eventually committed the unforgiveable sin of stealing TR's emergency bottle of whiskey so that the hunter returned to find the camp keeper drunk, the bottle empty. Roosevelt was nearly a teetotaler, but like many of his day, truly believed in the medicinal properties of liquor under certain dire circumstances. The theft was the last straw.

TR took just one horse of the five in camp and a very minimal assortment of gear and walked away, leading the pack animal, to hunt and camp on his own. Some would consider him to have been overly generous in leaving the majority of the gear and most of the horses with a man who did not deserve such kindness. But consider the wilderness environment and frontier ethics. To leave a man ill-equipped for the wilderness, without a horse to carry him, a rifle to sustain him, and a minimum complement of food, could be, in effect, putting him to death. Roosevelt was not going to risk such an outcome.

Billy and I did bump up against the limitations of a two-man camp, however. With all camp chores, cooking, and horse tending divided between just two hunters, time spent actually hunting is somewhat reduced. Outfitters, of course, keep paying hunters happy and maximize their time in the field by hiring full-time cooks and wranglers. But for self-guided hunts, Billy and I decided three hunters in rotation would be just about ideal, one each day doing the cooking and wood-gathering so that the other two could leave in the morning's darkness and not worry about returning until after shooting light, nor worry about horses left unattended on the highline. One day in three would be spent by each person enjoying camp, doing some reading, and hunting close by.

True, those who construct sociograms point out that three can be a bad number, that two of the individuals will tend to link up at the expense of the other. But it seems to me, that is most true when the three are all peers who tend toward a competitive nature. Age differences can dampen this tendency, as when an older man accompanies two younger ones, as can sex, a mix of men and women with defined roles. In any case, a rotation of tasks takes care of the problem. In the Big Horns with two sons and the friend of one of them (one old guy, three young guys), we quite deliberately rotated our hunting parties so that we didn't develop into two pairs of hunting buddies. It worked quite well. The variety of companions was enriching.

Severe weather adds to camp chores considerably. Military doctrine on winter warfare states that 90 percent of time and resources will be spent simply functioning, keeping people warm and fed, maintaining equipment, keeping vehicles and machines operating. Only 10 percent of time is left for actually fighting. The army with the guts to attack during severe winter conditions normally carries the day. Something similar can happen in a hunting camp. It takes a staggering quantity of wood fed into a voracious stove to keep a tent tenable when the thermometer hits zero or below, and in a wilderness area, all such wood must be cut or chopped by hand. If two-man camps become problematic, one-man camps become so survival-oriented that there is often little time left for hunting.

I once meticulously planned an elk-hunting trip for a friend and myself, a pack-in to a favorite drainage for a hunt of just three days and two nights. At the last minute a sudden conflict took my friend out of the picture. Always feeling that I would rather go by myself than with the wrong companion, and knowing that other compatible friends were unable to come on short notice, I packed up my horses and headed up the trail. I like my own company well enough, and I remember enjoying the ride, not intimidated in the least by the low clouds scudding ominously below the mountains nor by the scattered snowflakes that whipped horizontally past my horse's ears.

But, as too often happens, the packing up at the ranch, the readying of horses, and the drive to the trailhead had all consumed more time than scheduled. So when I reined Little Mack into a favorite camping spot by a crystal creek, a spot where I had once enjoyed a big, lively camp in the company of Emily, my three sons, and the new bride of one of them, it was already late in the afternoon. By the time I set up the tent, built a highline for the horses, picketed a couple of them out, and sawed enough wood to last through the night and into the morning, all hunting light was gone. The planned late-afternoon jaunt to check several favorite clearings was out of the picture. More snowflakes filled the air, and the wind whipped them into the cooking area, defying the tarp I had hurriedly rigged for an overhead shelter. I cooked myself some supper, and then sat on a stool and enjoyed an outside campfire until the wind and falling snow won out. I shook off the two inches of white stuff that had already accumulated on my hat, my shoulders, and my back, and retreated to the spike tent.

I do not recall the next two days as being miserable. I was well equipped, used to functioning in winter conditions (Montana ranchers do a lot of that) and Norwegian enough to consider a bit of suffering to be an essential ingredient in any worthwhile experience. The problem was simply one of time. Too much of it was spent fixing food, sawing wood, and keeping the horses fed and comfortable. Too little of it was available for hunting. I recall thinking that a second person would add little to the requirements for a comfortable camp but would split my workload in half. True, a younger, tougher man, willing to exist in a minimal camp, sleep in a bivy sack and eat nothing but freeze-dried foods, might have chased elk more successfully. But then, for me, a decent camp is an essential part of the experience, even if I could function with less.

Conversely, a solo camp I enjoyed on a moose hunt was beyond decent and well into the luxurious category. Drawing a moose tag in Montana can happen once in a lifetime or, equally likely, not at all. When I won this sportsmen's version of the lottery, I was determined to do it right. This was before wolves were brought in from northern Canada to feast on moose calves before moving on to elk, so it was still hard to ride up the Stillwater drainage in south-central Montana

without seeing moose. But I knew, too, that Murphy's law could
enter in: when one possessed a tag, the critters could suddenly be very hard to find. A rancher friend had once waited half
his life for a tag, finally drew one, and then hunted his heart
out to no avail.

So I was determined to do it right. Since my friends were
tied up with jobs, I would be going alone. Still teaching, I saved
up my personal leave so that, combining it with a weekend,
I could hunt for a five-day stretch. Then, since I wanted the
sort of camp that would let me come "home" in the dark, get
warm, eat, and prepare for the next morning, I enlisted Emily to help me pack in the same sort of camp I would have set
up for three or four hunters. She was teaching also, but relished the ride up her favorite drainage the weekend before
the September 15 opener.

The camp we set up by the Stillwater River included a twelve-
by-fourteen wall tent with stove, and, since we were on only the
fringes of grizzly country and food-storage regulations hadn't
yet been imposed, a pretty complete kitchen within the tent.
The camp rivaled a furnished wilderness cabin. The timeframe
(more than a month before general rifle season for deer and
elk) pointed to milder weather, and the setting was gorgeous
under tall spruce fringed by an aspen grove showing its first
touch of yellow. True, the tent partially blew down during the
intervening days before moose season began and my ride on
Major up the trail leading three packhorses. There was also
one stormy night, when a flash snowstorm blew in, the inadequate packable tent-pole set gave way, and I frantically circled the tent in my underwear making emergency repairs, re-
inforcing the tent with lines to surrounding trees.

But even that storm was a blessing, for it brought the moose
down out of the timber. I tracked a cow and a calf the next
morning in the inch of wet snow on the trail. Then, far up the
drainage, I encountered a small bull with cows in deep timber,

dropped to one knee, and shot him with my .35 Whelen improved. In a day and a half I had the bull's quarters packed out and in the hands of a fine meat cutter, and the next weekend, Emily and I packed out the camp. It was certainly one of the more satisfying hunts I have enjoyed, and a really first-rate camp that allowed me to concentrate on hunting had much to do with that.

• • •

After Billy and I made the decision to pull out of our camp on a tributary of Slough Creek, we worked hard for two hours. The drizzle was changing to snow. Before we locked the food into the bear-resistant panniers, Billy made four big sandwiches. We had an idea we would need them. I elected to ride Little Mack, the veteran, rather than force him into pack duty again. Manties tightly assembled, we basket-hitched them onto the Decker packsaddles, mounted up, took one last look around, and headed up the trail. Horses always know when you're going home, and the steeply ascending trail was just what they needed to dampen excessive enthusiasm.

I took no photos on the way out, my hands having been relatively full, and I regret that. I was too protective of my very expensive digital camera, a tendency I should have learned to avoid at all costs. In Vietnam I purchased through the PX system a Pentax single-lens reflex with several auxiliary lenses, truly a state-of-the-art outfit for its time, and I did bring home a reel full of decent slides. But I remember better the photos I did not take, the mental ones, not preserved on film because my camera was too well protected from dust and rain and thus inaccessible. Of course, there were other considerations. In commanding a convoy one has to be prepared to reach for things more life-preserving than a 35mm camera.

But perhaps it is the images indelibly imprinted on the gray matter of one's brain that are the most strongly preserved of all. I have several such from this pack-out through a snow-storm that edged nearly to blizzard level, then backed off to brilliance as the sun tried to push through light falling snow. Then we would have a blizzard again. It was beautiful. The new white contrasted with the dark timber that had survived the 1988 fires in scattered copses interspersed with open al-pine flats. The contrast of white and dark green kept the scene three-dimensional, fetching in a fairyland sort of way, even with snow blowing into our eyes.

Billy, watching the packs from the rear, warned me of a manty slung too low, just imbalanced enough to make the D-rings of the packsaddle list slightly to one side. We were in no danger of losing the pack, but for the benefit of the horse, we would have to make a correction. I stopped in a bad place, an open flat where the wind whistled and the snow stung my face. Sweat was frozen onto the horses' coats, decorating them with icicles, and their whiskers, too, were silvery with frost frozen from the clouds of vapor that rose above their nostrils. While Billy held the horses, I lifted the listing manty onto what I've come to call my "packer's shelf," a euphemism for my slight-ly protruding midriff, handy only on certain occasions. One of the beauties of Decker packing is that a manty slightly heavier than its mate can simply be slung a little higher on the horse, which moves it toward the center of gravity and thus compen-sates. I loosened the basket-hitch, raised the manty, took up the slack, retied the knot, and all was well.

And then there was one last ridge to climb, a steep but short one, the wind howling and the snow in our faces, Little Mack perceptibly tired under me but refusing to admit it, his rear legs piston-like as they drove us forward over the top to, surreal in the snow, a parking lot jammed with horse trailers and pickups but without a soul in sight. The entire surface of the clearing was glare ice. Our horses baby-stepped toward the horse trailer, afraid they would fall, and nearly doing so.

After we tied the animals to the trailer, first surveying tires, a habit, and sighing with relief that all on both trailer and pickup were still inflated, we dismounted on a surface so slick we found ourselves hanging onto the pickup's box as we shuttled between truck cab and trailer. Billy and I looked at each other and, tired of shouting over the wind, mouthed the same word, "chains." We would not tackle the steep descent without tire chains.

Horses unsaddled and loaded into the trailer, we eased the rig down the mountain at walking speed, the chains giving our brakes the necessary bite. We unchained, hit the pavement, and only then felt relieved enough to dig into the sandwiches Billy had made. We would not risk the Beartooth Pass at nearly eleven thousand feet during a snowstorm, and we suspected it would be closed, in any case. Instead, we would take the longer route out, down the canyon of the Clark's Fork of the Yellowstone, the route Chief Joseph and his Nez Perce used in 1877, the year after Custer died.

Facing increasing conflict with whites in Idaho, the Nez Perce staged their remarkable retreat through Yellowstone Park, where they shot a couple of tourists (yes, there were tourists in Yellowstone, even then—the Park had been established five years earlier), descended the canyon east of the Park, turned north (sending warriors southeast dragging small trees to raise a dust and confuse the army), then, in a running battle, fought their way north almost to the Canadian border, their destination. It was a tremendous feat. There are some inaccuracies in the way it has often been depicted. Joseph himself was more the spiritual leader than the tactician. He left most of the fighting to his son and other younger warriors. Further, it is often claimed that the Nez Perce retreated across country hitherto unknown to them, but that is not true.

The Nez Perce were friends of the Crows and had often come

east to stay on the Crow Reservation and hunt with their friends. Thus the leaders of the retreating tribe knew the country well. Further, they hoped for Crow support in their fight with the whites, but, in that, they were disappointed. The Crows had made their accommodation with the whites years earlier and had managed a treaty for a reservation (at the time) extraordinarily large, considering the population of the tribe. Hunting with their friends was one thing. Committing to help them in a military capacity was quite another, and they weren't about to jeopardize what they had gained.

The highway running east from Yellowstone Park, down the canyon and into Sunlight Basin, is staggering in its beauty. It now bears the Nez Perce chief's name. Unfortunately, the winding Chief Joseph Scenic Highway in darkness (it proved longer than I remembered) lacked visual appeal except when the weather cleared and we were granted a show of stars we could watch through the windshield. And, near the bottom of the canyon, I hit the brakes and hollered Emily's expletive, "Hold on, horses!" as three cow elk crossed the highway in front of us. "Well," Billy said, "No one can say we didn't see any elk on this trip!"

"No," I said, "and we dang near got one. On the hood."

But there was little lament at returning from this trip without elk quarters in the pickup bed. The general hunting season still lay ahead, and we'd had a good, rugged, wilderness trip, had proven ourselves and our horses up to the task, had seen grizzly sign and had laid plans for future trips. There are those who shoot wildlife from elevated blinds that are much like cabins on stilts, heated, tree stands run amok, with rifles over sandbags, the "hunters" sometimes between sightings watching television or talking on cell phones. The biggest whitetail buck (or bull elk or bear) would be a tasteless conquest indeed, for Billy or me, if taken under such circumstances. We had done the real thing, and eventually, on a similar wilderness trip, we'll return with elk quarters and antlers bas-ket-hitched to our packsaddles.

• • •

On the drive home from the high-altitude trailhead from which we had plunged toward Slough Creek, when the snow stopped and the stars broke through and Billy could point out Orion through the windshield, I thought of an earlier trip when we watched the stars. We were camped at a favorite spot where two small creeks come together, the same place I had enjoyed with Cliff and Roger on the bear hunt when Cliff's mule took a dive off the bluff, the place Emily and I have several times stopped for lunch under the aspens. Billy and I were on a brief elk hunt, too brief, on which we interacted with just one bull, a bull that slept in one morning while we rose in the dark dur-ing a wet snow, ate instant oatmeal by lantern light, and head-ed up the black trail.

The bull, meanwhile, stayed snuggled in his bed until the sun was up, had his morning coffee, read his newspaper, and then sauntered down the trail, his big round cloven tracks neatly overlaying those left by our horses. So, on the trip back to camp we could look at the tracks and lament that on this particular morning, rather than being such good and consci-entious hunters, we could have slept until daylight crept into the clearing, fixed bacon and eggs, and then, heading up the trail, met the bull as he took his morning constitutional.

But back to the stars. The word "brilliant" doesn't hack it when used to describe the display we saw that night in camp. The dome overhead, blackness overlaid by white fire, was a moving, living mass with shooting stars and sometimes an il-luminated cloud scudding across in the foreground, only brief-ly successful at masking some of the light behind it. I looked first at the Big Dipper, as I always do, the "drinking gourd" as it was termed by slaves fleeing north on the Underground

Railroad, slaves who knew to look where the two stars on the lip pointed, about four lengths away, to the North Star, their compass to freedom. Billy quickly found Orion, his favorite on any hunting trip. And then we just watched, eyes fixed upward until our necks ached. And somewhere along the line, when we had quit talking merely to watch and the only sounds were the horses munching on their picket lines and the pine crackling in the campfire, he said, "I just can't look at that without thinking of a Supreme Being behind it."

Billy is a scientist, a biologist and a medical doctor, and a Catholic. His science has never trumped his religion. Indeed, wonder at the universe and the Force behind it have for him simply been further elaborated by a study of science that compelled him from childhood. Maybe it is just in the genes for some of us, this belief, this spiritual context that overlays all else. And, I must think, too, of TR. Camped in a national forest supervised by an agency he created, hunting yearly on land he did more than any other individual to preserve, seeking animals whose existence today owes more to his early intervention, born of his own scientific acumen (for Roosevelt was a scientist long before he was a politician or cowboy or rancher) than to that of anyone else, I have to ask myself just where he was in this matter. What, or Whom, did he think of when he stood by a campfire in mountains near here by a crackling fire and looked upward at a Milky Way so bright it dazzled the eyes? I will get there. But first I think of another friend.

• • •

Dr. Dick Little Bear is Northern Cheyenne. I call him a friend even though the hours actually spent interacting with him could easily be counted on the fingers of one hand. With just the right person, that is all it takes. Many years ago he came into the Barnes and Noble store in Billings, Montana, when I was signing my book *Women and Warriors of the Plains* and offered me a compliment I'll never forget. "This reads," he said, pointing to his already well-thumbed copy, "like a Cheyenne history." And, if that were not enough, when it came time for a paperback reprint he wrote this dust-jacket blurb: "'Tse'tohe Ve'ho'e Dan Aadland tseheševeestse eohne' seomoxoe'êstone. Eevepêheve' me' esta Tsetsesêstâhase tse ohkemehaahe he˘sevo' êstanêhehevose.' This translates to: 'This white man named Dan Aadland writes truthfully. He tells very well about the dignity with which the Cheyenne people live.'"

When the publisher of the paperback edition told me he may not have room for the Cheyenne language on the back cover, only for the English, I told him that I would rather have him print the Cheyenne and forget the English. But please, I said, find room for both. The comment honors me in a way I've never felt I deserved.

When the paperback was released, Emily and I drove to Lame Deer to see Dr. Little Bear on his home turf at Dull Knife Memorial College (now Chief Dull Knife College), of which he is president. He flashed me a smile of immediate recognition when I walked into his office, a long room, his desk at one end facing a conference table. Picking up a ringing phone, he told me to take a seat, spoke quickly, then hung up, only to have it ring again. Covering the receiver with his hand he told me, "The buffalo man is coming. I don't have time to talk to the buffalo man. You talk to the buffalo man!"

And I did so. The "Buffalo Man," a tall Cheyenne rancher, entered the office, his lined face and Stetson framing good-humored eyes. I entertained him (or, more properly, he entertained me) for twenty minutes while Little Bear disposed of ringing phones, one after another. This supervisor of the reservation's bison herd was a good salesman, and he spent much of the time trying to convince me to sell our cattle and buy bison instead. When he learned that our ranch was a bit small for such an endeavor, he seemed disappointed, but he did not entirely give up. "Buffalo are no trouble at all," he said. "Except one day the herd will be in one place, and the next day they'll be twenty miles away."

Years passed before I saw Dick Little Bear again, this time at a group book signing for a charitable cause to which he had brought a new book he had edited, *We, the Northern Cheyenne People: Our Land, Our History, Our Culture*, a product of his college. Surrounded by lavishly decorated Christmas trees (for the charitable auction), and strolling shoppers, and with the background sounds of children's groups singing and dancing on stage, we had a nice chat. He was excited about having recently discovered another ancient Cheyenne creation story. He said, "In words that are just a little different, it really tells the Big Bang theory of the universe."

"And why not?" I asked. "That just means that modern science is beginning to catch up with the wisdom of your elders." So we discussed for a bit creation stories from Indian tribes, white religion, and modern science, and noted that they tend to be pretty similar. And I know from Little Bear's writings that although he may believe the universe started with a bang, he believes it was Maheo (Cheyenne for "God") who built the bomb and lit the fuse.

A postscript: I related my conversation with Little Bear a week later to another spiritual man named Dick—my friend Richard Hardel, a Lutheran theologian—and he quickly replied, "Well, you know, Adam in Hebrew translates into 'Red Man.'"

• • •

"I am Dutch Reformed." TR said it with straightforward innocence, I suspect, to the members of the Episcopalian church he attended while first at Harvard. The young Roosevelt had been unable to find a Dutch Reformed church near his new home on campus, so he had been worshipping at an Episcopalian church instead. He did not understand the High Church formality, the customs and liturgy, so he was asked whether he had some sort of problem with the mode of worship. Reading between the lines, I suspect the congregation had noticed that he was out of synch with their liturgy, and it's doubtful this brash young man would have been particularly subtle in this.

So, no, he answered, he had no problem with the service. It's just that he was Dutch Reformed, not Episcopalian. And he remained a member of this Calvinist body (whose name was changed to Reformed Church of America) his entire life, though other churches claimed him. During his presidency he slipped off to a little red brick Dutch Reformed church, while his wife and children went to the Episcopalian.

He did not wish to be photographed while attending church. We have come to expect presidents (and presidential candidates) to wear their religions (always a form of Christianity, in modern times) on their sleeves. I'm not quite sure when this happened. Always an election junkie, I remember all the way back to the hotly contested race between Taft and Eisenhower for the Republican nomination during the summer of 1952 when I was seven years old. My parents listened to the convention, every word of it, on the big console radio up in their bedroom, and I occasionally joined them. I believe I remember subsequent photographs of the Eisenhower family attending church, but focusing on the religious beliefs of presidents seemed to really begin eight years later when Nixon (raised a Quaker but attending mainline Protestant churches) and Kennedy (the first Roman Catholic candidate) squared off. The press, certain that JFK's religion would become a major issue, homed in on the candidates' church attendance, and it has done so ever since. Roosevelt was unabashedly Christian, openly so, but he considered worship a private matter, and he lived in an age when the press still honored privacy.

The Dutch Reformed Church was the primary seat of

Calvinism, and was often thought to be straight-laced and exclusive, but TR had no such tendency. He would happily worship in any church, and he counted many non-Christians among his closest friends. TR was tolerant of other religions in a way far ahead of his time, a tolerance he also showed regarding race. He took some flak for inviting Booker T. Washington to the White House, but in typical TR fashion, was completely unruffled by it.

Why are religious beliefs of concern in a book about outdoor adventures? Roosevelt's accomplishments as a conservationist are products of the whole man, his culture, his environment, his family, his country, his learning and his preoccupations from earliest childhood. Roosevelt's religion was as much a part of him as was his early fascination with the biological sciences. And it happens that his religion, indeed its larger context, the Judeo-Christian tradition, has taken a few hits lately from some in the environmental movement and from several prominent hunter-conservationists, including the editor of an otherwise conservative hunting magazine.

The reasoning is something like this: Biblical writings grant Man dominion over the earth and all creatures on it. Therefore, they seem to give humans the right to run roughshod over the environment. Thus, past environmental abuses must be laid at the feet of the religion dominant in Western civilization. This criticism is based primarily on just one verse in the very first chapter of Genesis: *And God said Let us make man in our image, after our likeness: and let them have dominion over the fish of the sea, and over the fowl of the air, and over the cattle, and over all the earth, and over every creeping thing that creeps on the earth.*

Whether the Judeo-Christian tradition justifies environmental abuse or whether it actually commands quite the opposite is the subject for treatises different from this one. I think Roosevelt believed the latter. First, the Genesis verse, it should be noted, describes a state before the Fall of Man. Secondly, it is one of myriad biblical references to humans' relationship with the environment and thus must be placed in a much larger context. Lastly, biblical writings develop the idea of stewardship, certainly the central concept of Roosevelt's conservation ethic. Currently, several conservation organizations fly the stewardship banner prominently. As I see it, the concept is simple. We are charged with caring for the "estate," but we do not claim to own it. Others will follow us in this role. With our authority comes responsibility. And that responsibility is to leave the estate, the garden, and the creatures in it, in better shape than we found them.

And if actions speak louder than words, Theodore Roosevelt became the ultimate steward. In his mind, stewardship was not simple preservation. It included some ideas not popular today, the improvement of "the garden" (thus his passion to irrigate the arid West via what became the Bureau of Reclamation). The garden is to be tended, nourished, cultivated, its resources used, yes, but used wisely.

And where does the hunter fit in? In several early biblical accounts God favors the hunter over the farmer, though that seems to change as the Judeo-Christian cultures edged toward a more agrarian existence. Roosevelt referred to Nimrod, the great biblical hunter, whose name, unfortunately, has since sometimes become a synonym for a foolish or ridiculous person, the transformation of the term traceable to Disney cartoons.

But Roosevelt did not over-intellectualize hunting. Sportsmanship, he defined frequently. But the drive among humans to hunt seems to have been simply a law of nature to be accepted as simple fact. He more than once decried its absence in some modern nations, fully believing that human character suffered without it. I suspect TR would have been comfortable with a statement by Ike McCaslin in Faulkner's story "Delta Autumn." Ike, the boy of "The Bear," now grown old, still accompanies men on their annual hunts, though the men are now the sons and grandsons of his earlier partners.

Ike says, "God created man and He created the world for him to live in and I reckon He created the kind of world He would have wanted to live in if He had been a man—the ground to walk on, the big woods, the trees and the water, and the game to live in it. And maybe He didn't put the desire to hunt and kill game in man but I reckon He knew it was going to be there."[3]

CHAPTER SEVEN

Gardiner, 2008 (and 1903)

Memories of Eagle Creek, boys, horses, and elk; TR in Yellowstone; Roosevelt, Burroughs, and Muir; a bull for Jim; a .38 on a .45 frame; spring bear plans

WE STOP TO LET THE HORSES BLOW. We are riding in deep, crusted snow, high above the Yellowstone River on the northeast side of the valley, looking down at the town of Gardiner, Montana. Although the weather is relatively warm for late November at this elevation, steam rises visibly far to the south, marking for us the spot where the hot innards of the earth bubble up at Mammoth, in Yellowstone Park. I have ridden here in extremely cold weather, when the steam from the hot springs looked more like smoke rising from a major fire. I have ridden here many times, usually with sons, each time in pursuit of elk—cows, because we were never lucky enough to draw the highly sought bull tags. But we were always thankful for the cows, for good experiences with sons and horses, and (usually, but not always) for good meat that winter in the freezer.

Billy and I are on a three-day road trip with a highly mobile outfit, the pickup camper and the two-horse trailer Emily and I used earlier in the year. We have come with no illusions about elk. Besides, Billy has already taken his, a five-point triumph high on a plateau to which he climbed, shot the elk, and then in many trips, descended with the meat. Afterward, the day of his last shuttle, he cut the meat up for the freezer. That's one very well-earned elk. So he has come along with his horse Smokey to lend me a hand, to see some territory he has not yet seen, and to carry a rifle on the chance we will run into a really good mule deer buck.

But we have no illusions about elk. The weather is too warm to kick what is left of the annual migration out of the Park, big bulls first, weakened by the rut and thus needing nourishment. Such bulls do still exist, and some do eventually exit Yellowstone's border, but the pool of possibilities has been decimated by predation, primarily by wolves, though grizzlies, too, have had a hand in it. The famous northern Yellowstone elk herd has shrunk considerably in recent years.

But we are here because, against all advice, I want this ride, an overnight camp in the Eagle Creek Campground, a circle on the high ground, an outside chance of catching a bull that had wandered this way during darkness, feeling out the dangers. Billy, too, had wanted to see this terrain. And it's true that even in scant times one never knows what he might run into in the Gardiner area. A mile above the campground, I once dragged a cow elk over the snow with my gelding, right through the middle of a herd of bison. Thankfully, they parted on each side of us and simply stared. Another time I looked up on a ridge and saw, a mere fifty yards above me, a magnificent full-curl bighorn ram.

We have recent intelligence from a man named Ron (we will meet him two days hence) via my friends Hopkins and Jim that the elk situation is nearly hopeless around Gardiner, that yes, it could change, but probably only if the weather takes a sharp turn downhill. Ron works in Gardiner daily. He has sent some tantalizing news of another sort: a five-hundred-pound grizzly is cruising the area. Ron, driving a pickup, saw him cross the county road. A man enjoying himself at one of

Gardiner's bars has seen the big bear under more potentially embarrassing circumstances. He stepped out of the bar at
closing time, and there was the grizzly. We know no details,
but it's easy enough to fill in the blanks.

When we pulled into the famed Eagle Creek Campground,
the dearth of hunters and camps was a good news/bad news
situation. It was nice that we had our choice of spots, but the
fact that we saw only one big outfitter's camp at the lower
end suggested that local knowledge about elk was negative.
The campground would fill rapidly, should a big storm come.
There was one other outfit, a camping trailer surrounded by
stacks of firewood and two tough-looking vehicles, along with
a snowmobile and assorted junk. Smoke rose from the trailer via a stovepipe punched through the roof, a conversion for
economy, no doubt, from propane to wood heat. Forest Service regulations prohibit camping in one spot for more than
sixteen days. This guy looked as if he were planning to stay
hunkered down all winter.

I have many memories centered on the Eagle Creek Campground at Gardiner. The first to come to me as we pulled in, I
related to Billy, probably for the umpteenth time, though he
was too kind to say so. It was after one of my earlier hunts in
this area. The parking lot was lined with vehicles and camps,
hunters everywhere, the surface glare ice. I had shot a cow
and hooked onto her in deep snow with my big walking horse
gelding Rockytop, a sorrel lit up with blaze and socks, taller than sixteen hands and almost always a handful. He was
the first horse I raised and trained from the day he was born.
His training to pull an elk with a rope dallied to the saddle
horn consisted simply of pulling an elk with a rope dallied to
the saddle horn, doing this when the time came with no real
preparation earlier. Bringing the big cow a mile through deep
snow, then another mile on a nice icy groove formed by the
dragging of earlier elk, had made him sweat but had done little to quench his spirit.

So we hit the upper end of the campground in a running walk, this big flashy horse dragging an elk with the same aplomb he would have exuded in a show ring, and we threaded our way on the icy surface through vehicles and horse trailers and hunters who stopped and quieted and stared. Reaching our trailer, I dropped the drag rope and hopped off. An outfitter sauntered over and asked, "What kind of a horse is *that?*"

Billy and I have parked our rig on the upper end of the campground, approximately where Rockytop and I entered the parking area so many years ago. Now we are circling the high ground above the camp, hoping our friends are wrong about the elk. It occurs to me that Little Mack, the horse I've brought on this trip in lieu of my young horse, Partner, is, in human terms, Rockytop's nephew. There is something fitting in that. But our friends are not wrong about the elk. The crusted snow, which deepens as we climb, gives us nothing fresh enough to be encouraging.

Mule deer abound, though without a buck of stature to tempt Billy. So we simply ride, Billy drinking in this country he has not seen since his arrival in Montana some years ago, I spending much time in the past, as older hunters tend to do, identifying ridges and basins and groves of timber with stories attached. Here is the ridge we crossed in deep snow, when Rockytop (ridden by Steve), sweated up and itchy, simply plopped himself down in a snow bank. Thankfully, he did not roll.

Terrain features, tempered and mellowed by the passage of time, shift slightly. The little basin where Jonathan and I each shot a cow is even smaller than I remember. In a display of lousy horsemanship, I managed to let Rockytop loose as I dismounted. I sat down, shot a cow elk, first telling Jon to dismount and hold onto Marauder for dear life, since Rocktop was loose. He did his best to hold onto Marauder's reins, but as Rockytop, spooked by the shot, charged downhill, Marauder, impersonating a discus thrower, whirled Jonathan in an arc, sending him over the edge into a snowbank, where he simply disappeared. He emerged, a slim snowman with a rifle, wiped off his scope, and dropped another cow! He was as competent as I was embarrassed at having to have my horses caught by a hunter downhill from us.

There is a south slope where Billy and I ride through deep snow, whipped by wind into crusty drifts. I am quite sure this was where my son Steve and I caught up with a scattered herd of elk bedded down in the snow. Several were nice bulls, the common scenario when you have only cow tags. I had shot an elk earlier, near home, so was strictly in the guide role, an enjoyable one. Steve knelt in the snow and dropped a cow with the .35 Whelen I'd made up by rebarreling my old, left-handed .270. (Steve shares the left-handed affliction.) The cow dropped promptly. We dressed her out in thigh-deep snow, and I hooked burly Major to her for his first experience of seeing out of his rearmost vision an elk on the ground chasing him along. He was spooky about it only for a short time. The deep snow soon took care of that, and he settled into a strong, steady pull.

But I remember most their first ones, Jon's and Steve's. As Billy and I have ascended the high ground we have followed a ridgeline where Jon and I rode many years ago. Looking east over a coulee, I see another ridge line, nearly three hundred yards away, timber on its flank that runs into scrub trees and brush, then a small clearing above. Jon and I had spotted movement in the timber. We dismounted and got into position. Animals emerged one by one out of the top of the timber and into the clearing. Counting them off, I said, "Deer—deer—deer—*elk*," Jon joining me on the last word as we spotted the final animal in line, what appeared to be a young cow but turned out to be a very large calf. (On these special, late-season hunts, in late January, the calves are nearly yearlings.) Jon squeezed the trigger on his 7mm-08, and the elk went down.

Steve took his first elk a couple of miles north of where

Billy and I ride, a big cow, again in deep snow. We were panting from a tough walk up a steep slope. I had brought just
one horse, Rockytop, and had left him in the trailer in case we
needed him for dragging. It was cold. When the time came,
though, Steve made a fine shot at about 250 yards with, I recall, his .270, shooting a cartridge I had loaded with the long
Nosler 160-grain semi-spitzer. After we dressed out the elk, I
hiked down across a flat so thick with bison droppings that for
a moment I wondered who had been feeding cattle at that particular location. It looked like a feedlot, but when I saw bison
in the distance it suddenly dawned on me that bovine poop
looks and smells pretty much the same, regardless of the species of "cow." I saddled Rockytop, rode up, and dragged Steve's
elk the relatively short distance down to the vehicle. The last
few hundred yards were over a sagebrush flat, tough going,
the elk snagging frequently on brush. Rockytop was lathered
and steaming by the time we got to the trailer, so I unsaddled
him and dressed him with a big insulated blanket.

There are other good memories, a cabin converted from a
railroad depot in which I stayed with Hopkins and another
friend, pine crackling in a red-hot stove, a side trip to a Gardiner bar. I shot my very first elk at daybreak the next morning,
a huge dry cow, aged by the wardens at the check station at
$3^1/_2$, that had never produced a calf. Hopkins and I had walked
in the dark against a powerful but warm chinook wind, and
I leaned over a huge boulder to take her with my .270 at long
range. The cow's meat turned out to be superb.

And there are others as well, many, a medley of recollections
centered in an area that for half a century has been a breadbas-
ket for human hunters. Billy comments that it must be neat
for me to see some of the places I've hunted earlier with my
boys, and, in saying so, shows that he understands my preoccu-
pation, my relative quiet, the look, perhaps, on my face. And I
suppose for me, too, there is a sense of loss, the usual one that

comes with recollections of sons now grown, but a feeling of loss, too, for the famous elk herd that once migrated through this area. Actually, in Montana generally, there are more elk now than there have been at any time during the last century. Many areas are overpopulated with elk, and, as access to private property becomes more limited, more ranches having become inaccessible trophies of the wealthy, controlling elk numbers becomes more problematic. But I still miss this region's herd, once numbering nearly twenty thousand, now reduced to a quarter of that. And I miss what the herd meant to many Montana hunters.

In the 1950s the Gardiner-area hunt was famous and infamous. The so-called firing line described a dangerous and inhumane mess, hundreds of hunters, thousands of elk pushing out of Yellowstone Park, hunters shooting, wounding, fighting over who shot what. Aesthetics and sportsmanship gave way to the psychology of a feeding frenzy. What I heard during my boyhood about Gardiner hunting left me with no desire to ever venture there, rifle in hand.

But Montana Fish, Wildlife and Parks got hold of the situation. To control the size of the northern Yellowstone herd, they instituted late-season hunts, primarily for cows, usually two days in duration, or four days if you happened to draw one of the rare bull tags. These hunts were scheduled after the regular season from early December until early February, when the migration of elk seeking better feed north of the Park was in full swing. Regulation was strict, with check-in on the way to the area, checkout upon exit. Game wardens, freed from policing their own regions during the regular season, converged for this late duty. With the number of hunters quite limited during any particular timeframe, these late-season events were now proper hunts, sometimes resulting in easy elk, but sometimes making you work very hard for winter meat. The Gardiner hunts were not sure things. Once Jon, Steve, and I

20. Cornerstone of the Roosevelt Arch, Gardiner, Montana.
Courtesy of Dan and Emily Aadland.

were completely skunked on a bitter weekend when we hunted hard for our two days.

Odds for drawing a late-season cow tag were quite good,
so for many Montana hunters, such a tag meant an elk to fall
back on. You hunted in your home region, knowing that if
you failed to find an elk, your late-season Gardiner tag meant
chances for meat were still good. It was a wholesome, if not
always a terribly aesthetic, hunt, often a family affair, often
the first experience for youngsters hunting elk in wild country with a relatively high chance of success.

It was good. Late-season hunting remains, but the number of
tags issued is but a fraction of what it was, as are the elk numbers. Many Montana hunters believe that wolves have been de-
clared by a federal government and a non-hunting citizenry

21. Gardiner, Main Street, 2009. Courtesy of Dan and Emily Aadland.

out of touch with Montana's hunting tradition to be more important than human hunters. And I have to wonder what TR would think of that. He saw national parks as breeding and production grounds for game animals, "great nurseries and wintering grounds, such as Yellowstone Park" being essential to preserve hunting, which, in turn, he considered crucial to maintain what he called "national character."[1] And Roosevelt made it clear that local residents, those most affected by Washington's dictates, should not be ignored, that respecting their way of life was essential to the success of his pet conservation projects. The presidency never erased the cowboy in TR.

• • •

Before leaving Gardiner, Billy and I drove up to view the famous Roosevelt Arch, the stone edifice at what was the first official entrance into Yellowstone Park. Built in 1903, the arch contains a cornerstone placed by Theodore Roosevelt during a visit that year. It is said to include a time capsule containing a Bible, local newspapers, and a photograph of Roosevelt. But laying a cornerstone was not his major purpose when he arrived in Gardiner early in the spring of 1903. A young president who had already established five new national parks, who two years later would create the National Forest Service, and who was responsible for many wildlife and bird refuges and the National Bison Range in northwest Montana, TR, in visiting Yellowstone, was more the extremely successful farmer smiling at the obvious growth of his crops.

He was delighted with what he saw, including the antelope grazing so close to the buildings in the town of Gardiner. (They still do that, the football field being a favorite feeding grounds.)

> On April 8, 1903, John Burroughs and I reached the Yellowstone Park, and were met by Major John Pitcher of the Regular Army, the Superintendent of the Park. The Major and I forthwith took horses; he telling me that he could show me a good deal of game while riding up to his house at Mammoth Hot Springs. Hardly had we left the little town of Gardiner and gotten within the limits of the Park before we saw prongbuck. We rode leisurely toward them. They were tame compared with their kindred in unprotected places; ... and though they were not familiar in the sense that we afterwards found the bighorn and deer to be familiar, it was extraordinary to find them showing such familiarity almost literally in the streets of a frontier town. It spoke volumes for the good sense and law-abiding spirit of the people of the town.[2]

TR continues with a description of antelope migration in and out of the Park and attributes their numbers to the lack of predators.

Although there are plenty of coyotes in the Park there are no big wolves [wolves in species, as opposed to coyotes], and save for the very infrequent poachers the only enemy of the antelope, as indeed the only enemy of all game, is the cougar. Cougars, known in the Park, as elsewhere through the West, as "mountain lions" are plentiful, having increased in numbers of recent years. . . . I found them feeding on elk, which in the Park far outnumber all other game put together, being so numerous that the ravages of the cougars are of no real damage to the herds. But in the neighborhood of the Mammoth Hot Springs the cougars are noxious because of the antelope, mountain sheep, and deer which they kill; and the Superintendent has imported some hounds with which to hunt them.[3]

The last line speaks volumes about TR's and the Park superintendent's attitudes toward national parks as wildlife preserves. There is no thought of creating a "balanced" ecosystem if "balanced" means *exclusion* of Man, the hunter and predator. Quite the contrary is true. The animals traditionally hunted by humans for food are favored over the animal predators that eat them, and when predators take too many, human control of the predators is routine. I can't help but think of a recent proclamation by a news anchor that a political candidate was obviously "bad for the environment" since she favored control of wolves preying on the caribou herds required for the subsistence hunting of Alaskan natives. TR is lionized today, but his beliefs are often cherry-picked (or unknown or ignored).

Roosevelt rejoices, too, at the success of the closely guarded bison being managed and supplemented from the few originally left in the Park: "Just before reaching the post the Major took me into the big field where Buffalo Jones had some Texas and Flathead Lake buffalo—bulls and cows—which he was tending with solicitous care. The original stock of buffalo in

22. A Yellowstone coyote. Courtesy of Dan and Emily Aadland.

the Park have now been reduced to fifteen or twenty individuals, and their blood is being recruited by the addition of buffalo purchased out of the Flathead Lake and Texas Panhandle herds. . . . The buffalo are now breeding well."[4]

The rest is, as they say, history, the Yellowstone bison herd having grown until it bursts its seams, controversy reigning because of potential for brucellosis spreading from bison to cattle. Montana has instituted a very limited hunt by drawing in areas adjacent to the Park. But few in the public are likely aware that the herd represents a genetic composite carefully tailored under TR's auspices from native Yellowstone bison injected with new vigor by animals from northwest Montana and from Texas. I've heard it claimed otherwise, that the Yellowstone herd is genetically unique, unaffected by outside influence.

The quantity of elk thrilled Roosevelt on his 1903 visit, and the migration patterns of the Park's two major herds was quite similar to that of today, their numbers comparable to those of a decade ago.

> In the summer the elk spread all over the interior of the Park. As winter approaches they divide, some going north and others south. The southern bands, which, at a guess, may possibly include ten thousand individuals, winter out of the Park, for the most part in Jackson's Hole. . . . It was the members of the northern band that I met. . . .
>
> From a spur of Bison Peak one day, Major Pitcher, the guide Elwood Hofer, John Burroughs and I spent about four hours with the glasses counting and estimating the different herds within sight. After most careful work and cautious reduction of estimates in each case to the minimum the truth would permit, we reckoned three thousand head of elk, all lying or feeding and all in sight at the same time. An estimate of some fifteen thousand for the number of elk in these Northern bands cannot be far wrong.[5]

Roosevelt's delight at these numbers is easily understood when we remember his earlier judgment while writing of his Medora experiences, that elk would soon be extinct or nearly so. He had seen them disappear on the plains, had hunted them in the mountains, but for many years was pessimistic about their prospects for survival. The first president to have devoted much of his attention to conservation and the survival of animal species must have felt sweet reward on Bison Peak watching thousands of elk through his binoculars.

But his interest lay not only in game species. His inventory of birds observed on this Yellowstone trip is thorough, the star being the water ousel, a bird I had seen on mountain trips as a boy but first heard lauded by a poet who taught one of my classes at the University of Utah.

23. Spike bull elk and cow near Eagle Creek.
Courtesy of Dan and Emily Aadland.

They are striking birds in every way, and their habit of singing while soaring, and their song, are alike noteworthy. . . . The ouzels are to my mind wellnigh the most attractive of all our birds, because of their song, their extraordinary habits, their whole personality. They stay through the winter in the Yellowstone because the waters are in many places open. We hear them singing cheerfully, their ringing melody having a certain suggestion of the winter wren's. Usually they sang while perched on some rock on the edge or in the middle of the stream; but sometimes on the wing; and often just before dipping under the torrent, or just after slipping out from it onto some ledge of rock or ice.[6]

24. TR and John Muir in Yosemite, 1903.
Courtesy of the Boone and Crockett Club.

Roosevelt goes on to credit John Muir with the best description of this captivating little bird, said to be the naturalist's favorite. Interestingly, it was in this same year, 1903, that Roosevelt traveled with Muir in the Sierra. Muir and Roosevelt's esteemed Forest Service director, Gifford Pinchot, had been friends, but then became bitter enemies in what could be called the beginning of a split in the conservation movement that persists today between "preservationists" (Muir and the Sierra Club, which he founded) and "conservationists" (stewardship, wise use of natural resources in a sustainable fashion, TR in the center).

But each side has learned from the other, and Muir convinced Roosevelt that federal protection of Yosemite Valley, and its inclusion into the adjacent park, was the only avenue for preservation. Roosevelt is said to have asked Muir to show him the "real Yosemite," and the two set off on a backcountry trek. The president of the United States, hero of San Juan Hill, and Muir, a Scottish-born visionary, a wilderness mystic, shared a campfire, slept on the ground, and awoke covered with a skiff of snow.

> When I first visited California, it was my good fortune to see the "big trees," the Sequoia, and then to travel down into Yosemite, with John Muir. Of course of all people in the world he was the one with whom it was best worth while thus to see Yosemite. He told me that when Emerson came to California he tried to get him to come out and camp with him, for that was the only way in which to see at their best the majesty and charm of the Sierras. But at the time Emerson was getting old and could not go. John Muir met me with a couple of packers and two mules to carry our tent, bedding, and food for a three days' trip.
>
> The first night was clear, and we lay down in the darkening aisles of the great Sequoia grove. The majestic trunks, beautiful in color and symmetry, rose round us like the pillars of a mightier cathedral than was ever conceived even by the fervor of the Middle Ages. Hermit thrushes sang beautifully in the evening, and again, with a burst of wonderful music, at dawn. I was interested and a little surprised that, unlike John Burroughs, John Muir cared little for birds or bird songs, and knew little about

them. The hermit thrushes meant nothing to him, the trees and the flowers and the cliffs, everything. The only birds he noticed or cared for were some that were very conspicuous, such as the water-ousels—always particular favorites of mine too. The second night we camped in a snow-storm, on the edge of the cannon walls, under the spreading limbs of a grove of mighty silver fir; and the next day we went down into the wonderland of the valley itself.

I shall always be glad that I was in the Yosemite with John Muir and in the Yellowstone with John Burroughs.[7]

What a trio: our greatest conservationist president (perhaps the best ornithologist of the three, though he envied Burroughs's eyes); John Burroughs, the great naturalist and essayist, a personal friend of Walt Whitman, Henry Ford, and Thomas Edison; and John Muir, the great preservationist, a friend of Emerson's, and so, like Burroughs, heir to the great poets of what has been called the "American Renaissance." Roosevelt's conservation ethic and agenda, already at full steam in 1903, took on an additional load of coal.

· · ·

Leg two of Billy's and my three-day road trip involves going north where, strange at it sounds, we will hunt elk in a subdivision. Most subdivisions are killers of habitat and hunting, and in time this particular one may kill them, too. But this subdivision is somewhat unusual in that people have bought relatively large tracts, eighty acres or so, inaccessible during the worst of winter, and have built summer cabins that rely on water hauled to cisterns. Thus, few people inhabit these cabins during hunting season, and resident elk commute through the tracts between Forest Service wilderness and a big ranch where hunting is forbidden. Further, since the cabin owners are not interested in agriculture, the land is not grazed, and

feed abounds, tempting the elk into close proximity to buildings and roads.

It's a "catch as catch can" proposition, hunting permission
available on only a few of the tracts, the elk either there or not
there. But if nothing else it's a chance to rendezvous with some
old friends. In late afternoon we drive past the private tracts
to a Forest Service trailhead where we unload the horses and
use the last hour of daylight to ride logging roads through old
clear-cuts among stumps and low second-growth timber, ideal elk habitat but with no sign fresh enough to be tempting
for our morning hunt.

After breakfast, through the mixed miracle of cell phones
we communicate with our friends Jim and Hopkins. We join
them, along with the aforementioned Ron, who has seen elk
the day before in the open on the posted ranch and has watched
them drift into the timber on one of the available tracts. Ron,
who took his elk the first day of the season, will guide us, and
Jim will walk a parallel route below us on the other side of
a tangle of buckbrush and timber. Hopkins stays on a stand
near a cabin below us.

Ron, slim, quiet, and long of stride, knows his business. He is
in outstanding condition. At one point we make a quick climb
up an extremely steep slope and, when I catch up, breathing
like a windbroke horse, I learn that he is recovering from a
knee replacement. Privately, I think that if he has the other
knee done, then a hip replacement, perhaps followed by in-
stallation of a pacemaker, I'll have a better chance of keeping
up with him next year.

We ease through timber to the edges of clearings, sniff the
wind, eyeball the dark timber, and finally prepare to pussyfoot
quietly down a two-track. Just as we reach it, a pickup truck
appears from nowhere and streaks past, its occupants throwing us a jocular wave. Ron, certain that we have sole permission to hunt here this morning, seethes. But there is nothing

25. Jim's bull. Courtesy of Dan and Emily Aadland.

we can do. We change tactics to parallel the road on the lower side, hoping that the pickup's blitz through the area has left something undisturbed. (We learn a week later that the vehicle's occupants, not serious hunters, spooked two bulls right off the road.)

It is a beautiful day, except for the powerful west wind. I've long thought that really strong winds are not all bad, that they can disperse and confuse scent and also cover noise, a fact we appreciate the many times when we have no choice but to bust through brush that crackles if you even look at it. And so powerful is the wind that we're startled by a signal from Jim that he's put a bull down only a few hundred yards from us, and we never heard the shot. Busting brush in the hope he would spook an elk to me, he had come face-to-face with a five-point bull at eighty yards. It fell to his .270. He says he really would have preferred I had shot it, and he's completely sincere, but I tell him it's okay, it's fine, it's hunting. The next time the bull will run my way.

So while Ron goes for the additional help of Hopkins and a neighbor, Billy and I watch Jim dress out the elk, helping when necessary by holding a leg in this way or that, ribbing him about his surgical style but being careful not to go too far: our hands are not thoroughly bloody, and we'd like to keep it that way. Billy does, though, give him a subtle poke. Jim is covered with blood to his elbows, his wristwatch scarcely visible under the gore. Billy asks, "What time's it getting to be?"

There is just one day left in our three-day saga, and this one we will spend near home riding mountains we know well, or think we do. But it has been good to rendezvous with these friends. Hopkins and Jim make an annual trek to the ranch to hunt whitetails and turkeys, and it was with the two of them that I made a memorable pack trip into the west side of the Absaroka range to look for a mountain goat. Hopkins (his first name is Steve, but with both a brother and son named Steve, our family has learned to skip it) had the tag. We packed into a high clearing for our camp, and after Steve and Jim spotted goats a couple of miles to the south, we rode hard. The result was a fine billy goat and much more material for the constant stream of ribbing among the three of us.

We also talk what Emily calls "code." Since I taught with Hopkins in eastern Montana many years ago, our interaction has been dominated by technical gun talk. A phone conversation soon turns to grains of powder, trajectories of various calibers, and the endless list of rifles and handguns we would love to have if only it weren't for the age-old problem repeated in the refrain, "So many guns, so little time and money."

Apparently, gun enthusiasts have always "talked code." TR was no exception. During his 1912 campaign for president, this time on the "Bull Moose" ticket, Roosevelt, while entering an

automobile, was shot in the chest by a would-be assassin. Instead of seeking medical attention, he went on stage and gave
a ninety-minute speech. In his autobiography he relates this
incident to a conversation he had with a cowboy, one of his
former soldiers in the Rough Riders, at a regimental reunion.
The cowboy told Roosevelt that he was grateful to have been
let out of jail in time for the reunion.

> I asked what was the matter, and he replied with some
> surprise: "Why, Colonel, don't you know I had difficulty
> with a gentleman, and . . . er . . . well, I killed the gentle-
> man. But you can see the judge thought it was all right
> or he wouldn't have let me go." Waiving the latter point,
> I said, "How did it happen? How did you do it?" Misin-
> terpreting my question as showing interest only in the
> technique of the performance, the ex-puncher replied,
> "With a .38 on a .45 frame, Colonel."
>
> I chuckled over the answer, and it became proverbi-
> al with my family and some of my friends, including
> Seth Bullock.
>
> When I was shot in Milwaukee, Seth Bullock wired an
> inquiry to which I responded that it was all right, that the
> weapon was merely "a .38 on a .45 frame." The telegram
> somehow became public and puzzled outsiders.[8]

One can imagine the consternation of reporters who thought
the telegram contained some sort of mysterious, coded message rather than a reference to a simple joke about a handgun
built on a large frame but chambered for a smaller caliber. Perhaps the press in those days, as today, considered ignorance
about firearms to be a badge of honor.

Roosevelt adds, as an aside, that none of his former regimental members or his western friends considered it remarkable in the least that he gave a speech before seeking medical attention, this with a bullet that could have killed him

lodged in his chest, a bullet that was never subsequently removed. All considered it perfectly ordinary that their former
commander would push on and continue the mission before
seeking help for his wound.

Back in our home country on the third day, Billy and I discover a trail loop through a draw we haven't before known,
and the wheels start turning. It's good bear country. We could
set up a spring bear camp just there, ride up each morning in
the dark, and glass in a spectacular 360 around us the dozens
of parks where hungry bruins out of their dens might cruise
looking for the first green stuff to emerge. On the county road
into this area, Emily and I once watched a huge blond bear (in
species, a black bear) lope across in front of us, muscles and fat
rippling under his hide. A rancher friend has told me the blond
genetics were not destroyed, as he had feared, by the huge fire
that rolled through here two years ago—he has seen three such
sows. And so, anticipation builds for something in the future,
and it dulls, even dissipates any disappointment we have at
not finding an elk. They say that in hunting the reward is the
journey not the destination. We are convinced of that.

PART III
The Home Range

CHAPTER EIGHT

Back at the Ranch, Thanksgiving, 2008

Gobbler on the porch; "It looks good enough to eat"; sportsmen; "real food" and "not real food"; a morning buck; "You *got* him!"

IT WAS A LITTLE HUNT, a sort of "subsistence hunt" (though no one could actually claim Reverend Richard and I *needed* the turkeys we sought.) But tags were burning holes in our pockets. Year after year I have contributed to Montana Fish, Wildlife and Parks the cash for two turkey tags, one for spring and one for fall, but I've taken only a very few of the birds. One time I did ambush a big gobbler that made the mistake of following a string of hens over a bridge right toward our corrals. I felt a little bad about it. He was very big and very proud, and my method—charting his daily feeding pattern and then bushwhacking him—had none of the ingredients of a classic turkey hunt. I did not wear camouflage, set up a blind, move stealthily, or call. I simply anticipated his next move, crouched in some tall grass, and waylaid him. But he tasted very fine.

During my work as a rancher I see turkeys often, enjoy hearing the big gobblers in spring, do my best to dodge with my mowing machine the diminutive offspring tagging their mothers through the hayfields in June. Wild turkeys of the Miriam variety thrive today, thanks to one of the most successful of Montana's wild game restoration projects. In some areas they have become pests, vast flocks actually perching on haystacks and eating them to the ground.

Our ranch has no similar problem with turkeys. The population is healthy and constant, and my aversion to filling my tags has nothing to do with my very real affection for the big, awkward birds. It is far more selfish than that. Truth is, I would far rather field dress an elk than dress out a turkey. Moreover, I could handle the elk in considerably less time. Reared on big game rather than birds, and lacking an old-fashioned farm background where routine tasks included butchering chickens, ducks, and turkeys, I've never developed the dedicated bird hunter's efficiency at converting feathered creatures to savory products for the oven, stuffed and browned, fodder for hungry boys.

Maybe there's something more, too, a Thanksgiving memory from my boyhood, involving another minister, my stern but soft-hearted father, and a gift given him by a parishioner when we lived in South Dakota. In the early 1950s butchering and dressing skills were simply assumed. No man or woman with a well-rounded education could have failed (in the eyes of South Dakota farmers or Montana ranchers) to learn such basic skills. So during my boyhood my dad received gifts of food that were virtually on the hoof. I remember opening our chest freezer (this was later, in Montana) and meeting the eye of a dressed and scalded pig. He was incised neatly down the middle, split at the backbone and right up through the head, and it was his right half that stared up at me, this frozen half-model of a pig. I'm sure the parishioner had asked Dad if he liked pork, if he'd like half of the pig scheduled to be butchered, and Dad, with many mouths to feed, had jumped at the offer and had replied with profuse thanks. And I'm equally sure that Dad had imagined his freezer would receive neat white packages marked "pork chops," "bacon," "shoulder roast," and "ham." Instead he got, literally, "half a pig," exactly as promised. He was plenty grateful notwithstanding, and with Mom's help the good pork did end up cycling through their (at the time) eight children.

Earlier, in South Dakota, I had returned home from the second grade, skipping along the cold cement sidewalk toward the parsonage and its front door, which was centered in a screened porch. I opened the door and had the wits scared right out of me by a huge ugly bird that rose into the air, beating its wings, cackling as it attempted to launch itself through the screen, shedding feathers as it did so. I screamed, slammed the door, and sprinted past the lilac bushes to our back door, where I learned from my mom (who was manning the wringer washer) that a nice farmer had given us our Thanksgiving turkey. "Wasn't he a beauty?" I don't recall thinking there was one beautiful thing about the feathered prehistoric monster to which I'd nearly lost my life seconds before.

It is interesting what I remember and what my siblings do not, and vice versa. One brother remembers with almost photographic detail things I've long forgotten (or never observed in the first place). I seem to remember things subtle and poignant. So I do not remember eating that turkey (though I'm sure we did so). I do remember two solemn trips toward the porch my father made after retrieving from the shed out back his double-bitted axe, the one remnant he owned of his young man's dream to homestead in Alaska. He first touched up both edges of the axe, seeming to take longer than usual to do so. Perhaps Mom kept us out of the picture, because I don't recall seeing him dragging himself with the steps of a condemned man (rather than with his accustomed forty-inch strides) all the way to the front porch and its captive bird. But I do remember his coming back at least twice, and my disappointment—hoping as I was for restoration of safe passage through the porch—to still hear, as I approached, the clucking of the big, feared bird.

The incident did not create a lifetime trauma, just perhaps negative vibes whenever I think of the whole procedure of rendering a turkey into a form ready for the oven. Once I tried plucking a turkey in the kitchen at our riding arena. Soon the air was filled with floating feathers, and I ejected myself outdoors to a picnic table, where things scarcely went better. Since then I've elected to skin the creatures, but still have trouble cleaning off the myriad tiny feathers that cling to the bird and defy the faucet. In this butchering process, Emily comes into play. Retired now from teaching, Emily was raised by a mother who routinely butchered and dressed two chickens prior to Sunday morning's church service, chilled them in the sink, then, after church, began frying them for Sunday (midday) dinner. Town relatives routinely arrived on Sundays to feast on Nora's famous fried chicken. What they got was very fresh.

So on a bitterly cold morning when my friend Richard took me up on my earlier offer to hunt for a turkey on the ranch, I decided to take a gun myself. After all, Emily was home. That is what made the difference. Maybe I would cash in on my fall turkey tag, which, in Montana, allows taking a turkey of either sex with the firearm of one's choice, rifle or shotgun. Dick deals with a malady that renders his legs nearly devoid of feeling, but he copes quite well with a cane. He had earlier taken two whitetails on the ranch using what might be the most productive method of all, sit and wait. Now we would look for cooperative turkeys, a flock of which I had often seen feeding just into the edge of a cottonwood grove. Our strategy was simple—I spotted them and drove right past within fifty yards, Dick and his son following in another vehicle, figuring the turkeys would not be spooked by a vehicle as long as it stayed moving.

Then, hidden by a mini-ridge, we got out, got ready, and eased our way over the rise. It would be all or nothing. They would be there still feeding under the cottonwoods, or, having decided our vehicles weren't harmless work trucks heading for the gravel pit, they would have hustled their way into the brush like so many penguins, but faster, in that ground-covering waddle of which they are capable. They were there. One fell to Dick's twelve gauge, another to my little .17HMR-caliber rifle. It was another not-so-classic turkey harvest, but Thanksgiving had reminded us of the taste of turkey. These ranch-fed residents, both three-fourths grown, would be good, indeed.

Emily seemed happy I had shot one, and told me she would join me out at the arena shortly. "Hey, maybe we'll want to eat it tonight," she said. I doubted that. Elk tenderloins eaten the day you kill the animal are fine. As I've said, for some reason, turkeys turn me off. I told Emily that by the time we got the critter freezer-ready, we would probably want to defer the next stage for at least a few days.

So I laid out the critter on a bed of newspaper atop the Formica table in our arena kitchen, its ungainly bleeding head on one end, its prehistoric three-toed feet on the other. At first the bird seemed anything but pretty. But I lifted its feathers, straightened those on the wing, admired the subtle colors mixed with the dominant black and brown. These wing feathers were the ones I knew to be coveted by traditional bowhunters who fletch their own cedar shafts. Oh, yes, the bird was pretty.

Emily arrived, tolerant and half-amused at my scant progress thus far. We went to work, agreeing that the biggest problem was that we infrequently tackled turkeys (or any other sort of bird). But Emily, up to her forearms in the gut cavity, soon repeated my thoughts. "No, we probably won't want to eat this tonight."

Since the tiny .17-caliber bullet had caused a small amount of bloodshot, we decided to simply extract the good meat rather than cutting out the bad. And with that the transformation began. A stainless steel pan on the counter began receiving washed portions of breast along with legs and wings. The plan was to collect these into a plastic bag for vacuum sealing and freezing and, eventually, the deep-fat frying that seemed increasingly appetizing. It did not take long. We began to speculate that, as young as the bird was, Emily could possibly tackle it with a method she calls "oven frying." Then I recalled that we had stashed away some poultry seasoning we had never used. Soon we were openly discussing cooking the bird for that evening's supper. Finally, we were relishing the prospect. It had been "a turkey." Now it was "turkey." I rubbed the seasoning into the meat for a half-day's repose in the refrigerator. Later, Emily did her magic. It was very fine.

• • •

A few days after taking and eating the turkey, I received in the mail my new issue of *Traditional Bowhunter*. I've come to increasingly enjoy this magazine and also one called *Primitive Archer*, and although I don't anticipate ever selling my rifles, I'm spending more time with my longbow. I grew up with bows and arrows, home-built ones we boys whittled out of willow staves, building arrows for them from hardware store dowels, fletched with split chicken feathers scavenged from a neighbor's henhouse, points whittled sharp and fire hardened. In my renewed boyhood as an archer, I have killed my first deer, a whitetail doe, and plan to kill more. There is something elemental and thrilling about close proximity to game while holding in your hands a weapon that has been used for thousands of years, basically a sophisticated version of a bent stick and string weighing a mere pound and a half but so efficient that it can bring down a moose.

In the current issue of *Traditional Bowhunter*, E. Donnall Thomas tells of a hunting trip to Labrador on which he never releases an arrow and does not try very hard to do so. Instead, he spends his time helping other hunters and finds much satisfaction in that role:

"I am reminded of the five phases in a hunter's development as outlined in standard hunter education texts: the shooter, limiting out, trophy, method, and sportsman stages. Having reached the fourth such stage (that's what limiting oneself to traditional archery tackle is all about), I admit that I once found the fifth a bit sappy, the kind of thing that gets inserted in texts to make everyone look good even though nobody means it. That was a mistake; the idea of limiting one's own "success" in the field in order to enjoy helping others is the real deal. As a kid I remember my father telling me he'd rather see me catch a trout or shoot a grouse than do it himself. It took some maturity on my part to appreciate how much he really meant it."[1]

I'm too many years separated from my boyhood hunter-safety instruction to recall whether these stages of hunter development were taught those many years ago. Certainly they're useful. Certainly it's also quite normal for many hunters to move freely back and forth among the stages. I'm in the "method" stage when I take after antelope with my .45-70, deer with an iron-sighted .30-30, or any game with my longbow, and in the "sportsman" stage when I take joy in guiding a family member through a hunting opportunity, quite forgetting my own tag and rifle; and, I freely and unabashedly descend into the "shooter" stage when I find the woodchuck holes too numerous in my alfalfa fields or when an errant coyote edges too close to our calving ground.

But there is a "stage" not mentioned, one never to be despised, the origin of all hunting and, in a sense, its most honorable objective. Hunting involves killing an animal and converting it to digestible protein. This side of hunting may not be its most romantic, but it is certainly its most elemental and, in many ways, its greatest strength against those who would attack it. Surveys among non-hunting Americans consistently

232 THE HOME RANGE

show very strong approval for hunting that garners meat, but consistently weak approval for trophy hunting.

Things were somewhat different a century ago. The term "meat hunter" was often pronounced with a certain disdain. One primary reason was the rise of market hunting, shooting wildlife in order to sell the meat. Market hunters rendered the passenger pigeon extinct and nearly sent most of the continent's big game animals in the same direction. What they did to bison need not be reviewed. The game laws pushed by Roosevelt and other conservationists were aimed primarily at such commercialization of wildlife, not at the individual who hunted to feed his family. Roosevelt himself during his western years was hunting for meat at least as often as he was hunting for trophy heads.

But class and wealth entered in as well. Wealthy Americans had not completely shaken the European (particularly British) aura of hunting as an activity for those who did not need the meat, of hunting with hounds for a fox or for a dog-mangled deer. Hunting for reasons other than garnering food came to be considered superior. There was both good and bad in this. We "senior" hunters, like Thomas, have come to recognize that hunting is both complex and basic, its rewards many. If the term "sportsman" works for conveying recognition of these larger rewards, so be it. My only problem with the term has been with the connotations carried by the first syllable—competition, Super Bowl glitz. I find application of any vestige of arena sports to hunting completely inappropriate, just as I'm turned off by the high fives and shouts of glee exhibited by most of the "successful" hunters on outdoor television upon the death of the creature they've killed.

The term "sportsman" was used liberally by Roosevelt, and both his objections to converting hunting to competitive sport and his zeroing in on market hunters seem extremely modern:

True sportsmen, worthy of the name, men who shoot only in season and in moderation, do no harm whatsoever to game. The most objectionable of all game destroyers is, of course, the kind of game butcher who simply kills for the sake of the record of slaughter, who leaves deer and ducks and prairie-chickens to rot after he has slain them. . . . To my mind this is one very unfortunate feature of what is otherwise the admirably sportsman-like English spirit in these matters. The custom of shooting great bags of deer, grouse, partridges, and pheasants, the keen rivalry in making such bags, and their publication in sporting journals, are symptoms of a spirit which is most unhealthy from every standpoint. . . .

But after all, this kind of perverted sportsman, unworthy though he be, is not the chief actor in the destruction of our game. The professional skin or market hunter is the real offender. . . . The professional market hunter who kills game for the hide, or for the feathers, or for the meat, or to sell antlers and other trophies; the market men who put game in cold storage; and the rich people, who are content to buy what they have not the skill to get by their own exertions—these are the men who are the real enemies of game.[2]

The very day I read this, the *Billings Gazette* reported the discovery of two bull elk killed out of season and left to rot, the antlers cut off. It's a scenario too common. Market hunting (or more properly, poaching for market), in this case to sell horns rather than meat, still exists and still plagues our wildlife.

But back to the importance of meat, taken legally in season by the true sportsman of TR's definition. I suppose a vegetarian could legitimately be a hunter if his or her diet were a medical compulsion or if the hunting were done to feed someone in need. Otherwise, the juxtaposition would seem hypocritical. The same issue of *Traditional Bowhunter* containing Dr. Thomas's article has one on hunter's intuition, by James A. Swan, PhD, which underscores the oneness of Man the hunter and Man the meat eater. It contains a quotation with which to tease vegetarian friends (if they have a sense of humor). We're told that, in the Blackfeet language, "the term for 'meat' is *nita'pi waksin*, which translates as 'real food.' All other food is called *kistapi waksin*, which translates as 'not real food.'"[3] My kind of people, those Blackfeet!

And, from TR himself: "A man doing hard open-air work in cold weather is always hungry for meat."[4]

• • •

It is not correct to say that she was slaving in the kitchen, because that would imply that what she was doing was a chore instead of a joy. Having her entire family home for Thanksgiving, three sons, their wives, and the six grandchildren (including the baby, Evan), cooking the favorites of the entire crew, was something she lived for. So there was steak and ham and turkey and turkey enchiladas (the next day), along with brunches consisting of eggs Benedict one morning, pancakes another. In between, the Christmas cookies began to appear. And I kept saying, "Hon, you have two deer tags yet to fill, and the season ends Sunday." We weren't really concerned about taking two more deer. One would do. One, combined with the modest whitetail buck I had shot earlier, would be adequate to spice the spring and summer's diet with venison loin and cubed round steak and to keep the smoker going on my best product, summer sausage, along with several newer concoctions.

I had shot my buck almost accidentally in that I was out to enjoy myself early that morning, not to actually work at hunting. I had dived quickly into the woods, making a good deal of noise in the process, on the aspen and cottonwood leaves crisped between the remaining patches of snow. Better to make all your noise at once, I've always thought, even ignoring the flash of the tails on deer you've scared from their beds, and then get by the river, where its noise, and that of the wind in the trees, supersede yours, especially if you just stop and sit down and let the woods return to normal and forget you are there. Then walk into the wind slowly upriver, enjoying the smell of fall leaves and running water as the morning light cracks over the eastern hills, stopping more than you walk. And if you do it just right you see the deer even before it sees you.

The buck crossed the river, while I quit breathing and dropped to one knee. He moved in quick bursts but so smoothly I scarcely saw what he did to get suddenly twenty yards ahead of where he had been. And then he stopped broadside to me in a clearing about 125 yards away, looking my way, curious and suspicious but not quite ready to spook. The brush between him and me, branches from deadfall, and the tall grass the cattle had left, were too high for my kneeling position. I rose in very slow motion, giving the deer a chance to spook, and half hoping he would. I've noticed that when you only half want to shoot something, you're positively deadly. It was too easy, this hunt, and not very satisfying, except for anticipation of the meat. The shot, however, offhand at that distance and perfectly on the mark, was one of which I could be proud. The buck was hog fat.

So with Emily, the season running out, the larder not yet full, I finally put my foot down. "You need to get out of the kitchen. Go hunting with your son. C'mon, I'll get your rifle."

"I'll interfere with Jonathan's hunting," she protested. Her middle son still had an antlerless whitetail tag. Earlier he had taken a nice mule deer buck, not trophy-sized but very respectable, on our east range. I had enjoyed playing guide, or at least keeper of the pickup, my insulated coffee cup in hand. We spotted the buck and jockeyed the rig to be hidden from him by a low rise. Jonathan started his stalk. Twenty minutes

26. A long-range muley. Courtesy of Dan and Emily Aadland.

or so later, I heard his big rifle crack just once and knew that
would be the end of it. The buck, four hundred yards away
across open ground, vindicated Jon's penchant for super-
accurate rifles and .300 ultra mags. That range, to him and his
rifle, is a surer thing than two hundred yards to many hunters, so I couldn't fault him.

"Jon will love every minute of it," I insisted, and able to
see that she was weakening, I walked to the gun safe and re-
trieved her little Remington Model 7, a youth model, cut down
in length and perfect for Emily's five-foot-one frame. In the
first year she owned the rifle, she killed a fine whitetail buck.
I had studied the heavy antlered buck by the creek behind our
house, surprised to see such a nice rack combined with only
three points plus brow tines on each side, an eastern eight-
pointer, a western three-point in the old days before western
hunters started counting brow tines. I ran to the house and

hollered, "Get your vest. There's a nice buck by Butcher Creek and he may just stay there."

To our surprise he did just that, sticking tightly to the creek, more interested in the does in the field than he was in any activity behind him at the ranch headquarters. He seemed reluctant to venture toward the does, though, and I wonder to this day whether a buck larger yet, claimant to this harem, was bedded in the slough to the east. But I looked afterward and never saw him. Emily hustled along with me, both of us ducking low, keeping the cottonwood grove between the buck and us until the last moment when, at 150 yards, we eased to the right into the clear. On one knee she aimed carefully, almost too long. I held my breath, she squeezed, and the buck went down.

Arthritis in Emily's arms makes holding her rifle in certain positions difficult, so this year we had added a bipod, something I've never mounted on my own guns. Now, as I thrust the rifle into her hands, encouraging her to get out of the kitchen, I had to admit the bipod made the little rifle look jaunty and ready. So there they stood, both clad in orange, the little blond mom and her middle son, a Boeing engineer, a technician when it comes to shooting, one who plays with big, super-accurate rifles shooting steel gongs at a thousand yards. And it was the ultimate role reversal. She had gone with him more than once during his boyhood to help drag and retrieve deer, of which he was proud. Now, like E. Donnall Thomas, he would discover the fulfillment involved in this "sportsman's" stage, in being the guide, the mentor, because now it was his turn. And he would say later that although it was just a little hunt on the ranch, just a couple of hours, it would be one of his most unforgettable.

So they went together and walked the river bottom, the edge of the woods, then looped back for the vehicle, and she walked well and carried her rifle, and in spite of the wind she

27. Jon and Emily, the son now as sportsman and mentor.
Courtesy of Dan and Emily Aadland.

enjoyed this time with her son. And later, on the east side of
the valley, where our dryland pasture slopes up to a sort of ter-
race before sloping up again, they spotted a rutting whitetail
buck, distracted but still wary. Jon "ranged" him. Too far.

Getting low, using the open terrain as best they could, they
got to three hundred yards, the buck holding position, the
ground between the hunters and the buck completely naked
of brush and flat as a pancake. There was no way to get closer. So the mentor—instructor put his mother through the se-
quence. Prone position, bipod down, bolt worked once, aim in.
"How is your rifle sighted in?" he thought to whisper.

"I don't know. Dad checked it." She had fired her rifle at
the range, but after a slight change in the powder charge of
the cartridges I was handloading for her, I had shot a group

to make sure the rifle was still zeroed. Jon knows my habits. He was sure I would have kept the rifle shooting between two and three inches high at a hundred yards.

In Emily's Burris scope there are additional dots below the crosshairs for long range. "Use the first dot below the crosshairs, and squeeze." She did so. The little .260 Remington barked, and the buck leaped into the air, heart shot. And Jon, too, went airborne, more tickled at his mother's shot than at any of his own. "You *got* him!"

And it was my hunt, too, mine to enjoy, mine to live with them and to know every second of it even though I spent it in my recliner with a grandkid on each knee. Being an old sportsman is not that bad.

CHAPTER NINE

The Western Star

Cows and corrals; the end of the Elkhorn; the solitary singer; Hamlet
and Fortinbras; the curlew and the thrush

THE HEAVY, ROUGH-SAWN PLANKS of Montana fir diluted with
a fresh, mountain smell the less pleasant odor of creosote still
lingering from the railroad ties I had set into the ground with
the backhoe. The October bite in the air, too, did its job, cutting, when I raised my sweaty face to the breeze, the lingering
heat of a summer so dry it had stolen the hay from our fields,
the second crop of alfalfa I had recently baled a laughable excuse for a proper hay crop, not worth stacking. I had brought
the dozen or so round bales into the barn. High in protein,
they would jumpstart the weanlings, newly deprived of their
mother's milk, seven or eight walker colts along with a Bel-
gian crossbred and Billy's and my first two mules.

Luther had stopped to visit with the weanlings, especially
Ruthie, my molly mule, who always noses her way to the front
when there is petting or a handful of grain to be had. Then he
walked over and said, "Figured you could use some help."

"I never turn it down." Few words were needed to line him
out. Like all five of my minister father's sons, Luther, my youngest brother, is a builder. All of us have discovered, as life has
moved on, just how strong was the influence of our father,

who never bought anything he could build, who turned out in his parsonage basement shop bright varnished wood, often salvaged from unlikely sources—and with beautiful and solid workmanship wrought it into lamps, shelves, whatever was needed—and eventually, built piece by piece, pipe by pipe, an eight-rank pipe organ for his church.

But, by profession, Luther is a fisheries biologist for the state of Minnesota. And, of course, he is a hunter. A family move meant that his later growing up was in walnut groves broken by cornfields rather than in the dryland western hills. He carried the .22 rifle I had carried, and like me, always had a dog along. Now he spends much time restoring trout habitat, removing abandoned dams, and fighting the political battles invariably associated with such efforts. He had come to hunt with me and our brother Steve, and, restricted to an antlerless whitetail tag, has quickly "limited out." There would be more hunting for him, with rifle, bow, and shotgun, back in Minnesota.

He had accompanied me on a day ride in the mountains looking for elk. Before season, when my bear tag was still valid, I had ridden the same route alone, the octagon-barreled .45-70 in the saddle scabbard riding lightly under my knee. Partner was at his best, five years old, filled out with muscles under his black hide, most of the training kinks out of his mind. Alas, shortly afterward he came up with an unexplainable cut on a hind leg that sidelined him for the rest of the season. So I rode Little Mack with Luther, who was mounted on Redstar, and we rode over a pass through crusted snow, hoping to find elk sign that would justify my setting up a hunting camp in a favorite valley, near a clear creek under tall trees that had survived a recent fire. But we found nothing to motivate me, only two flat tires on the horse trailer upon our return. Luther was better humored about that than I was.

Today I was building a cattle-loading chute, the solid edifice up which cattle are driven to be loaded into the rear of a cattle truck. During our last overhaul of the corrals I had torn our old one down. Whether it was built by Elmer or by Magnus before him or by both together I do not know. I'm sure the fir used for its floor and the newly peeled poles used for its sides smelled good, too, in the October air when they first built it. But after half a century or more, its uprights were rotten. I had rebuilt the floor of the chute at least once, but it wasn't worth doing again. Besides, since low-to-the-ground gooseneck trailers have become the rancher's transport of choice, loading chutes have become less necessary, and I thought we could do without one for a while.

But a big semi would be coming soon. And a ramp expected to bear the weight of half a dozen jostling cows at once must be built well. And whether this chute was to be used once or a hundred times, no half-assed attempt would do. I would build it well. So Luther helped me, and we worked hard, and when I walked away from it later that afternoon I could look over my shoulder and see the chute's new bright wood contrasting with the grayed-out planks of the older portions of the corral, and grunt to myself a grudging satisfaction.

Two weeks earlier I had rounded up our cattle from the east range. I went alone, on Little Mack, my best cowhorse, loping the good old guy the first quarter mile, for him a necessary preamble to cattle work. But it took less to settle him down than in the past. Game as he is at sixteen, there is a little stiffness in front when you first ease him into a lope, the first touch, I'm afraid, of arthritis. I could have had help, but I did not really need any or want any. By western standards our six-hundred-acre east range is small.

We climbed the trail on the south side of "Indian Coulee" where it cuts through sandstone, a trail worn deep over time by the passage of thousands of bovine feet, then through young Douglas fir growing well on this north-facing slope in spite of the drought. In places the small trees now crowd the trail, and their new branches reached out and rubbed me as I rode by. Then we were on top, finding a few of the cattle immediately. We ignored them and rode on east through thick sage until we could see our border fence on the far side of the range and be satisfied that there were no cattle there. We would make a counter-clockwise circle, kicking the cows toward home as we found them, then cutting back for another bunch. So long after breeding season, the cattle were well scattered.

The first group did not understand. I sent them toward home with short loping charges from Mack and my usual high-pitched hoots, but they looked confused and moved out only reluctantly, then turned north as I circled back away from them to look for others. No matter. They would herd up when we found the rest of them. Perhaps the warm wind blowing, the summery weather, kept them from believing that it was time, time to come down to the irrigated land they normally coveted. Could they know, too, that this annual ritual meant the weaning of their calves? I've never wanted to think so.

Soon I had the rest of the bunch, and then the mooing started in earnest, the constant communication between cows and their calves whenever they are being moved, the vocal link that to humans sounds the same from all of them, but to the cow is as individualized as a person's voice calling your name. Once they herded up it did not take long, the cow-calf pairs beginning to spill over the hill into the valley. But I did have to ride hard to the north where one of the bulls was hanging out with several pairs and saw absolutely no reason, breeding season long past, that he should have to accompany the herd. It took a little loping and a little shouting, and a couple of rides back around him before he trotted down the old wagon road that cuts through one of the coulees toward home.

Once at the bottom of the hill, the herd lined out nicely along the fence toward the gate, and I held Little Mack back a ways out of the dust. And I banished as best I could, all through this small roundup, voices that said "last time," last ride on this gelding after cows, last roundup, last chance to cuss these good old cows. The decision to sell them a couple of weeks after we shipped the calves was a rational, sensible one, made after considerable deliberation. Hay was scarce and expensive, so the cost of wintering them would be great. By selling them we would gain that back, have the money to reinvest in other projects, and have the option to lease grass to others or to run yearlings through the summer. Freedom from daily winter feeding and calving in the spring would mean more time to write, to see grandkids, to work in my shop on the sailboat that has lingered half-finished for more than a decade.

But what is rational is not always enough. When the day came a neighbor helped Emily and me. We pushed the cows up the new chute into the great truck, the back door slammed shut, and I held open the gate to the field so that the trucker could turn the big rig around in the pasture. He waved as he went by. Emily and I walked away from the corrals toward the house. It was some time before we spoke.

• • •

The winter of 1886–87 was a bitter assault of ice and snow and blizzard after blizzard; it was a winter so terrible that dead cows were found afterward in the crotches of trees, where they had floundered in high drifts and attempted to eat the small twigs; coulees were piled high with dead cattle as the snow receded; the Little Missouri was choked in front of TR's Elkhorn cabin with bloated carcasses. Every rancher on the river lost at least half his herd, and Roosevelt lost more than that.

It was the end of a dream. Raising cattle on the fat of the land, on the high-protein prairie grass, with relatively little tending and no major hay production for feed in winter, worked for a while. Then nature made a correction. Roosevelt, with his usual resiliency, threw himself in other directions. During the December of that terrible winter, he had been in London (after losing a three-way election for mayor of New York, but claiming he had a "bully time"), where he had married his childhood friend Edith Carow. He was writing at a prodigious rate. But his status as but a part-time rancher who lived at the same time in several other worlds must not be thought to have dampened the blow of this winter that killed his cattle and sent his ranching business into ruin. His letters, written when he returned to Medora, convey shock.

> You cannot imagine anything more dreary than the look of the Bad Lands [he wrote Sewall]. Everything was cropped bare as a bone. The sagebrush was just fed out by the starving cattle. The snow lay so deep that nobody could get around; it was almost impossible to get a horse a mile.
>
> In almost every coulee there were dead cattle. There were nearly three hundred on Wadsworth bottom.

Later, in another letter, he wrote, "I am bluer than indigo about the cattle. It is even worse than I feared."[1]

The Medora experience did not end abruptly for Roosevelt, but the winter of blizzards was a demarcation. During the fall of 1887 he returned to help round up many of his remaining cattle and place them on a train, sold at a loss. The next fall the Elkhorn served as home base for a hunting expedition that took him to the Selkirks of northern Idaho. In 1890 Edith came out with him for a stay at the cabin, and the following year Roosevelt hunted near Two Ocean Pass in northwestern Wyoming.

In 1892 the Merrifields moved out of the Elkhorn ranch house, and Roosevelt closed it. Hagedorn wrote, "A year later he returned to Elkhorn for a week's hunting. The wild forces of nature had already taken possession. The bunch-grass grew tall in the yard and on the sodded roofs of the stables and

246 THE HOME RANGE

sheds; the weather-beaten log walls of the house itself were one in tint with the trunks of gnarled cottonwoods by which it was shaded. 'The ranch-house is in good repair,' he wrote Bill Sewall, 'but it is melancholy to see it deserted.'"[2]

A couple more times he saw the country where he said the romance in his life began, reliving the western experiences that, without which, in his estimation, he would never have been president. As governor of New York, whistle-stopping as candidate for the vice presidency of the United States, the now-decorated hero of the Rough Riders stopped in Medora in 1900, swapped stories with his old friends, and galloped a cow horse past the bluffs, excitedly pointing out landmarks of his former life.

And there was one more time, on the train trip in 1903 to Gardiner, Montana, with John Burroughs, the naturalist. President Roosevelt was greeted as a conquering hero at each stop, old friends crowding to see him. In an extensive letter to John Hay, he recorded interaction with cowboys he had known on the roundups, friends and guides from his hunting expeditions, each crowding toward him to recall an experience they had shared. Roosevelt seems to have relished each of these contacts, commenting on the friendliness shown by all, even former rivals. At Medora, he wrote, "they had all gathered in the town hall, which was draped for a dance—young children, babies, everybody being present. I shook hands with them all, and almost each one had some memory of a special association with me he or she wished to discuss. I only regretted that I could not spend three hours with them."[3]

TR's last touch with his rancher past came on the visit to Billings, Montana, in 1918. Refusing to give in to illness and to the crushing grief at the loss of his son Quenten, he took the tour mentioned earlier in this book to raise money for war bonds. Like the old gunfighter that he was, TR had been obsessed with raising a military unit and leading it into battle.

President Wilson had turned him down flat. TR never sulked. Again, he turned with all he had left to a cause bigger than himself; if he could not fight in the war that had taken his son, he could raise money to help the cause.

So it was in Billings, on the visit when my father-in-law and his father may have seen him, that TR talked for the last time with one of the cowboy bunch from Medora. According to Hermann Hagedorn, TR met an old friend, George Myers, and offered to share his room so that they could talk about old times. Three months later, home at Sagamore Hill, Roosevelt died.[4]

• • •

On April 25, 1865, the funeral procession of Abraham Lincoln moved with somber grandeur along the streets of New York City. With his brother Elliot and Edith Carow, the childhood friend he would someday marry, peering through the window of his grandfather's house, the six-year-old Theodore Roosevelt watched.

Walt Whitman, like hundreds of thousands of others, watched as well. "Oh Powerful, Western, Fallen Star," he called Lincoln in "When Lilacs Last in the Dooryard Bloomed." The poet picked a sprig of the spring flower, a piece of nature he shared with his idol as a symbol of immortality, and likened Lincoln to a solitary singer, the hermit thrush.

The child Roosevelt must have been awed by what he saw below him in the street, and the fact that his father and Lincoln were good friends can only have intensified the sorrow felt in the Roosevelt home. The connection continued throughout TR's life. John Hay, Lincoln's young private secretary, later in life became secretary of state for both President McKinley and his successor after the assassination, Theodore Roosevelt. On the eve of TR's inauguration, Hay is said to have given him a "mourning ring" containing a strand of Lincoln's hair.

Whether the little boy watching the procession already

28. The president. Courtesy of the Boone and Crockett Club.

harbored high ideals, ambitions even, at such a young age, we cannot know. We can wish he could somehow now know that his likeness on Mount Rushmore flanks that of Lincoln and inclines toward him rather than toward Thomas Jefferson, on his right, whom he held in lesser regard. But I take with me from this association between two great men something simple given me by the poet. The western star that burns so brightly just before dawn is as fitting a symbol for the New Yorker who became the rancher, the hunter, and the western horseman as it is for the great president from Illinois.

• • •

One does not lightly undertake exploration of a man about whom new biographies appear yearly, a president a century past whose association is so sought by current political candidates, an outdoorsman whose adventures still spawn bestselling books such as *The River of Doubt*. My journey has included riding and hunting some of his favorite ranges and haunts, living with my family a life enriched by the hunting legacy he did so much to preserve and ensure, looking perhaps with new appreciation on the sight of a curlew, and hearing in the song of the meadowlark hints of the tragedies that sometimes touched this great man.

Fascination with Roosevelt today is an interesting thing. Conservatives claim him, overlooking his belief in a strong central government as the only tool capable of controlling capitalistic excesses. Liberals claim him, ignoring a militaristic foreign policy that was not above preemptive war on those who would threaten our nation. Environmentalists claim him, looking the other way at Roosevelt's penchant for huge engineering projects designed to improve what nature had given us, projects they would sue against and march against with religious fervor, were such to be proposed today. (Building the Panama Canal is the first of those that comes to mind.)

Indeed, I am sometimes surprised at Theodore Roosevelt's rise today in the minds of many Americans to a position so close to the top of the presidential pantheon. He was an aggressive, powerful, decisive human being, unafraid to advocate such qualities (now considered by some to be anachronistic) as "manliness." And he was, after all, a hunter, a member of a class of people frequently derided by the mainstream press but still sought (in sometimes ridiculous fashion) by politicians who want their votes. Perhaps the answer lies in our craving for leadership, for Whitman's constant western star, the bright light we can count on in the cold that leads to the dawn. Never did anyone question where Roosevelt stood. And those who served under his leadership would (and did) follow him to hell and back and sorrow when the mission was done.

And perhaps, too, Roosevelt's complexity better reveals itself once the "bully" stereotype is penetrated. Of all our presidents he perhaps most deserves the term "Renaissance man." Our most published president and perhaps the most voracious reader among them, digesting a book a day even while in the White House, TR went nowhere without a book to read and a writing project to pursue.

Once, during his early Dakota days, Roosevelt rode off looking for a lost horse. He chanced upon a cowboy who was also searching for a stray animal. The two made friends, spent the night at a ranch house, and then set off on their mission only to be caught in a heavy snowstorm.

We were soon completely turned around, the great soft flakes—for luckily it was not cold—almost blinding us, and we had to travel entirely by compass. After feeling our way along for eight or nine hours, we finally got down into the broken country near Sentinel Butte and came across an empty hut, a welcome sight to men as cold, hungry, and tired as we were. In this hut we passed the night very comfortably, picketing our horses in a sheltered nook nearby, with plenty of hay from an old stack.

To while away the long evening I read Hamlet aloud, from a little pocket Shakespeare. The cowboy, a Texan—one of the best riders I have seen, and also a very intelligent as well as a thoroughly good fellow in every way,—was greatly interested in it and commented most shrewdly on the parts he liked, especially Polonius's advice to Laertes, which he translated into more homely language with great relish, and ended with the just criticism that "old Shakspere saveyed human natur' some"—savey being a verb presumably adapted into the limited plains' vocabulary from the Spanish.[5]

What a picture. Two cowboys marooned in a line shack reading, critiquing, and enjoying one of Shakespeare's most complex plays. Jedediah Smith would have been proud. And it seems to me that Roosevelt combined in rare measure the qualities of that play's two most compelling characters, Prince Hamlet, the intellectual, the introspective one, and Prince Fortinbras, the decisive Norwegian warrior. Each admired the other. Fortinbras honors Hamlet in death and recognizes that, had circumstances been different, the prince would have "proved most worthy." Hamlet refers to Fortinbras as a handsome and delicate prince who is willing to risk all "even for an eggshell," and with his dying breath he chooses Fortinbras as the future king.

It is not the big stick that distinguishes Theodore Roosevelt. It is the vast repertoire of human qualities behind the hands of the man holding that stick, a medley of some of the very best that can be expected from any man, packaged in an almost superhuman bundle of energy and determination, that makes his star continue to rise nearly a century after his death. And we have the testimony of those who knew him directly, who were awed by his energy, the sheer force of a personality that

29. The author and Partner, 2009. Courtesy of Dan and Emily Aadland.

even after brief exposure stuck with one forever, an electricity that somehow has been capable of conducting itself, transcending time, to anyone who studies him.

• • •

And what of me, the other character in this book, the hunter, the rancher, the horseman who has spent a couple of years, now, focusing on shared experiences with that far better known hunter, rancher, and horseman? This is not a project one quietly puts to bed. Ride with Roosevelt, shoot with Roosevelt, share campfire tales of horses and hunts with Roosevelt, and he will, I believe, be always with you.

And so, I expect to think of him when I see between my horse's ears the herds of "prongbucks," when I hear the curlew's cry, when I seek (but usually fail to find) the bugling elk.

I will take time on the next ride along the rapids of the Still-water River to enjoy the water ousel, and I hope to hear a hermit thrush. I will get through the short, dark days of winter by anticipating the warbling arrival of the sandhill cranes, the promise of foals to be born, the plans I make with friends for a spring bear hunt when the snow recedes to reveal the green. And every moment I have enjoyed reading Roosevelt, knowing him, will simply make all of these things better.

In 1914 Theodore Roosevelt lay close to death, wrapped in a waterproof poncho that did little to protect him from the steaming Amazon downpour. On the infamous expedition down the "River of Doubt," he was fighting malaria and a horrible bacterial infection in his leg. By any measure, he should have died. According to Candace Millard, Roosevelt's temperature skyrocketed, and his companions took turns watching him during the night: "Roosevelt fell into a trancelike state, and he began to recite over and over the opening lines to Samuel Taylor Coleridge's rhythmic poem "Kubla Khan": 'In Xanadu did Kubla Khan a stately pleasure-dome decree. In Xanadu did Kubla Khan a stately pleasure dome decree. In Xanadu . . .'"[6]

Perhaps had he been given the choice of dying then and there, in a tent on a wilderness expedition, his rifle within reach, he would have preferred it to death in bed by coronary embolism five years later. In any case, it is best to leave him here with the words of Horatio in the Shakespearean play enjoyed by TR and the cowboy in the snowy line shack: "Goodnight, Sweet Prince."

Notes

1. Pronghorns on the Powder

1. Hagedorn, *Roosevelt in the Badlands*, 179.
2. Morris, *Rise of Theodore Roosevelt*, 205–6.
3. Morris, *Rise of Theodore Roosevelt*, 220.
4. Morris, *Rise of Theodore Roosevelt*, 241.
5. Roosevelt, *Outdoor Pastimes*, 147–48.
6. Roosevelt, *African Game Trails*, 534.
7. Roosevelt, *Outdoor Pastimes*, 175.
8. Roosevelt, *Hunting Trips*, 417.
9. Roosevelt, *Outdoor Pastimes*, 181.

2. The Elkhorn Ranch

1. Roosevelt, *Ranch Life*, 74.
2. Roosevelt, *Ranch Life*, 59.
3. Roosevelt, *Ranch Life*, 59.
4. Roosevelt, *Hunting Trips*, 18–19.
5. Roosevelt, *Hunting Trips*, 391–92.

3. Horses, Rifles, and a Man Named Magnus

1. Roosevelt, *Outdoor Pastimes*, 175.
2. Roosevelt, *Outdoor Pastimes*, 177–80.
3. Roosevelt, *Hunting Trips*, 39.
4. Hagedorn, *Roosevelt in the Badlands*, 310–11.
5. A Sam Stagg rigging anchors the cinch of the saddle to straps

that run over the horn. A Cheyenne roll is a flat, horizontal edge on the rear of the cantle.

6. Roosevelt, *An Autobiography*, 49.

7. Hagedorn, *Roosevelt in the Badlands*, 473.

8. Hagedorn, *Roosevelt in the Badlands*, 107.

9. Roosevelt, *Hunting Trips*, 426.

10. A Running-W is an old-timers' device that, when pulled, deprives a horse of the use of his front legs.

11. Hagedorn, *Roosevelt in the Badlands*, 17.

12. Morris, *Rise of Theodore Roosevelt*, 68.

13. Roosevelt, *Hunting Trips*, 693–94.

14. Roosevelt, *Outdoor Pastimes*, 205.

15. Roosevelt, *An Autobiography*, 107–8.

16. Roosevelt, *Hunting Trips*, 41–43.

17. Roosevelt, *Hunting Trips*, 169.

18. Roosevelt, *Ranch Life*, 102–3.

19. Hagedorn, *Roosevelt in the Badlands*, 251.

20. Roosevelt, *Outdoor Pastimes*, 176.

21. Hagedorn, *Roosevelt in the Badlands*, 404–5.

22. Morris, *Rise of Theodore Roosevelt*, 637.

4. The Big Horns

1. Roosevelt, *Hunting Trips*, 268–69.

2. Roosevelt, *Hunting Trips*, 268–69.

3. Roosevelt, *Hunting Trips*, 271.

4. Morris, *Rise of Theodore Roosevelt*, 287 (quoting from Hagedorn's *Roosevelt in the Badlands*).

5. Roosevelt, *Hunting Trips*, 275.

6. Morris, *Rise of Theodore Roosevelt*, 285.

7. Faulkner, "The Bear," 448.

8. Roosevelt, *Hunting Trips*, 536–37.

9. Roosevelt, *Hunting Trips*, 304–5.

10. Roosevelt, *Hunting Trips*, 306.

11. Faulkner, "The Bear," 329.

5. The Absaroka

1. Brown, *Plainsmen of the Yellowstone*, 17.
2. Brown, *Plainsmen of the Yellowstone*, 261.
3. Linderman, *Plenty-coups*, 156–57.

6. Slough Creek

1. Roosevelt, *Hunting the Grisly*, 67–68.
2. McMillion, *Mark of the Grizzly*, 172–73.
3. Faulkner, *Go Down Moses*, 348.

7. Gardiner, 2008 (and 1903)

1. Roosevelt, *Outdoor Pastimes*, 252.
2. Roosevelt, *Outdoor Pastimes*, 294.
3. Roosevelt, *Outdoor Pastimes*, 204–5.
4. Roosevelt, *Outdoor Pastimes*, 298.
5. Roosevelt, *Outdoor Pastimes*, 301.
6. Roosevelt, *Outdoor Pastimes*, 309.
7. Roosevelt, *An Autobiography*, 333–34.
8. Roosevelt, *An Autobiography*, 128.

8. Back at the Ranch, Thanksgiving, 2008

1. Thomas, "Lessons from Labrador," 24–25.
2. Roosevelt, *Outdoor Pastimes*, 292.
3. Swan, "Hunter's Intuition," 51.
4. Roosevelt, *Ranch Life*, 118.

9. The Western Star

1. Hagedorn, *Roosevelt in the Badlands*, 440–41.
2. Hagedorn, *Roosevelt in the Badlands*, 458.
3. Hagedorn, *Roosevelt in the Badlands*, 472.
4. Hagedorn, *Roosevelt in the Badlands*, 473–74.
5. Roosevelt, *Ranch Life*, 75.
6. Millard, *River of Doubt*, 297.

Bibliography

Brown, Mark H. *The Plainsmen of the Yellowstone*. Lincoln: University of Nebraska Press, 1961.

Faulkner, William. "The Bear." In *Six Great Modern Short Novels*. New York: Dell, 1967.

——. "Delta Autumn." In *Go Down Moses*. New York: Modern Library, 1942.

Hagedorn, Hermann. *Roosevelt in the Badlands*. New York: Houghton Mifflin, 1930.

Leforge, Thomas, and Thomas Marquis. *Memoirs of a White Crow Indian*. Lincoln: University of Nebraska Press, 1974.

Linderman, Frank B. *Plenty-coups, Chief of the Crows*. Lincoln: University of Nebraska Press, 1957.

Little Bear, Dr. Richard, ed. *We, the Northern Cheyenne People*. Lame Deer MT: Chief Dull Knife College, 2008.

Louv, Richard. *Last Child in the Woods: Saving Our Children from Nature-Deficit Disorder*. Chapel Hill NC: Algonquin, 2008.

McMillion, Scott. *Mark of the Grizzly: True Stories of Recent Bear Attacks and the Hard Lessons Learned*. Guilford CT: Falcon Guides, 1998.

Medicine Crow, Joe. *From the Heart of Crow Country: The Crow Indians' Own Stories*. Lincoln: University of Nebraska Press, 2000.

Millard, Candice. *The River of Doubt: Theodore Roosevelt's Darkest Journey*. New York: Broadway, 2005.

Morris, Edmund. *The Rise of Theodore Roosevelt*. New York: Ballantine, 1979.

Roosevelt, Theodore. *An Autobiography*. 1913. Reprint, New York: Da Capo, 1941.

——. *Hunting the Grisly and Other Sketches*. 1889. Reprint, New York: Barnes & Noble, 2003.

——. *Hunting Trips of a Ranchman and The Wilderness Hunter*. New York: Modern Library, 2004.

——. *Outdoor Pastimes of an American Hunter*. 1893. Reprint, Mechanicsburg PA: Stackpole, 1990.

——. *Ranch Life and the Hunting Trail*. 1888. Reprint, Lincoln: University of Nebraska Press, 1983.

Russell, Osborne. *Journal of a Trapper*. Lincoln: University of Nebraska Press, 1965.

Thomas, E. Donnall. "Lessons from Labrador: The Sportsman Stage," *Traditional Bowhunter* (February/March 2009).

Also by Dan Aadland

The Best of All Seasons: Fifty Years as a Montana Hunter
(University of Nebraska Press, 2007)

Sketches from the Ranch: A Montana Memoir
(University of Nebraska Press, 2008)

Women and Warriors of the Plains: The Pioneer
Photography of Julia E. Tuell
(Mountain Press Publishing Company, 2000)